MONEY MAKERS

THE STOCK MARKET SECRETS OF BRITAIN'S TOP PROFESSIONAL INVESTORS

Updated 2nd edition

Jonathan Davis

HARRIMAN HOUSE LTD

3A Penns Road
Petersfield
Hampshire
GU32 2EW
GREAT BRITAIN

Tel: +44 (0)1730 233870
Email: enquiries@harriman-house.com
Website: www.harriman-house.com

First published in Great Britain in 1998 by Orion Business, an imprint of The Orion Publishing Group Ltd.
This edition published in 2013.

Copyright © Jonathan Davis

The right of Jonathan Davis to be identified as the author has been asserted in accordance with the
Copyright, Design and Patents Act 1988.

ISBN: 978-0857191434

British Library Cataloguing in Publication Data
A CIP catalogue record for this book can be obtained from the British Library.

No responsibility for loss occasioned to any person or corporate body acting or refraining to act as a
result of reading material in this book can be accepted by the publisher, by the author, or by the
employer(s) of the author.

Printed and bound in the UK by CPI Antony Rowe.

WARNING
Stockmarket investments, and income, can go down as well as up. They may also have poor marketability.
The shares referred to in the text of this book are for illustrative purposes only and are not an invitation
to deal in them. Since this book was completed market conditions have changed. Neither the publishers
nor the author accept any legal responsibility for the contents of the work, which is not a substitute for
detailed professional advice. Readers should conduct their investment activity through an appropriately
authorised person.

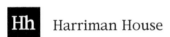

CONTENTS

eBook edition

As a buyer of the print edition of *Money Makers* you can now download the eBook edition free of charge to read on an eBook reader, your smartphone or your computer. Simply go to:

http://ebooks.harriman-house.com/moneymakers

or point your smartphone at the QRC below.

You can then register and download your eBook copy of the book.

www.harriman-house.com

 Harriman House

ACKNOWLEDGEMENTS

I owe thanks to a great number of people for help in bringing this book to fruition. First, and most obviously, I am grateful to the eight professional investors who spared me the time to talk at length, and uncomplainingly, about their activities. As I note in the Introduction, collaborating on this book has led on, in many cases, to further fruitful professional contact over the years. Colin McLean's senior colleagues gave me a long and fascinating tutorial on his (and their) investment appraisal methods. Robin Angus has given me many insights into the character and achievements of his friend and colleague, Ian Rushbrook, as have Ian Hamilton Sharp and others. Mark Slater shared some fascinating thoughts on his father. My colleagues at Genagro Ltd have done the same. The following also proved invaluable in hunting down background material for the first edition: Paul Kafka and Jo Roddan (at Fidelity); Helen Tweddle (Scottish Value Management); Patricia Riddle (Foreign & Colonial); Claire Pallen (St James's Place Capital); Linda Macfarlane (ABN Amro Carrington Pembroke); and Graham Quick (Hemmington Scott, publishers of Jim Slater's *Really Essential Financial Statistics*).

Among those who provided invaluable comments on the first edition text were Vivian Bazalgette, Rupert Morris and Mike Mitchell and. It is impossible to list all the fund managers, brokers and investment advisers who have shared their insights on the investment business over the last few years. They will, I hope, know who they are and accept my gratitude accordingly. Some of those I have relied on most can be found mentioned on my website **www.independent-investor.com**, and in my blog

blog.independent-investor.com. Sandy Nairn, the CEO of Edinburgh Partners, and co-author of my most recent book, *Templeton's Way With Money*, has been a particularly productive source of ideas and inspiration over the past 15 years. Readers of my columns in *The Independent* and *Financial Times* have made many valuable suggestions.

I am grateful to Martin Liu at Orion Publishing for originally commissioning the book, to his two assistants, Louise Radford and Claire Christian, who helped to shepherd the first edition through to production and to Adele Linderholm for editing the text. For the new edition, my thanks are due to Myles Hunt, the Managing Director of Harriman House, who suggested reissuing it, and Nick Read, who enthusiastically incorporated all my many suggested changes into the revised manuscript. Christopher and Linda Davis provided an invaluable 'safe house' where a good chunk of the original text was written, and Kristin van Santen, now my wife, has been a constant source of inspiration and advice. She has more than earned a dedication in the new edition.

INTRODUCTION TO THE 2013 EDITION

When asked his opinion about what the stock market would do next, the banker J.P. Morgan replied, briefly but pointedly: "It will fluctuate." Ben Graham, the leading stock market authority of his day, searching for an appropriate theme for his last and probably his greatest book, *The Intelligent Investor*, turned to Virgil's epic poem *Aeneid* for the inscription: *Per varios casus, per tot discrimina rereum tendimus.* This he translated as: 'Through chances various, through all vicissitudes, we make our way.'

Since 1997, when the first edition of *Money Makers* was written, events have amply justified the wisdom of these two great investors in affirming the essential changeability of the stock market. The fifteen years that have elapsed since have been marked by some extraordinarily violent fluctuations. The Asian crisis of 1998, the extraordinary Internet bubble of 1999-2000, two severe bear markets during which share prices fell by around 50% from peak to trough (2000-03, 2007-09), followed by the global debt crisis and subsequent recovery; it has certainly been a rollercoaster ride.

As I write this introduction, the timeless cycle of rotation from fear to optimism and back again is once again at work. For most of the past year markets have been spooked by well-justified fears about the consequences of the unprecedented build up of debt in many Western countries. The Eurozone has struggled for months to contain fears that it was about to break up. Pundits everywhere have been warning bleakly of hard times ahead, sending investors scurrying into supposedly "safe haven" assets, such as bonds and gold. Then suddenly a few weeks ago the mood changed once more and many so-called risk assets, including shares, recovered strongly, rising by an average of 20% in a matter of weeks.

Faced with such dramatic reversals of fortune, it is not surprising that many people seem to have given up on trying to understand, or benefit from, an investment in stocks and shares. There is no doubt that we are living through a period of relatively poor stock market returns, as always occurs after such extreme bubbles as we witnessed at the height of the Internet boom, when many investors lost all touch with reality and pushed share prices to absurdly high levels that were quite unjustified on any fundamental grounds – a mania as dramatic and as extraordinary as anything in recorded financial history. Such long cycles of market booms and busts have happened throughout history.

From 1982 to 2000, so we can see with hindsight, stock markets rose at an unprecedented rate, averaging annual after-inflation gains of 12% per annum, well above their long run average return. It was a period in which, notwithstanding such dramatic interludes as the 1987 stock market crash and the 1990-91 recession, making money from shares was as easy as it has ever been. Many people came to the stock market for the first time and prospered from the experience. A powerful combination of new technology and deregulation led to the rapid growth of new stock exchanges around the world and the advent of round-the-clock, real-time global trading.

Now, however, in the less favourable environment of the early twenty first century, the going has become much tougher. The best-known US and UK stock market indices, the S&P500 and FTSE All-Share, both finished the first decade of the new century lower in capital terms than they started it. Even allowing for dividends, investors in mainstream shares have suffered a largely barren decade. The severity of the banking crisis in 2008 and the periodic outbreaks of volatility since have heightened risk aversion. Interest rates have slumped to unprecedentedly low levels, dragging down the returns on many different types of investment, not just shares.

It is important however to draw the right conclusions from this generally unproductive period. The premise behind writing *Money Makers* the first time round was that there was much that investors could learn from studying the ideas and methods of the best professional investors of the day. Since the crazy market peak in 2000, with the search for successful investments becoming harder, the need to understand how the markets work continues to grow. In fact, in a period of low and declining nominal returns, I would argue that there has never been a greater need to learn from wise and impartial professional opinion, where it can be found. Today's investing conditions are difficult and challenging for professional and private investors alike.

The past fifteen years have certainly been a period when it has paid to be selective in deciding where to invest. While the UK and US stock markets have struggled to make ground since 2000, the same has not been true for example of gold, of emerging markets or of bonds. Gold has completed eleven straight years of annual increases, rising eightfold in value over the period. Emerging markets funds, such as the investment trust run by Mark Mobius, one of the investors featured in this book, has doubled in value over the past twelve years. The annualized rate of return on government bonds since 2000 has meanwhile been around 7.6% per annum, against just 3.2% for shares in the UK. (Please don't assume however that the superior performance of bonds can be repeated in future. It cannot and it won't be).

Many of these trends were spotted well in advance by those I write about in this book. In truth there is always money to be made if you know where to look – the question is: do you? If not, where can you learn how to do better? That is one reason for reissuing a new and updated version of *Money Makers*. A number of the professional investors I profile are sadly no longer active. Two of the wisest, Ian Rushbrook (who correctly forecast the onset of the 2008 global banking crisis), and Nils Taube (who had done the same for the 1987 stock market crash), have died since the first edition appeared. Two others, Michael Hart and John Carrington, have retired. The chapters on these four investors I have therefore left largely unchanged, with only a brief note at the end to update their personal biographies. Their wisdom and insights remain as relevant as ever.

For the other four, all of whom are still very much actively engaged in looking after their own or other people's money, I have made more substantive revisions, updating and revising the chapters as appropriate. In the case of Anthony Bolton, I have updated the chapter to take his story to the end of 2007, when he retired from running his main UK equity fund, with his reputation as the outstanding fund manager of his generation securely in place. I have not sought to look in detail at his subsequent post-retirement reappearance in Hong Kong as the manager of a Chinese equity fund, since it is too early to pass a definitive judgment on his performance in that interesting new venture (it has made a disappointing start). In the interests of readability, I have maintained the present tense for all eight of the profiles. I have also left the original Appendices unchanged.

One happy consequence of the first edition of *Money Makers* is that I have been able to deepen my knowledge of several of those I profiled at the time. Jim Slater, for example, knowing of my interest in the commodity cycle, persuaded me to become a founding shareholder and advisor to a Brazilian farmland fund, Agrifirma Brazil (now renamed Genagro Ltd), which he helped to set up in 2008. Shortly before that, I completed a full-length book about the methods of Anthony Bolton, based on further extensive conversations about his experiences and ideas. I have subsequently written a third book, this one on the methods of Sir John Templeton, published in 2012, for which Mark Mobius, one of his disciples, has provided several useful insights.

It has been a pleasant surprise to discover how little I have had to change my personal judgments as a result of these more extensive contacts. I have also felt little need to change the conclusions of the original edition. It remains the case that the basic principles of investment – buy low, sell high, spread your risk, acknowledge your limitations and tailor your methods to your temperament and experience – do not change with the passage of time. Attempts by academics to introduce more scientific methods to investment practice were all the rage in the 1990s, but the results have, by and large, been disappointing. The search for psychological and behavioural explanations for market movements has turned out to be a more productive line of enquiry than the assumption that investors are driven by rational expectations.

If I had to add any emphasis to my original text, it would be to say that the case for using low cost index funds for building exposure to core assets in an investment portfolio is much stronger than I gave it credit for in the original edition. It is a well-documented fact that the great majority of professional fund managers and investment advisors fail to deliver consistent outperformance of their benchmarks over time. Index funds, which passively seek to track the performance of well-known market indices, have meanwhile become both much cheaper and more widely available, making them an increasingly attractive building block in any investor's portfolio. Any newcomer to the investment field should start in my view by reading the wonderful books of Jack Bogle and Charley Ellis which make the case for indexing and cost minimization as core disciplines in your investment portfolio.

That general principle does not in any way however invalidate the case for studying the methods of the most successful market practitioners, or indeed investing in their funds. It merely makes it imperative, as in any professional enquiry, to seek out the very best of the bunch. That is what I set out to do when I first wrote *Money Makers*. I know that my own portfolio has benefited hugely from what I learnt. It is gratifying to know that others have also profited. One pleasing example concerns an up-and-coming fund manager by the name of Sebastian Lyon, who so liked what he read in one chapter of the original edition that he subsequently travelled up to Edinburgh to meet and seek advice from its subject, Ian Rushbrook. The two men found they shared the same philosophy and remained in regular contact. When the board came to appoint a new Investment Adviser to Mr Rushbrook's investment trust Personal Assets after his untimely death, they had no hesitation in appointing Sebastian's firm Troy Asset Management to do the job, with what so far has been very satisfactory results.

Most investors are guilty of serial offences in their behaviour, not least in chasing what is popular rather than what is objectively good value. The best and most profitable way to invest is of course exactly the other way round: trim and protect your profits when markets are overvalued and look for new opportunities when the reverse is true. Don't be afraid to think for yourself – and, most importantly of all, don't be deterred by the inevitable reverses. A fascinating new field of scientific enquiry, behavioural finance, has started to chronicle the many emotional biases which prevent human beings from doing the most rational things with their money. "Investing is not a smooth graceful progression to wealth," observes the American authority Charles Ellis. "It is a bumpy road and requires persistence and constancy of purpose."

The long-term case for investing in the stock market remains robust; and to the extent that shares have recently become cheaper the current difficulties may already be creating more favourable opportunities for the future. (My personal view is that we are not yet quite through the long and painful adjustment that became necessary after the excesses and policy errors of the past decade, but it will not be that long coming). In order to profit, however, it is necessary to understand exactly what successful investment in practice entails.

There is no escaping the fact that active fund management is a little like professional golf – a field where the mediocre can earn handsome rewards, but where true champions, who can raise and keep their game at a higher plane for years at a time, are few and far between. It takes rare gifts to sustain success in this business over more than a few years, but the challenge to a certain type of individual is irresistible. It is evident that someone like Anthony Bolton has an ideal temperament to pursue his contrarian investment style; dedicated, unflappable, thoughtful, somewhat obsessed. It takes courage and commitment to go on, year in year out, taking a different view to everyone else in your profession. As the author John Train says in his outstanding study of successful professional investors of the modern era: "Although a professional investor can sometimes strike it rich with a big coup, there's no luck in professional portfolio investing, any more than in master chess. It's a skilled craft, involving many decisions a week. The year-in, year-out manager of a large portfolio can no more pile up a superlative record by luck or accident than one can win a chess tournament by luck or accident."[1]

The point that both Morgan and Graham were at pains to make all those years ago is that it is the nature of the stock market to go up and down. You cannot have the periods of gain without the equivalent periods of retreat. It you don't like that fact, you shouldn't be in the market at all. The good news is that there are more up periods than down periods and it is the down periods that create the best buying opportunities. But never forget, either, that successful investment is not as easy as it is often made to appear. It pays to be forearmed – and to have wise and experienced counsel at your shoulder. I hope you will find just that in this book.

Jonathan Davis
February 2013

---

[1] John Train, author of *Money Masters of Our Time.*

1. INTRODUCTION

This is a book about some of Britain's most successful professional investors – who they are, what they do and how they think. It is designed to appeal to anyone who shares my interest in the stock market and wants to know how the experts go about making money from it. It is, thank goodness, no longer politically incorrect, as it seemed to be thirty years ago, to believe that the stock market fulfils an important function in the working of an efficient economy, nor to suggest that there is anything wrong in people trying to maximise their wealth through buying stocks and shares. For good or ill, we are all capitalists now.

The stock market does enjoy one huge advantage over most other ways of risking your money. Unlike say, gambling on the horses, or buying a National Lottery ticket, stock market investment is an activity where the odds actually favour the ordinary investor making money over the medium to long term. There is no certainty about it, but the balance of probability is that anyone who invests sensibly over a period of years with some idea of what they are doing will earn a significant real return from their investment. "The stock market is a casino," says one of the professionals I quote in this book, "but it is also a very nice casino in which everyone can get to go home with a return of 10% *after* the house take." This book is designed for anyone who finds that thought appealing and would like to make some capital from it.

Over the past few years, I have been fortunate to spend a lot of time talking to those lucky few who are able to make their livings purely from their stock market expertise. Through my work as a columnist on a national newspaper, and my consultancy work for large companies, I have been privileged to share the thinking of many of the sharpest investment minds in this country and watch them go about their work. This book is the result of many hours of conversation and research. It is my attempt to pass on to the general reader some of the professionals' insights into the art of investment.

It so happens that investment is something at which Britain is rather good. Although we still lag a long way behind the United States in our popular enthusiasm for the stock market, as a nation we are undoubtedly blessed with some of the most talented professional investors anywhere in the world. In a typically understated way, we have been managing money and investing on behalf of others longer than almost anyone in the world. London and Edinburgh are both established centres of excellence in the investment management world. Investment expertise is also one of our leading export industries.

An official report in 1996 estimated that fund management, although it employs no more than 35,000 people, contributes 0.4% of the country's Gross National Product. It brings in £425 million a year of income from abroad. This is one reason why so many of our best fund management firms are now being bought by large foreign banks, which want access to our long-standing expertise in this field. One of the benefits of Big Bang, the act of deregulation which swept away many of the restrictive practices in the stock market in 1986, is that it has opened the business of investment management to much greater completion than before. There had been an all-round improvement in professionalism and standards.

The effects have not all, admittedly, been for the good. The 1990s witnessed some deplorable cases of dishonesty and incompetence at some the largest and best-known City firms: Barings and Morgan Grenfell to name but two. The new century has produced other examples, calamitously in the great banking crisis of 2008. There have been worrying signs of the emergence of a 'star system' in the investment management business. Cut-throat competition to secure the services of the best fund managers has led to an unhealthy spiral in the rewards paid to top names and a dangerous obsession with short-term performance. Some of the biggest players in the business seem to have forgotten that, however highly rewarded, they are ultimately paid to manage other people's money, and not merely to enrich themselves. While there are plenty of honest and competent investment managers around, there are only a handful of exceptional ones.

What I have attempted to do in this book is to take a detailed look at a number of professional investors who I believe can with justice be called 'stars' of the investment business. These are investors who are held in the highest regard by their professional peers, not just for their performance over a period of years, but for their commitment to the art of investing. Apart perhaps from Jim Slater, none is a household name, yet all eight share the experience of having made a lot of money from practising their skills. Between them, I calculate that they manage something like £15 billion of other people's money, and earn their employers over £100 million a year for doing so. But for most of them the financial rewards have long ceased to be their primary motive. They carry on because they are hooked on the business of stock market investment itself.

Investment managers are also, of course, commercial animals. Fund management is a business like any other. It is not enough to be good. You have to convince others how good you are as well. According to Warren Buffett, the legendary American investor, the business of investment management is '25% performance, 75% marketing'. One has to allow for the fact that few professional investors are as good as their marketing departments would have you believe. Beating the market averages is a much tougher business than their seductive advertisements suggest. Academic research has demonstrated quite conclusively that only a small minority of professional investors consistently do better than average over a period of years and even in these cases, it is difficult to prove conclusively that this is the result of skill rather than luck. But while consistent outperformance is rare, it *can* be achieved; and those in this book have all done it for protracted periods. This is the reason why they are worth listening to.

Despite the advent of investment consultants whose sole function in life is to analyse the performance of professional fund managers, there is no one way of measuring success in investment. It is not just about making the most money, but doing so with an acceptable level of risk. There is little point in trying to rank the performance of someone running a hedge fund – a highly geared specialist vehicle for professional investors, of the kind run by George Soros – with someone running a general unit or investment trust targeted at ordinary investors. As a matter of policy I have only included in this book those who operate in the mainstream of investment management. Explaining how the masters of the hedge fund business make their money is a fascinating subject, and one where the financial rewards can literally be fabulous, but is a subject that I have left for another time and place.

Although I have screened the performance figures of all those profiled here, I have allowed myself to be influenced by subjective factors as well in deciding who to include. Twenty years of working in and around the City have allowed me to consult many of the top names in the business about who, in their opinion, are the best professional investors. There is a surprising degree of consensus about the names, as there is also about those whom the experts regard as the most overrated. I am grateful to all those who have let me tap their brains and experience so exhaustively.

Apart from track record and the respect of their peers, one other criterion I have insisted on is that those profiled must have something of value to say about the craft of stock market investment – and be prepared to say it, since this book could not have been written without their co-operation. Deep Blue, IBM's chess computer, may have beaten the world champion Gary Kasparov for the first time, but would still make a very dull interviewee. In the same way there is no obvious correlation between being successful as an investor and having something of interest to say about it. In fact, as Ian Rushbrook pointed out to me, one of the great things about the stock market is precisely that it is oriented towards results. You don't have to be able to articulate why what you have done works and a number of experts who failed this test have been excluded for that reason. It ought to be said here that while the subjects of the book have all had the chance to correct factual errors, the final judgements are mine and mine alone.

The format of the book has deliberately been kept as simple as possible. Each chapter consists of a detailed account of one professional investor. It describes his background, personality and views about investment. In the final chapter, I pull together the common threads that run through the previous chapters and make some observations about what lessons can be drawn from them. This is not a 'how to' book, but I will be disappointed if anyone who reads it does not come away with some valuable insights into how to improve their own investment performance.

A SHORT NOTE ON INVESTMENT TERMINOLOGY

The business of analysing investment performance has become a growth industry of its own in recent years, with a concomitant increase in new vocabulary and jargon. There is no reason why readers should bother themselves overly with it, but you may find some of the basic concepts helpful in differentiating between the investment styles of the investors described in this book.

Bottom up investment is the term used to describe those who base their choice of investments on the merits of individual stocks and shares rather than on broader economic or business trends. There is a parallel to the way that economists distinguish between *microeconomics*, the study of the behaviour of particular firms and individuals, and *macroeconomics*, the study of the behaviour of whole economies.

Top down investors, by contrast, believe that the most important decisions to make are not which particular shares to buy, but which stock markets, which currencies and which types of financial asset they should be invested in. The main classes of investment assets are: equities (shares), bonds (fixed interest securities), cash, property and index-linked gilts. For large investment institutions, in particular, these *asset allocation* decisions can often be the primary factors that determine their investment performance. The sheer size of their portfolios means that they cannot rely on just a few stocks and shares to determine their results, as individual investors can.

Active fund management is what most professional investors are paid to do. It is the business of trying to outperform the market by buying and selling shares or other investments which are expected to provide an above-average return over a given period of time. A share's return each year is measured in two ways: by the income it pays and by the extent to which its capital value rises or falls. A share whose price rises from 100 pence to 120 pence during the year and pays dividends of 5 pence is said to have produced a *total return* of 25% (20 pence of capital appreciating plus 5 pence of dividend, expressed as a percentage of the 100 pence purchase price).

Passive fund management is an alternative approach which has grown in importance over the last ten years. The premise here is that, for many investors, the odds of consistently outperforming the main stock market indices are not good enough to justify the cost and effort involved. Better in these circumstances to buy a fund whose sole purpose is to mimic the performance of the main stock market indices (a policy known as *index tracking*). The market indices play another role in the life of professional investors. They are the *benchmarks* against which an investor's performance is measured. An investor that invests solely in UK equities will typically assess their results against one of the main UK stock market indices; either the FTSE Index (popularly known as Footsie) which records the performance of 100 of the large quoted companies, or the FTSE All-Share Index. The latter measures the performance of around 900 shares and gives a broader picture of the market's movements, including as it does many small and medium-sized companies. For international investors, there are any number of global, regional and country indices to choose from.

Of the two poles in the investor's universe, return is the easy one to measure. *Risk* is a much harder animal to pin down. In the absence of an agreed definition of what investment risk is, the measure most commonly adopted is that of *volatility*. This is a statistical measure of how far a fund's returns have deviated from the norm over time. In this narrow sense, a fund which demonstrates high volatility is deemed to be riskier than one with lower volatility. It makes more sense however to think of the risk as the probability of permanent capital loss.

Among active fund managers, a traditional distinction is between *value* and *growth investors*. *Value investors* are primarily interested in buying shares that they judge to be 'cheap'. That is, they appear undervalued when measured against one of a number of different criteria, such as the stock market value of companies in similar lines of business, or their own share price history, or the value of other competing types of security (for example, government bonds or gilts). The kind of shares that value investors look for typically have relatively low price/earnings (p/e) ratios or relatively high dividend yields. *Growth stock investors*, by contrast, are primarily interested in buying shares in companies whose businesses are growing rapidly. The shares may not necessarily appear cheap at the moment, but their growth potential is expected to produce an above-average growth in share price in the future.

These are some of the standard valuation tools that investors look at when judging the merits of a particular share.

Yield (or dividend yield). The value of a company's annual dividend payments, expressed as a percentage of the current share price. For example, a company with shares priced at 100 pence and paying dividends of 5 pence a year would have a dividend yield of 5%. (This is the gross dividend yield; it is also possible to refer to a share's net dividend yield, that is after the deduction of income tax.)

Price/earnings ratio. (Also known as *P/E ratio*, or *earnings multiple*.) This is a company's share price expressed as a multiple of its earnings (or profit after tax) per share. A company which has reported earnings per share of 10 pence and sells at a price of 100 pence has a *historic p/e ratio* of 10 (100 pence/10 pence). A company which is forecast to report earnings per share of 10 pence in its next year end statement and sells at 100 pence has a *prospective p/e ratio* of 10.

Return on capital. A company's profitability expressed as a percentage of the amount of capital invested in the business. There are a number of different ways of calculating this figure. A related concept is *return on equity*, which measures a company's profit as a percentage of the capital that shareholders have subscribed or ploughed back in to the business (i.e. excluding capital raised in the form of debt).

Price to book value. The ratio between a company's share price and the company's net worth, as recorded in its balance sheet and expressed as a per share value. Thus, a company with a net worth of 100 pence a share, and whose shares sell for 150 pence, has a price to book value of 1.5 (150 pence/100 pence).

Net worth. Is calculated by taking the balance sheet volumes of a company's assets and subtracting all its liabilities. This figure is also known as shareholders' funds. Because accounting conventions record assets at cost, rather than at current market value, a share's book value will usually understate the current value of the business.

Price to sales ratio. The ratio between a company's share price and its sales, expressed as per share value. A company with sales of £100,000 a year and 100,000 issued shares has sales per share of £1. If the share price is £2, its price to sales ratio is 2.0 (£2/£1).

Real and nominal returns. All professional investors need to isolate the effect that inflation has on the investments they make. To make a real return, a share has to grow in value by more than the rate of inflation. If inflation is 3% a year, a share that returns 6% a year has produced a real return of approximately 3% (6% – 3%).

All the investors profiled in this book are active investors, but their styles are strikingly different in important respects. This is reflected in such things as the length of time they tend to own particular investments (the *holding period*), the rate at which they change their holdings (their *turnover* rate) and the range of markets in which they are prepared to invest.

2. ANTHONY BOLTON:

The professional's professional

AN ORDERLY MIND

To find Anthony Bolton's London office, you take a trip to the heart of the City, to a large modern office block that overlooks St Paul's Cathedral. The site formerly housed a large American bank whose global ambitions proved to be greater than its capabilities. It is unquestionably his employer Fidelity's grandest office yet, with a marbled entrance hall and a selection of David Hockney prints on the walls, reflecting the success of the firm's foray into Europe. Bolton's office is located on the second floor, where he sits at a standard issue desk, facing away from the view of Sir Christopher Wren's glorious creation outside. On a shelf behind his desk is a row of books that contain, in date order, his notes on all the meetings with companies that he has recorded and kept over the years. (There are over sixty in all, of which more than 80% concern his meetings with UK companies.) There is a computer screen in the corner, and on the walls family photographs, cartoons and a handful of the numerous industry awards his efforts have won over the years. The overall impression is strongly reminiscent of a university professor's office. This is orderly, functional space, and not much more. There is little to indicate that this is where arguably the best money manager the UK has ever produced goes about his business.

To meet, Bolton is a slim, unobtrusive figure with bright eyes and slightly curly, now greying hair. He speaks quietly and suprisingly haltingly, but mostly in complete sentences, the telltale sign of an orderly mind. He gives off an image of cool and quiet efficiency, is unfailingly courteous in company, and would certainly not look out of place in a serious university. You gain the impression that there is little he does with his life that is not deliberate. But that, intriguingly, proves not to be entirely the case. This is someone who had to be kicked out of bed by his father to get a job on leaving university, and who drifted into the City by chance rather than from any lifelong conviction that he was destined to make money from buying and selling shares. This leisurely start to life has not stopped him becoming one of the most highly sought-after fund managers in a highly competitive, well renumerated business whose top performers can earn multiple millions in a single year.

Quiet and thoughtful, and anything but flash, Bolton is a model of what the modern professional investment manager should be: clear-sighted, disciplined, hardworking and conscientious, with a track record of consistent outperformance in all his funds. Although the business of investment can never be reduced to a science, Bolton's career has demonstrated how a mixture of flair, common sense and hard work can be profitably applied to the art of picking stocks. He is a contrarian investor, someone who takes positive delight in scouring the bargain basement areas of the stock market, looking for shares that are damaged or unloved, but capable of redemption. The strategy has its risks, even for a diversified fund, but it has worked like a dream over the 28 years that his funds have been on the market, and that is what ultimately counts for any professional fund manager.

The two funds that have occupied the bulk of his career, Fidelity Special Situations and Fidelity European, have both achieved a compound annual rate of return of 20% while under his management, comfortably beating the market and their peer group in both cases. The funds and their manager have won a stack of industry awards, too numerous to mention, and both command best-of-class ratings from Standard & Poor's, Morningstar and other leading independent fund rating services. Serious observers have described him in print as Britain's answer to Peter Lynch, the legendary Irish-American stockpicker who for thirteen years ran the world's largest mutual fund, the Magellan fund, for Fidelity in the United States. More significantly perhaps, in a poll of leading fund managers conducted by *Sunday Business* in 2003, when asked to nominate the competitor they most admired, no fewer than five out of the ten named Bolton.[1]

In his own view, as well as those of his admirers, Bolton's great strength as an investor is that he is an emotionally placid individual, more than capable of taking setbacks with fortitude. "You have to be a fairly calm person to be a fund manager" is his own assessment. "The great thing about him," says Peter Jeffreys, a former colleague who went on from Fidelity to co-found the ratings firm Fund Research, "is that everything he does is completely straight up and down. There is absolutely no side to him, none at all." Sir Charles Fraser, a fund director, asked to provide an anecdote about Bolton, replied simply: "I have none. He is not an anecdote sort of person." Less immediately obvious is the high degree of commitment and organisation that Bolton brings to his task. Like the majority of successful professional investment managers, he believes that to be a professional investor, you have to be wholly absorbed by the markets. "I think you have got to be fanatical about it", he says, "because investing is continuous and intangible. There's no beginning or end to it, and there is always something new that needs delving into. I think you have to be completely taken by it to do well. If I look at the investment managers I admire, none of them do it part time."[2]

He concedes that it may be different for those, such as George Soros, the hedge fund speculator, who specialise in making big bets on the macroeconomic outlook. For those two or three decisions a year, assuming they are the right ones, and they are backed heavily, can be all the

---

[1] It is an indication of the unassuming way that Bolton works that three of the five who nominated him said that they had never met him.

[2] Unless specifically attributed to another source, all the direct quotations in this section are from interviews with the author.

difference between success and failure. But for investors who specialise in picking stocks, as Bolton does, there is no alternative to being fanatical. When he started, he had only 20-30 shares to look after. But now, thanks to the success of his funds, which have grown two hundredfold in size since 1987, there are nearly two hundred stocks to track in his various portfolios. It requires not just hard work, but the support of a large team of analysts to keep tabs on what they are all doing. At the last count, there were more than 50 analysts at Fidelity in London whose work he could call upon. Bolton has helped to train many of them himself in the art of stock analysis, Fidelity style. They know what he wants and he has faith in what they produce.

DEVOTED TO DETAIL

Bolton's working week is a long one. Given the emphasis that Fidelity places on in-depth research, the amount of paperwork and electronic material he has to shift through every day is formidable. A typical day for Bolton begins with him leaving home in West Sussex at 6.30 a.m. to catch a train to London. He reads the *Financial Times* on the train and also does his homework on one or more of the companies he will be seeing later. On the way to and from the station he also catches up on the forty or so voicemails he has each day, many of them from colleagues reporting back on recent meetings with potential or current holdings. His working week revolves around company meetings. When he was covering both UK and continental companies, it was not unknown to do as many as five or six a day, and there are many others for which a colleague will provide a report. Fidelity as a group sees an average of fifteen to twenty companies a day in London, sometimes more, either in its offices, at the companies themselves or by conference call. This commitment to face-to-face meetings is, Bolton has no doubt, one of its main competitive strengths as a firm.

Each company is analysed beforehand in detail by the in-house analysts, and becomes the subject of a detailed pack of information, several pages long, covering the key financial data, plus brokers' views and any other relevant material, such as press cuttings and so on. The meetings are an opportunity for Bolton and his colleagues to ask questions of the management and keep up to date on how the business is going. All these meetings are written up afterwards. Bolton himself takes his own hand-written notes, usually two or three pages long, which he files neatly away in the books behind his desk. He brings them out later to check that companies have not changed their tune since he last saw them. Browsing through them gives an insight into the austerity of his methods: in the dozen or so volumes I looked at one day, there was not a single anecdote, piece of gossip or personal remark to be found (and not even a doodle, for that matter). It requires, not least, an ability to concentrate intensively on the task in hand.

Unusually, in addition to Fidelity's own analysis and research bought in from brokers and others, Bolton also likes to look at a number of share price charts before seeing companies, in order to see what their recent price action has been. Add all this up, and you have a pile of daily paperwork that would make Sir Humphrey Appleby, the mandarin in the television series 'Yes Minister', proud. It is one reason why he normally gets home at eight in the evening, and says he dreads the end of holidays because of the huge pile of files that he knows will be awaiting him on his return. One way he escapes from the pressure of work is by composing classical music, an activity he has recently resumed after having been very keen as a child. It leaves little time for socialising with his professional peers, or even his Fidelity colleagues. He is not by his own admission "a going out for a beer person. I commute in from the country. I don't do a lot of evening things. I like to get home."[3]

"There is an awful lot of reading", he says. "One reason I commute by train is that I can kill off quite a lot of it that way. You have to know what you are looking for because you can become mesmerised by the sheer volume of it all, and lulled into complete inactivity. I like to screen a lot of things and most of the broker material is frankly unnecessary, at least for my purpose. There are certain analysts whom I rate, and I know to look out

---

[3] *Daily Telegraph*, January 10th 2004.

for their stuff. If the note is a sell and it's a company I don't own, I won't even look at it. If it's a sell and I do own it, then obviously I'll want to have a quick look. But you have got to weed out the dross."

The background briefing material that Fidelity analysts prepare on each company is presented in a standardised house format. Even so, the sheer weight of material means, says Bolton, that "you have to have a system to get through, otherwise you are sunk". Some of his fund manager colleagues survive by ignoring all the brokers' research, preferring to stick to in-house material alone. But this is not Bolton's style. "I don't have that approach. You never know where the next idea is going to come from." An eclectic mind, he insists, is needed to make his style of investing have any chance of working.

When companies come to visit, as they do in ever growing numbers, Bolton says that what he is mainly looking for is evidence that the managements know their business. But he is far from starry-eyed about the importance of management in the success of a company. "While some investors put a lot of emphasis on the quality of management, I'm more of a Warren Buffett follower in that I would rather have a good business run by average management than the other way round. I find that people who impress you in meetings are not necessarily the best managers." He mentions John Gunn, who was widely lauded for a while in the 1980s as the best manager in the City. A few years later, his company, British & Commonwealth, was bust.

"I like managements who are consistent in what they say. I dislike hyperbole, managers who consistently overegg the pudding." He is more concerned to see what companies are saying about their products: "If they put great emphasis on one product when they come to see us, and next time fail to mention it at all, we will obviously start to get worried. You are obviously looking to read between the lines." If a competitor says something positive about a company's product range, it counts for twice as much as the company saying the same thing itself.

A CHANCE BEGINNING

Given such a highly formalised approach to his work, it comes as something of a surprise to learn that Bolton only drifted into the business of investing by chance. His early experience was gained at a small and rather risqué merchant bank called Keyser Ullmann. In its heyday in the early 1970s, it enjoyed a reputation for adventurousness, later somewhat tarnished by a number of unsuccessful and controversial deals that eventually resulted in the bank disappearing as an independent entity. Bolton went there as the bank's "first and last graduate trainee". He had studied engineering at Cambridge, but says that after two years of the subject the "one thing I was pretty certain of was that I didn't want to become an engineer". When the time came to leave university in 1971, he did so without having a job lined up.

About three weeks after the end of his final summer holidays, Bolton's barrister father, who had previously encouraged him to take his time over deciding what to do, suddenly began to apply pressure on him to make a more positive attempt to find a job. A businessman friend of the family suggested he think about the City, and another family friend, a stockbroker, gave him an introduction to Keyser Ullmann, which at the time was still growing fast and had decided (according to Bolton) that "this graduate training business sounded a good idea". By such strange quirks of chance are successful careers often launched.

Unlike many other successful investors, Bolton did not set out to find a job as an investment manager, nor did he arrive in the business with any burning ambition to make money from the markets. As he points out, amongst his peer group at university, corporate finance was still very much the 'in thing' for those who went into the City. Investment management was regarded as second-division stuff. "Corporate finance had the glamour attached to it", he recalls, "and investment management was hardly known as an industry." He himself had no prior interest in the markets, and knew nothing about them. Not for him a history of trading stamps, or other moneymaking schemes, while he was a child. Unlike many of the greatest investors, whose motivation to succeed often stems from a poor background, Bolton had a conventional and comfortable middle class upbringing.

Bolton spent five years at Keyser Ullmann, and reckons he got good training while he was there, despite the bank's subsequent problems. He started as a general trainee, "behind the tills, doling out the money, trooping off to the money markets, where they all went around in top hats in those days". After a brief stint in administration, he spent a little time on the investment side, and it was there that he finally "picked up the bug of stocks and shares". He was offered a job as a research assistant in the investment arm of the bank. It was here that his career as an investment manager began. The investment side was separate from the rest of the bank and most of the money it managed was in investment trusts. This meant, says Bolton, that when the bank got into difficulties and depositors started taking their money away, his side of the business remained largely unaffected.

DEVELOPING A STYLE

Three things about the way that Keyser Ullmann managed money proved influential in the development of Bolton's style as an investor. One was that they specialised in smaller companies, something that remains one of his trademarks today. The second was that they went out and visited the companies they owned. This was rather novel at the time, when most investment managers still relied heavily on stockbrokers to bring them information and ideas. Third, one of the directors was interested in technical analysis, or the use of share price charts, to supplement conventional fundamental analysis of shares. This too remains one of Bolton's interests.

His job as an assistant to one of the fund managers included writing a few paragraphs on each company's half-yearly and annual results, saying whether or not the shares still looked reasonable investments. He remembers the fascination of discovering the Datastream machine, then something of a novelty in the City, which allowed him to search ('screen') the universe of stocks and shares looking for those which met common specified characteristics.[4] Nevertheless, he says, it took him quite a while before he fully understood how the business worked.

Bolton had to cut his teeth as an investor in the scary markets of 1973/75, when the secondary banking crisis was at its height, and the stock market endured its worst decline in living memory. He remembers lunches at which all the other fund managers spent their time boasting about how little money they actually had invested. Instead they seemed to be competing against each other to see who had most of their money in cash. "There was a feeling of: What have I got into? Is the whole world going to end? Would the stock market ever stop going down?" It did, but it was not long before Bolton had decided that, with all the problems at Keyser Ullmann, now was a good time to move on. After a few interviews, he was offered a job as a fund manager by the Schlesinger group, which was owned by a wealthy South African family with property and financial interests in London. Among them was a unit trust company, run by Richard Timberlake and Peter Baker.

Both men proved influential in the development of Bolton's career as an investor. Baker was the one with most of the investment ideas, while Timberlake, something of a pioneer in the modern fund management business, concentrated on the marketing. The former, says Bolton, had a very objective view of investment and was always willing to judge an idea on its merits. "If you could make a good case for something, he would look at it. I always felt that if the tea lady came in and said you ought to buy ICI and these are the reasons why, he would be prepared to listen."

Baker was also mathematically minded, with an interest in how to price options using mathematical models. He was one of the first people in this country to take an interest in the quantitative techniques associated with

---

[4] Datastream is an information service whose extensive database allows the user to trawl through a huge raft of historical information, including share prices, bond prices, economic data and company results. Thanks to the internet and improved telecommunications, allowing fast data transfer, such information is now virtually a commodity for any professional working in the City or the West End.

modern portfolio theory. Noting how academic research had demonstrated the difficulty of beating the market averages, he also launched an index-tracking fund, a concept that in those days was well ahead of its time. During this period Bolton had a hand in running seven or eight different funds, doing "a bit of everything". One of these funds was a 'special situations' fund, a type with which Bolton has been closely associated ever since.

Schlesingers was not all that stable an environment however. There were constant rumours that it was for sale. South Africans, says Bolton, are "very much dealers, they like to buy and sell things, not to hang on to them". So when the second of his bosses, Richard Timberlake, was recruited by Fidelity to help set up a UK operation for the first time in 1979, Bolton let him know that he was interested in following him there. At the time, he says, he did not even know who Fidelity were. When he discovered that they were the biggest independent investment management firm in the United States, with a reputation for consistent performance based on in-depth fundamental analysis, it clearly helped. As a result, he became one of the first two investment managers that Fidelity International recruited. He was 29, with only limited experience but the great advantage of being known to the new managing director.

STARTING OUT AT FIDELITY

While from today's perspective opting to join Fidelity may seem like an obvious career move, that was not the way it appeared to many at the time. The Department of Trade, says Timberlake, had never authorised a foreign group to run retail funds in the UK before, and insisted on several conditions before allowing Fidelity even to set up its stall. Big Bang, the act of deregulation which was to sweep away many of the cosy closed shops and restrictive practices that had long prevailed in the Square Mile, was still seven years in the future. Exchange controls had only been lifted a few months before and business sentiment remained fragile. Inflation was in double digits and seemingly out of control. The pro-capitalist government of Margaret Thatcher was still very much feeling its way after the Conservative Party's election victory earlier in the year.

Few in the City had heard of Fidelity, and those who had were often not impressed by the workaholic methods of American business. "My brother worked for Fidelity's auditors and I was told all sorts of horrific things about hiring and firing and what Americans were like", recalls Timberlake. Bill Byrnes, the Fidelity man charged with overseeing the launch of its UK operations, says; "We were a fledgling investment management company struggling to establish itself in the United Kingdom, operating in a recessionary period of soaring inflation, sky-high interest rates and wobbly equity markets. To top it off, Fidelity International had an association with an American company at a time when American invaders were viewed (not entirely unfairly) as short-term opportunists who fled the scene at the first indication of adverse circumstances." It therefore took some courage to join this unknown ship: indeed, he recalls, it was only after prompting by his wife that Bolton finally picked up the phone and confirmed his interest to Timberlake.

Timberlake asked Bolton to run a special situations fund, as this was the one that he had most enjoyed when he was at Schlesingers, though it was not top of Fidelity's priorities in the early years. (Byrnes and Timberlake in fact tried to persuade their new recruit to run a Japanese fund for them, an invitation that was politely refused.) Ironically, in view of what was to happen later, Special Situations proved the hardest of Fidelity's original funds to sell. The fund struggled along at around £2-£3 million in size for quite some time. At one stage, the sales team were even offered double commission to help get sales moving. It was only in the second half of the 1980s, when the fund appeared at the top of the five-year performance tables for the first time, that investors began to buy the fund in substantial volumes.

What, exactly, is a special situations fund? At one level, the answer is obvious. It is a fund that looks to invest in companies which are facing unusual and exceptional circumstances, and where any turnaround in fortunes can be anticipated to produce a profit within a relatively short time. "Almost any share at a particular time can be a special situation", is how Bolton described it in his first manager's report on the new fund. "In general it will be a company attractively valued in relation to net assets, dividend yield or future earnings per share, but additionally having some other specific attraction that could have a positive short term influence on the share price." This might be a takeover, a new issue, a change of management, a recapitalisation or some other triggering event — over the years, as we shall see, Bolton has refined and analysed what he does in some detail.

But at the time he started his Fidelity fund, one of its greatest advantages, he admits now, was precisely the fact that hardly anybody was actually quite sure what the term meant. There was, he recalls, a general perception that it was an 'aggressive' (i.e. risk-seeking) fund which looked for capital growth opportunities outside the ranks of the blue chips. Tipping potential takeover candidates was one of the routes that investors found relatively easy to grasp. The initial reports emphasised that Bolton was looking for quick profits, and willing to live with above average volatility. But beyond that, there was – and remains – plenty of scope to experiment. The flexibility of the 'special situations' concept has given Bolton the leeway over the years to develop his own distinctive style of investment. It is the kind of fund that appeals to those who believe that investment managers with exceptional talent can make a big difference, whatever the academics may say about the difficulty of finding a manager who can beat the market consistently over time.

The association with Fidelity has clearly worked out well for both parties. It is difficult for anyone unfamiliar with the American investment scene to conceive of the huge influence that Fidelity enjoys in the United States. It is not only the world's largest independent investment management company, but has long been prominent in helping to shape the way that both the marketing of the investment business and professional standards in investment management have developed since World War II. Fidelity was one of the first firms to invest heavily in fundamental research, one of the first to see the need for recruiting and training the best brains to a business previously regarded as something of a backwater in the financial industry, and also one of the first to pioneer the direct marketing of collective investment vehicles to ordinary investors.

The great bull market of the 1980s and 1990s put vast amounts of money in its hands. The rapid growth has created periodic adjustment problems, but the company rolled on like a juggernaut through the bear market of 2000-2003. In 2004, Fidelity Management and Research, the Boston company, was running over 180 different funds and had more than $1 trillion in funds under its management. This, to put it in some context, is equivalent to around 40% of the entire capitalisation of the London stock market. So large and influential has the firm become that the US now boasts newsletters that do nothing but monitor what is happening to Fidelity's army of funds. Its international affiliate, Fidelity International, of which the UK office is a part, has also grown steadily with more than $180 billion in assets under management. Its fund range today includes more than 30 UK retail funds and more than 250 offshore funds.

Despite its many years of growth, the original Fidelity business in Boston remains a private company controlled by the Johnson family, which started it in 1946, and other senior management. Although there are overlaps among the shareholders, Fidelity's International arm is set up to operate as an independent business. Ned Johnson is the second generation of the family to preside over its operations and, unusually for such family dynasties, his tenure has been every bit as successful as that of his father, a charismatic figure known to everyone inside and outside the industry simply as 'Mister Johnson'.[5] Unusually also, for a family firm in the fund business, the investment methods favoured by father and son are rather different. Whereas Mister Johnson liked to give individual fund managers their heads to invest in whatever personal style suited them, however idiosyncratic, his son has shaped the modern firm around a belief in the overriding importance of research, both fundamental and technical. He also takes a ruthlessly utilitarian approach to his employees. While Fidelity's fund managers are paid handsomely, and enjoy high quality technical support, those who fail to deliver sustained performance are ultimately shown the door.

---

[5] Ned Johnson's daughter Abigail is now President of Fidelity Management and Research.

The highly competitive environment and cohesive culture does not suit every kind of fund manager, but those who like it tend to like it a lot and prosper, as Bolton has done. A key feature of the Fidelity approach is that the fund managers are left to get on with running their funds, largely unhindered by other responsibilities. The running of the fund management team and investment process is left to the chief investment officer, while more recently, in response to the growing emphasis placed on corporate governance, another director handles the routine (though sometimes delicate) business of managing relationships with the companies in which the firm's funds own shares. The marketing and administration of the business is run from a separate office outside London. Whereas at many investment banks, a spell in investment management is seen merely as a stepping stone on the ladder to the top of the bank, at Fidelity fund management is the end itself.

"The Peter Lynch mould at Fidelity", says Bolton, "is that you've got to let the investment people spend all their time running their investments. If you mix in other things as well, the investment is likely to suffer." The round of daily meetings with companies leaves little time for anything else. It is an article of faith that the Fidelity way is the best, an attitude that prompts some outsiders to accuse it of insularity. Rather than recruiting from outside, virtually all the firm's portfolio managers, and a number of its analysts, are trained from scratch in-house to ensure consistency in the firm's investment approach. Again it may not be everyone's cup of tea, but for those who enjoy the discipline of being part of a tightly managed family, it works. The recruitment process is undoubtedly helped by the power of the Fidelity brand. In a survey of 500 investment professionals reported by the *Financial Times* in 2003, Fidelity topped the list of most highly regarded fund managers for the fourth year in a row.

ONE SIMPLE INSIGHT

Bolton started managing his Special Situations fund in 1979. In 1985 he took on the management of Fidelity's first European fund as well, and ran it and its sister investment trust until 2001, when he began the handover to a colleague, Tim McCarron.[6] For a number of years he also managed an offshore European fund based in Luxembourg. In 1994 he added a UK investment trust, Fidelity Special Values, which mirrors the investments of the Special Situations fund, to his portfolio. At one point Bolton had overall responsibility for some £10 billion of other people's money, a prodigious sum for one individual to manage. His two pools of money – Europe and UK Special Situations – are properly judged in isolation, but there are some common underlying principles that have governed the way he has managed all the money entrusted to him. Most of these principles can be clearly traced back to the ideas that Bolton identified as having force in his very early years at Keyser Ullmann and Schlesingers.

The big insight that Bolton has carried with him throughout his career can be easily summarised. It is simply this: that in order to achieve better results than other people, you have to do something different from everyone else. Or in his words: "If you want to outperform other people, you have got to hold something different from other people. If you want to outperform the market, as everyone expects you to do, the one thing you mustn't hold is the market itself. You certainly shouldn't hold the market and do lots of dealing as well, because the transaction costs will punish you. You have got to be different." In his case, this has pushed him first in the direction of small, rather than large, quoted companies; and then towards companies which for a variety of reasons are unloved and unfashionable, but where it is possible to foresee a positive change in the near to medium-term future.

"I manage my funds with an above average risk profile, based on contrarian type stocks", is how he sums up his approach. "My ideal is a

---

[6] McCarron took responsibility for the investment trust first, and after that went well took on the unit trust as well, completing the transition in January 2003. Another Fidelity fund manager, Graham Clapp, took on the offshore European fund at that point.

company where things have gone wrong, but where it looks as if things may be changing. I am looking for stocks that are unfashionable and cheap, but where there is something which will recapture investors' attention before too long." The idea of looking at shares which are out of favour is not of course new. In the UK, it is almost seventy years since M&G, the pioneer of the unit trust industry, launched its first Recovery Fund. That was based on the idea that you could do well out of buying shares in companies which were recovering from recession or some other setback, either external or self-inflicted. Conventional recovery stocks of this type have always been a big component of Bolton's special situation portfolios, and indeed have become more prominent in the last few years.

But they are not the only types of special situation he looks for. He also looks for companies which are under-researched, and which are therefore unlikely to be properly valued, and for companies that have growth potential that nobody else has yet recognised. In fact, Bolton's main achievement is to have taken his basic concept of being different from the pack and pushed it further than M&G, or any other mainstream fund management company, has so far dared to take it. There is a price to be paid for this in terms of risk. Although he has always insisted on a well-diversified fund, it means he has found himself holding a lot of stocks that most people would think twice about owning. That doesn't always play well with the armies of consultants who these days routinely pore over the statistical properties of every fund: one of the measures that most excites their attention is the extent to which a fund's holdings deviate from those of the market as a whole (its so-called 'tracking error'). Bolton's funds have one of the highest 'tracking errors' of all UK equity funds.[7]

Whether or not contrarian stockpicking of the kind that Bolton goes in for is in reality unusually risky is a moot point. What it does mean, unquestionably, is that it places an onus on the fund manager to pick his stocks with more than average care. Mishaps and the occasional disaster

---

[7] Calling deviation from an index 'tracking error' is evidence of how far the concept of indexing has advanced in modern investment management: for an index fund, which is specifically designed to match the performance of an index, such deviation is indeed reprehensible. For an actively managed fund such as Special Situations, the reverse is often the case.

are an inevitable consequence. Bolton has had his fair share of disasters along the way, including such horror stories as Polly Peck, Mountleigh and the Parkfield group, all of which either went bust or had to be rescued while in his ownership. A similar experience threatened to befall him more recently when Railtrack, the rail network operator, was threatened with effective renationalisation, a situation that was only redeemed when Fidelity and other leading shareholders banded together to take legal action against the Government. Without the strength of a broadly diversified fund, and the market clout of Fidelity behind him, these bad experiences might have proved too much for a less highly regarded manager, but Bolton is now sufficiently well established to be able to shrug off the occasional failure. He is playing a numbers game, and is confident that the gems will, on average, outnumber the duds.

THE SHARES HE LIKES

Being an analytical sort, and being constantly required to justify his methods to potential investors in his funds, Bolton has broken down the types of special situation he wants to buy into a number of different categories, all in the general category of 'unfashionable or undervalued' stocks. This has shown some subtle changes over the years, though the underlying philosophy is unchanged. In his early reports to investors, Bolton listed eight categories: small growth stocks, recovery shares, asset situations, new issues, companies involved in bids, energy and resource stocks, companies reorganising or changing their business, and new technology companies. Now in his presentations, he has refined the list to cover six generic types of situation. The headings are recovery, unrecognised growth, valuation anomalies, corporate potential (mainly shorthand for takeover prospects), asset plays and industry arbitrage. The philosophy behind this categorisation is set out in more detail by Bolton himself in his book *Investing Against The Tide*.

Of all his many early successes, Bolton is particularly proud of his success in finding the Mersey Docks and Harbour Board. This was a classic example of a business that conventional opinion thought to be a disaster, but which turned out to be what Peter Lynch liked to call a 'tenbagger' (a share which makes investors ten times their money). For years, the Board had been lumbered with the cost of enforcing the disastrous dock labour scheme introduced by the Labour government. This guaranteed employment to all dockers in the area, whatever the state of demand. Mrs Thatcher's government ended the dock labour scheme, but left most of the companies which operated the docks with the burden of meeting the resulting redundancy payments to dockers.

What Bolton saw, but which many others did not, was that the company was sitting on a highly valuable property portfolio. When the Conservative government privatised another docks company, Associated British Ports, it wrote off most of the company's liability for its redundancy payments in order to make sure the issue was a success. Bolton took a bet that something similar would happen with the Mersey Docks and Harbour Board. He was proved right: in fact, the government wrote off 100% of its liabilities for redundancy payments, leaving a business that was both asset rich and, for the first time in years, capable of making a worthwhile profit on its activities. The shares rose tenfold in just a few years.

The 'corporate potential' category is also of note. It is not quite right to say that this is purely a euphemism for 'takeover prospects', but Bolton has never disguised his interest in trying to spot companies that are likely to experience a change in management or control. He regards this as a legitimate activity for a professional fund manager, and one that many of his professional peers unwisely neglect. He had spectacular success in buying independent television companies in the 1990s. Five of the six he bought shares in were later taken over, reflecting the industry-wide consensus that the small regional monopolies originally set up by the government could not survive in the modern age of satellite and digital technology. (He was later to play a pivotal and unexpectedly high profile part in the merger that combined the last two surviving ITV companies, Carlton and Granada, in 2003.) Privatised electricity firms were another case where he found it was possible, on general principles alone, to foresee an industry-wide round of takeovers well in advance.

The general moral for investors in his approach is that there can often be something remarkably fragrant lurking behind a bad smell, provided you are prepared to go and sniff it out. Not all companies that perform badly are necessarily beyond redemption. The trick for a contrarian investor is to put yourself in the way of interesting ideas of this kind, where you can see the potential for change and also have a chance to get in early enough to take advantage of the change before it is fully recognised by the market as a whole. "My experience", says Bolton, "is that most investors tend to avoid companies that have not done well recently, and this reaction creates the buying opportunity." More recently, the much increased size and clout of the fund means that Bolton's emergence on a company's share register often now leaves him in a powerful position to promote or block changes in a company's ownership. In underperforming companies, where he has a major stake, he has become more of an agent for change, and less of a passive investor.

CASTING THE NET WIDE

In his early days running the fund, Bolton had little internal research to fall back on and says that most of his ideas came from brokers, something that his early notebooks reflect. Early reports to fundholders note approvingly that Fidelity had relationships with more than fifty London and regional stockbrokers, the latter especially useful for analysing small local companies.[8] Even then, however, he liked to cast the net quite widely. "I have always worked on the basis of having lots of ideas put to you from many sources and then choosing quite selectively from them. It is like a big sieving process. You get all these ideas brought to you, and then you choose just a few of them." He still uses a lot of broking material now, despite Fidelity's own extensive in-house research capability. That is partly because it is impossible to cover every stock across such a wide universe,

---

[8] For example, the Special Situations Trust's report May 1981.

but it also stems from an innate belief that it pays investors to expose themselves to as many new ideas as possible.

The trouble with relying on brokers is, says Bolton, that "they tend to be good at getting you into something but aren't so good at getting you out of it. If they get you into something that doesn't go that well, then they tend to lose interest in helping you to follow it. Time was when they thought something was a buy, they would tell a few of their favoured clients first. Now the regulators insist that they have to tell everyone at the same time, so there is a sort of scramble and if it is a very good idea, a few people get in and the bigger clients don't." The trick for a big investor such as Fidelity, even when it has a good idea, is therefore to find a way of getting in, and getting out of, shares earlier than the market as a whole. These days the firm has a dedicated trading desk to execute the orders that Bolton and all the other fund managers place, but the issue of managing liquidity remains an ever present one – not least because, given the scale of its operations today, Fidelity can quickly become the largest single shareholder in the small and midcap companies that he favours.

HOW FIDELITY SPECIAL SITUATIONS HAS GROWN
Total net assets 1987-2006

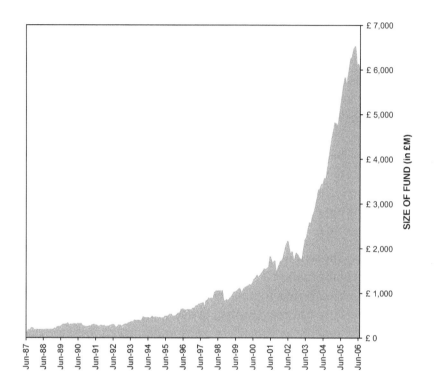

As a result, moving in and out of stocks is no longer as easy as it once was for Bolton, at least in the UK market. As his funds have grown in size, his choice has been between sticking to his last, hunting for small out of fashion stocks and simply looking for more of them, or changing his approach and looking for value among bigger quoted companies instead. Since the mid 1990s, when the fund catapulted in size to become the largest single fund of its kind, he has opted to take both approaches. In the main he continues to prefer to stick in the small and midcap area of the market, partly because that is the way that Lynch and others in Fidelity have tended to do it. But he is equally happy to own more stocks in the upper reaches of the market when valuations appear attractive, as they began to do, for example, he found, towards the end of 2003. For the last few years, his fund has owned what for him is an unprecedented number of large capitalisation stocks, even though in percentage terms his combined holdings in this segment of the market still account for under half the weight they have in his benchmark, the FTSE All-Share Index.

Why does investing in recovery stocks, and all the other out of favour categories he likes, seem to work so well? It comes back, in Bolton's view, to the herdlike behaviour of the market. "You have got to use the excesses of the stock market to your advantage. Looking at recovery stocks forces you to go against the herd. Most people feel confident doing what the herd's doing. If everyone tells them Vodafone is a good company, then they want to believe that Vodafone is a good company. If three brokers ring me and tell me something is a buy, then I normally say 'that doesn't look too good'. The market is excessive. It gets too optimistic on things and then gets too pessimistic on things. I also think it is quite short term and won't look at things like the longer-term dynamics of a business."

The key thing any serious investor must have is an information advantage over the rest of the market. "Generally I would feel uncomfortable taking a view on some of the macroeconomic stuff, and on things like oil prices. Why should I have a better view than hundreds of other people on them? But if you are looking at a small company in particular, there are times when you come out of some of our meetings with companies, and you can say, 'Gosh, I probably know more about this company than anyone else at this moment'. It is Jim Slater's Zulu Principle at work: if you are the expert on something, however small it may be in the broader context of things, you have an advantage over other people.[9] I want to put my bets on things where I have some advantage over others. We're also using the power of Fidelity as one of the biggest investors in the world to get access to companies and information. I am not talking about inside information, but about lots of little bits of things that when you put them together gives you a better informed view than the average investor."[10]

---

[9] Jim Slater was a high-flying financier in the bull market before last, the one that ended in the late 1960s/early 1970s. His credo, dubbed the Zulu Principle after a remark by his wife, has always been that the way to success is to know a lot about a little. See chapter 8.

[10] Under modern insider trading laws, it is illegal to buy or sell shares on the basis of information which is not publicly available.

PROSPERING IN EUROPE

One of the notable things about Bolton's career is that he has managed to demonstrate that his stockpicking methods can work in two distinct investment arenas. Very few fund managers succeed in running an active equity portfolio in both the UK and European markets simultaneously, as he has done. (Nils Taube is one, but there are not many others.) Bolton's early interest in European stocks can be explained in part by his desire to be looking for shares where other investors are not. "I started getting interested in Europe in the early 1980s. For somebody who likes unresearched stocks, Europe was amazing at that time, because it was completely undercovered. The stock markets were very unsophisticated in the way they reacted to news. Now that has changed dramatically; not completely, but it has changed dramatically."

Traditionally, fund managers had tended to regard the UK and Europe as quite distinct sectors. "You put your linguists onto Continental Europe", he recalls, "but it was very much the poor relation. Your best people were in the UK, America and Japan, and then Continental Europe was last." The combination of unsophisticated markets and limited competition made Europe look a good bet at the time, though Bolton adds: "As I was useless at languages, I was probably the last person who should have been put onto Europe. But at least I knew a bit about investment, so I was able to spot things that others had not."

There are good reasons why European stocks are harder for investors trained in the UK to analyse than their American or British counterparts. Accounting conventions are different, for example; the level of information disclosure has historically been less good; and in countries such as France, there are often complex cross-holdings and ownership structures to resolve as well. If you think earnings figures are unreliable in the UK, then the figures reported by Continental companies are much worse. Bolton therefore prefers to rely on other types of valuation ratio, such as the ratio of enterprise value to cash flow, in preference to conventional price/earnings ratios.[11] This, he points out, is how most companies value each other when weighing up whether or not to make a takeover bid which makes it a useful tool for investors too — especially ones who, like Bolton, are interested in spotting potential bid targets.

FIDELITY EUROPEAN 1985-2002
Value of £1,000 invested at launch

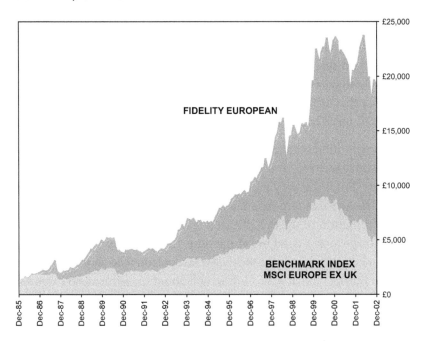

The way Fidelity goes about analysing European shares is to compare sector valuations from one country to another. "Someone will look at, say, the food retailers here, Sainsbury's and Tesco, and then compare the valuations with the Carrefour, and so on, on the Continent. I believe that

---

[11] To work out an enterprise to cash flow ratio, you take the economic value of the company - the market capitalisation of its shares and its net debt, added together – and divide it by gross cash flow (roughly speaking, operating profit plus depreciation).

if you are looking at an Italian insurance company, you want to look at it first through the eyes of someone who knows about insurance, and only later through the eyes of someone who knows all about Italy. The things you have learnt in the more sophisticated markets such as the UK and America help you to spot anomalies and opportunities in Europe. That is generally what I try to do." Sometimes the trend actually works the other way round. Bolton bought shares in British Energy, the privatised company which runs the country's nuclear power stations, not just because other investors were reluctant to buy – 'nuclear' being a classic 'bad smell' word – but because similar European utilities were trading on higher multiples and there was less of a 'nuclear discount'.

Wherever he is investing, Bolton has always been careful not to base the case for owning the shares he buys on broad macroeconomic grounds alone. (In the same way he makes little attempt to try and time the market.) In economic terms, he once told me, the macro argument for being an owner of European equities, for example, was "not that great". He reckoned that the drive towards federalism in Europe was actually quite negative for growth. But that was counterbalanced in the early years by the structural changes which have made equities more popular on the Continent, and companies much more open in the amount of information that they will disclose to investors. German companies, says Bolton, are the only ones which still adopt the traditional Continental habit of refusing to see investors who want to come and visit them, but even that is now slowly changing for the better.

Bolton's European portfolios were run on broadly the same principles as his UK ones, but with a greater bias towards larger companies. The primary emphasis was still on small and medium-sized companies, with a market capitalisation in the £50 million to £500 million range, but there was a large leavening (about 25% of the portfolio) of leading companies too. He says he found there were fewer turnaround situations than in the UK but more companies selling at a discount to their asset value. One reason for this is that the potential for takeover has historically been much greater in the UK than in most European countries. Companies which sell at a discount to their asset value for too long are liable to find themselves bid for in the UK market. By contrast, contested takeovers are much rarer on the Continent, where banks, rather than institutional investors, are the dominant shareholders. The main thing that differentiated him from the competition was that his approach was resolutely bottom-up. Many other European funds are run on asset allocation grounds — so much in France, so much in Germany — but Bolton's funds are driven almost exclusively by where he finds the best value.

As a result, the shape of his funds looked very different to that of his average competitor: for much of the 1990s, for example, they were heavily weighted towards Scandinavian countries. This is partly, he says now, because companies in the northern countries of Europe are more willing to talk to investors, and to take shareholder interests into account, than they are in, say, France or Italy. But it also reinforces the basic premise that Bolton brings to his investment approach: namely, that if you do the same as everybody else, then you will end up performing just the same way. In fact, it would be an affront to Bolton's entire philosophy if he found that his portfolios had the same weightings as the rest of his competitors. They rarely do, as the analysis by outside fund analysts repeatedly demonstrates.

He does however keep an eye on the overall balance of the portfolio to make sure that it has not become too reliant on any one theme or market; in his European funds, for example, with the exception of the major markets (Germany, France, Switzerland and Holland), no other country ever exceeded 20% of the total. The same goes for his UK funds, where his weightings in the various market sectors, regularly recorded in his funds' annual reports, bear only a tangential relationship to the market as a whole. He sees no point in trying to stack the odds against himself by filling his funds with shares in one sector, just because that is what everyone else is doing, when he would rather be buying more attractively priced shares in another. Except in very exceptional circumstances, however, such as the height of the bull market in 1999-2000, when he owned virtually nothing in the modish TMT sectors, it is rare for him to have no exposure at all to a sector. The main way that Bolton manages risk in his portfolios is by making sure that no single bet can put his whole fund at risk: it is unusual for any holding to exceed 3% of the total fund, or for him to be more than 30% 'overweight' in any one sector.

LOOKING BEYOND THE UK

Although he gave up his European responsibilities between 2001 and 2003, the legacy of Bolton's time running money outside the boundaries of the UK persists. The UK Special Situations fund has a remit that allows him to invest up to 20% of the fund outside the UK; and the opportunity is one of which Bolton has regularly taken advantage. Indeed, although he only occasionally approaches the 20% threshold these days, in the 1980s he sometimes had as much as 25% in holdings classified as being outside the UK at balance sheet date. The early reports by the Special Situations Trust are punctuated by the sudden emergence of obscure overseas companies that subsequently disappear as fast as they appear. In September 1981, for example, he had more than 5% of the fund in both Norway and Australia, mainly in the form of oil and mining stocks. Five years later a crop of Italian shares appear fleetingly in the portfolio. At another point he is reported to have been buying Eurobond warrants. In the 1990s Bolton again built up positions in Norwegian oil companies; and more recently, he has taken advantage of the economic boom in China to invest in a number of companies there.

Although it inevitably confounds the 'thought police' in the investment consultancy world, whose sophisticated analytical models depend on the funds they analyse displaying so-called 'style purity', the ability to invest in other areas adds a further moneymaking dimension to Bolton's armoury. His rationale is simple: "Investing in other countries is something that I have always done. It fits in with my style and has served the fundholders well. There is no reason not to go on doing so, particularly where I have a special knowledge of a market or industry."[12] That said, he emphasises that the overseas stocks he buys are almost always those that aren't well followed by other analysts, or ones where he believes he can bring some kind of personal competitive advantage to bear. Although he has occasionally owned some American stocks they won't be well-known names, but smaller companies that typically may have a particular British angle – for example, Cadiz Inc, a Californian company that owns water

---

[12] That said, the non-UK exposure makes it harder to make fair comparisons between his fund and that of other UK equity funds, which may be 100% invested in the UK.

rights in the United States and is listed on an American stock exchange, but was mainly financed by British investors and is run by a British CEO. By the same token, when he owned shares in TNT, the Australian transport company, 80% of its business was in Europe at the time.

His years of tramping round Europe, calling on companies means that he still has a solid core of knowledge on which to draw, and he has increased his holdings of European shares in his UK funds since giving up responsibility for Fidelity's European funds. They continue to add a bit of spice to the portfolio. His interest in China, meanwhile, is driven in part by a bargain-hunter's sense of value, but also by a feeling that this is now the most promising part of the world for any investor to be looking for new stocks. In the autumn of 2004, he spent two weeks in China and Hong Kong, visiting some forty companies. Shortly afterwards he also paid a visit to India. His verdict: "China interests me for three reasons. One is that it is one of the most exciting places that I have come across in recent times to find new stocks. The second is that China has become such an important factor in determining what happens to the rest of the world from an investment perspective. Going there and finding out what is happening on the ground gives me a good chance of establishing an advantage over other investors. Finally, having given up my European responsibilities, learning about a new area is itself a new mental challenge, something to keep me interested and on my toes."

Fidelity has a local research team based in the Far East, and Bolton has been using his experience of watching the European markets develop to help them spot the companies that he believes have the greatest potential for the future. The biggest risk for investors in China is not finding attractive buying opportunities, he says, but the corporate governance system (that is, the answer to the question "Will you get your money back?") is not as certain as it could be. This is one reason why the few investments Bolton has made to date are mostly in firms that have established Western partners. The Chinese stocks remain a modest proportion of his overall portfolio. He says, surprisingly, that he has never stopped to work out whether his overseas holdings have contributed materially to his performance over the years. The chart below, which measures the size of his non-UK holdings over many years, underlines the important role that they have played in the fund's history.

MORE INTERNATIONAL THAN IT LOOKS
Proportion of assets in Fidelity Special Situations by location

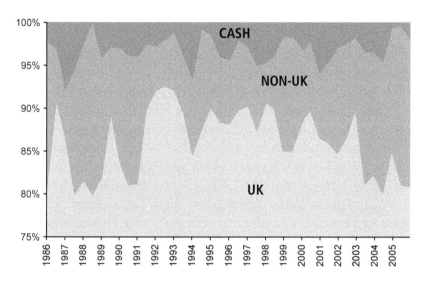

WHERE THE IDEAS COME FROM

Bolton says that his ideas rarely come as bolts from the blue, but accumulate in his mind until he has a conviction that something is the right thing to buy or sell. You need both knowledge of what constitutes a good company and an insight into how a company of its type should be valued. It is then a question of spotting anomalies, assimilating new information as it comes in and waiting for convictions to develop. "Conviction waxes and wanes and a lot of the time you're uncertain about everything, but when you do get a strong conviction, then it is important to back it strongly." In other words, when he feels strongly that he has found a winner, he will put a lot of money behind it, even if that means making his funds more heavily concentrated than many of his rivals. Even so, unless a large line of shares suddenly becomes available, his normal style is to build his positions in stages, testing the water with an initial purchase and then, if the market action supports his idea, to add to it as his conviction grows. He freely confesses that he is not always sure, even after making a sizeable investment, that he has done the right thing. "Some seem to think people like myself are hugely sure about what they are doing all the time", he told an interviewer in 2002, "but this business is not like that. You are in a constant state of questioning your convictions."[13]

Unlike 'buy and hold' investors, who like to hold shares for long periods, Bolton's policy is normally to sell shares as soon as they have become fully valued. At that point, it is time to move on to something else. His normal time frame for an investment is one to two years, though in exceptional cases it may be much longer. That helps to explain why turnover in his portfolios is reasonably high: something like 70% of the portfolio turns over every year. This is what comes from being an investor who looks for pricing anomalies and draws his ideas from so many sources. It is not the style of, say, Ian Rushbrook. Nevertheless, when I asked Bolton who had influenced him most as an investor, the first name he mentioned was Warren Buffett, even though the latter's style as an investor could not be more different. Although he owns nothing like as many stocks and deals only rarely, Buffett was responsible, says Bolton, for implanting in him two ideas: the value of companies with strong business franchises, and the value of businesses that are capable of generating free cash flow.

He also says he takes on board 'a lot of the Peter Lynch approach', which he defined as 'hands-on investment, seeing the companies, the strong view that if you predict earnings, you predict share prices'. Finally, he also echoed Nils Taube's view that, in one sense, the game of successful professional investment is also about plagiarism: looking for good ideas that other people have had, and copying them like mad when you find them. Rather like the stocks he buys, which come in all shapes and sizes, Bolton has something of a 'Smorgasbord approach' when it comes to

---

[13] Citywire Funds Insider April 2002. He also said in this interview: "Investment is a funny combination of being flexible and open-minded at times, and at others having the conviction to back something you feel is mis-priced and undervalued."

articulating the major influences of his investment style. There is, for example, an obvious tension between his desire to be a contrarian and his willingness to look at charts to see what other investors have been buying and selling. And although he is known, and regards himself as a 'value investor', he clearly also has a keen eye for a company that others might more readily classify as 'growth stock'.[14]

USING TECHNICAL ANALYSIS

Bolton is unusual among top-class investors in admitting quite happily that he has always used a lot of technical analysis, or charts, to support his investment analysis. A chartist in investment terms is someone who attempts to predict future winners and losers in the stock market by analysing the past performance of shares, using a variety of techniques which vary, quite literally, from the sublime to the ridiculous. The rationale for technical analysis is that it is possible to make deductions about the next movement in a share's price from the information contained in its recent price history. From the early days of Mister Johnson, Fidelity has always recognised that technical analysis has a place in an investor's armoury, so much so that all its investment management offices, including the London one, have chart rooms where scores of printed charts, some almost as big as plate glass windows, are displayed on banks of wooden screens ranged around the walls.

What chartists look for, typically, are common patterns which they believe signal a future change in a share's direction. Many investors regard this form of investment analysis as dangerous nonsense, although it has a long history and has proved remarkably resilient. The American writer and investment counsellor John Train speaks for most of the sceptics when he

---

[14] In reality, the line between 'growth' and 'value' is a blurred one – a fast growing company can offer value by being too lowly rated, even though it fails to meet the conventional value stock criteria such as an above average dividend yield, or a low price to book value. One of Bolton's greatest successes was spotting Nokia long before it became a world leading mobile phone company.

says, "I find charting as a matter of practical experience to be useless." Thirty years ago, Jim Slater won an easy laugh from his audiences by observing that chartists usually had "dirty raincoats and large overdrafts". The conventional thing to ask is: 'When did you last see one who looks rich?'

But Bolton is not so sceptical.[15] He uses charts to help screen out possible buying ideas, and as an early warning signal that something may be going wrong at a company he already owns. He finds technical analysis particularly useful when looking at large companies, as he increasingly has to do, given the size of his funds. GlaxoSmithKline is a good example. It is a world-class drugs company, and a leading blue chip share, but its shares, Bolton notes, are unusually volatile for such a large company. It goes from being "very in favour to very out of favour", even though the fundamentals of the business are well known. Looking at the charts on companies such as Glaxo often gives Bolton a first clue about when it is about to move into a new phase of its cycle. He has experimented with a number of different services over the years, but now relies mainly on Fidelity's own in-house technical analysts and an American service, QAS, for international stocks. The great advantage of the American service is that it routinely classifies where in the cycle the charts suggest each of the leading stocks in its universe has reached.

One day when I was in his office, Bolton gave me two topical examples of how charts had helped his thinking. One was the French computer company Axime, which he had owned for some time. It looked reasonably valued compared to other international computer companies. As he liked the sector, it was a stock he would normally have been looking to buy more of, but the charts suggested that the shares were in the process of 'topping out' on technical grounds, and this had made him cautious instead. A second example was the French television company TF1. Having owned

---

[15] Nor actually now is Slater. He too says there is value to be had in looking at charts to see how the balance between buyers and sellers is shaping up.

it for ages, not only had the Fidelity in-house analyst turned negative on the shares, but the charts were also suggesting that the technical position of the shares was deteriorating. So Bolton sold out of his position completely. The reason why charts do have some value, he explains, is that they give important clues about the current balance of advantage between buyers and sellers: they are the footprints which investors have left behind them.

COPING WITH SETBACKS

Despite his spectacular long term record, life has not always gone smoothly for Bolton as an investor. His biggest setback came in the 1990-91 recession, when his funds suddenly started to perform very badly. His run until then had been quite spectacular. In its first ten years, the Special Situations fund clocked up a cumulative return of more than 1,000%, a pace that was clearly unsustainable. The fund recorded nine years of positive returns out of ten: not only that, the nine good calendar years all delivered an annual return of more than 23%, an incredible run, even for a roaring bull market (not least because the decade included 1987, the year when Wall Street fell by a quarter in just a few days). Ironically enough, because the fund's reporting period never ran to the end of the calendar year, and the movement in the fund's asset value was quite volatile, Bolton's reports to shareholders are surprisingly often taken up with explaining away shorter periods of relatively poor results. By chance, one of the fund's reports appeared in October 1987, only days before so-called 'Black Monday', with this hapless statement: "Although valuation levels are high and the poor performance of gilts is a cause for concern, at the moment we believe the bull market is not yet over." In one sense, this was correct: the market did make a strong recovery from the October 1987 crash and the bull market powered on for anther two years, but the timing, to put it mildly, could have been better.[16]

---

[16] The statement nonetheless underlines the dangers in making forward market projections, something Bolton usually tries to avoid wherever possible.

By the start of the 1990s however, a recession did hit both the UK economy and the financial markets hard. In 1990, the fund lost 28.8% of its value in a year, a bad hit. In 1991, the return was a positive one, but only just (3.0%). A number of Bolton's holdings, instead of recovering from the economic downturn, as he had expected, simply went bust on him instead. Fund management, being a highly competitive business, can also be rather bitchy, and there were a lot of mutterings around the City that the great Bolton, whose reputation as the best performing manager in his sector was by then already known, had lost his touch. For the first time in its history, the fund's five-year performance record fell behind that of the FTSE All-Share Index. In its October 1991 report, Fidelity reported: "The last six months have continued to be a very depressing period for investors in this Trust and they are owed a detailed explanation of why this was the case and what went wrong. In the last report we wrote that we believed a new strong upward trend or 'bull phase' had started in the UK market and that – as in past cycles – it had started in the recession and before the recovery is clear..... We were too early in identifying a better environment for the type of company which accounts for the majority of the portfolio." One shareholder was so disgruntled at the decline in the fund's fortunes that he wrote to tell Bolton that his performance was so bad that he ought to be outside "sweeping the streets", a comment that is now immortalised in a cartoon on the wall of his office.

MOSTLY, NOT ALWAYS SUPERIOR
Difference in rolling one and three year returns
Fidelity Special Situations vs FTSE All-Share Index

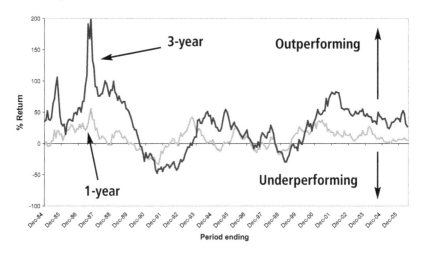

Bolton, his own harshest critic, conceded later that this was his toughest period. In hindsight, the downturn of 1990-1991 can be seen for what it proved to be, namely an 18-month setback on the way to a renewed long run of future superior performance. At the time it was nothing like so obvious. "I did a lot of soul searching in the early 1990s, when I had a bad patch", he told me in 1998. "If you hit a bad economic recession, it is obviously bad for my type of investing. But the question was: should I change my approach or not? Thank goodness, I didn't because that would have been the kiss of death. If you start doing a type of investment that you don't feel confident in, that's where you become completely unstuck." Since then, he and his colleagues at Fidelity have put a lot more effort into tracking 'z scores' and other tools used by credit analysts for spotting potential corporate failures.[17] The implication at the time was that Bolton had been skimping a bit on his homework. He denies that charge, but admits that he has learnt a lot from his experience at the time.

---

[17] 'z scores' are composite ratios which analyse the strength or weakness of a company's finances and have been shown to be successful at highlighting impending insolvencies.

His argument was then, and has been ever since, that the above average-volatility of his funds is something that both he and his investors simply have to learn to live with. "In recession, the kind of medium-sized companies that I invest in will often fall further than the big cap companies. It is a price that I have to pay. There is little I can do about it." His attitude now, he told me, is: "I don't mind buying a high risk, badly financed company provided I know the business well. It was the few where the finances were far worse than we realised that hurt us. We don't want to make that mistake again. That is why we do a lot more balance sheet work now." Another reason why his shares underperformed so badly during the 1990-91 recession may ironically, he thinks now, have been a result of the Fidelity policy of staying close to the companies they own. What made that particular recession different from previous ones was that even the companies which suffered most from the economic change were taken aback by the scale of the downturn. There was, for example, no cluster of share sales by directors which is what you would normally expect if the companies had been fully aware of what was about to hit them.

But while he is open about the above average volatility of his funds, he has come to the conclusion that "I have an approach that delivers in the medium and longer term. Why mess it up because once in a while people have an uncomfortable period?"[18] In any case, he says, good investment managers should not be over sensitive about their failures. Taking their lumps is part of the business. "You have to be comfortable in taking a different view from most other people. Most people like it if five people tell them they're right – that makes them feel more confident. I am not a very emotional person, and I think that's the only way you can run money. You've got to be very unemotional about stocks, and you have to be prepared to say you were wrong. This is the sort of business where you get bitten by the bug. It's constantly changing, constantly challenging. You must change with the changing climate, and not fall in love with what worked last year or the year before. Just as importantly, you need the support of an employer who is prepared to ride over the lumpy periods."[19]

---

[18] Interview with *Bloomberg*, January 1997.
[19] Quoted in *Financial Adviser*, October 1991.

THE BULL MARKET AND BEYOND

In the event, the 1990s proved to be a good, though not the best, decade of Bolton's career. Perhaps it had something to do with the fact that he was by now running two large pools of money, one for European stocks and the other his UK funds, but there were times when Bolton's UK funds, measured by their rolling three and five year performance, for once failed to beat their benchmarks by a handsome margin. True, investors in the Special Situations fund still had good cause to be happy, as their absolute returns were invariably positive. The average five-year return on the fund for investors who joined since January 1990 has been 106%, against 65% for the FTSE All-Share Index. But style trends in the market do not always favour Bolton's approach, and his relative performance, in the UK at least, suffered for a while, not least towards the end of the bull market when euphoria reached a new and unsustainable peak.

In 1998, Bolton told me in an interview for *Institutional Investor* magazine that he could not recall a time in his career when small and medium company shares, of the kind he favours, were so shunned by other investors – or so attractively valued for a bargain-hunting investor. He was right, but the market being as always a slave to fashion, and soon to be bewitched by the wonders of the internet craze, investors studiously ignored him for nearly 18 months. The discount on his investment trust, a barometer of his fund's standing in the eyes of the market, widened to an unprecedented 25%, creating a rare (and so far unrepeated) opportunity for savvy investors to buy into his stockpicking skills on the cheap. Shares in the investment trust, which owns almost exactly the same shares as the Special Situations unit trust, went to a premium in 2001 and have rarely gone to a discount since. Over the five years to the end of 2003, the unit trust produced a return of 120% and the investment trust 168%, in a period when the market itself, reeling from the bear market, lost 5% of its value.

In fact, the way that Bolton's funds have performed since the end of the great bull market has revealed another side to his talents as an investor. While he made his name by outperforming the market on the way up, his performance since the market peaked in March 2000 has, if anything, been even more impressive. It has certainly reinforced his reputation. As we now know, the pricing of the internet bubble, and the associated fashion for 'TMT stocks' (telecom, media and technology shares), was followed by the severest bear market for a generation. From its peak in March 2000 to its nadir in March 2003, the UK stock market, as measured by the FTSE All-Share Index, fell by nearly 50%. The great majority of actively managed equity funds tanked with it.

Many of the managers whose funds had soared in the last stages of the bull market turned out to be paper tigers, or one-trick ponies; scores of aggressively managed funds lost 70% or more of their investors' money. By rights Bolton's fund too, being of above average risk according to conventional classifications, should have suffered more than the market. Yet Fidelity Special Situations, while not immune from the market decline, has suffered nothing like as much, as these figures show. In fact, his was one of only a handful of funds that managed to produce a positive return over the period March 2000 – March 2003.[20] When the bull market resumed in the spring of 2003, the fund resumed its superior winning ways, outperforming the market once more on the way up, as it had done on the way down.

	BOLTON	MARKET	DIFFERENCE
MID 1990s BULL MARKET March 1993 - March 1996	73.2%	48.5%	24.7%
LATE BULL MARKET March 1996 - March 1999	40.3%	71.2%	-30.9%
LAST YEAR OF BULL MARKET March 1999 - March 2000	29.3%	9.9%	19.4%
BEAR MARKET March 2000 - March 2003	3.8%	-39.3%	43.1%
RECOVERY March 2003 - August 2006	144.8%	93.8%	51.0%

[20] The difference between the fall in the FTSE All-Share Index of nearly 50% and the total return loss of 39.3% shown in the table is accounted for by dividends. In this book all comparisons between the performance of Fidelity Special Situations (which does not pay a dividend) and the FTSE All-Share Index (many of whose component companies do) are adjusted for dividends to ensure a like-for-like comparison.

There are a number of reasons, Bolton says, why his performance has continued to be so strong. One can be traced back to the months before the market peaked, when shares in three sectors of the market, telecommunications, technology and media, all loosely and indiscriminately linked to the emergence of the internet, were so 'hot' that their valuations lost all touch with reality. At one point these three sectors accounted for some 40% of the entire value of the UK stock market. Yet Bolton owned virtually none of them: refusing to abandon his value disciplines, he was quietly loading up on scores of other shares whose prices had been untouched by the market bubble, and indeed were trading at what, historically, were absurdly low ratings.

That led his fund to lag the market at the time, but ensured that once the bubble burst, his performance would recover strongly. Alex Hammond-Chambers, the chairman of Fidelity Special Values, thinks this was one of Bolton's finest hours. "At the time, there was nothing unusual about having nearly half your portfolio in the TMT stocks, because that was where the index was and everybody else was doing it. But if you want to be a special investor, and you are naturally risk-averse, you have got to do what you believe is right, and absolutely not be swayed by the herd. Most fund managers are lemmings, and Anthony is the absolute antithesis of a lemming." In particular he did not fall into the trap of thinking that just because a stock in the most favoured sectors was trading on half the price-earnings multiple of the market leaders, it had therefore to be cheap. As it turned out, even the 'cheapest' stocks in the TMT arena were grossly overvalued.

A second reason why the UK funds have done so well since the bull market ended is that value investing as a discipline, having been increasingly overlooked as investors chased ever more improbable technology-fuelled growth stories during the boom, came back into fashion. Almost overnight, shares that paid dividends and enjoyed high dividend yields, or traded on low multiples of earnings or book value, the classic value criteria, started to come back into favour. As a value-minded investor, Bolton was always likely to do relatively well in this climate. At the same time, the period since 2000 has been one in which small and medium-sized companies as a group have, for the most part, outperformed larger stocks. This too has helped Bolton's performance, as did the fact that in 1999 an exceptionally large number of stocks in his portfolio were taken over.

Even so, to outperform the market and his peers so handsomely during the bear market underlines that his success is anything but a bull market phenomenon. Although he insists that he is primarily a stockpicker, not a market timer, Bolton has since shown too that he has developed an informed better nose for the currents that are running through the market. In the spring of 2003, to the surprise of his audience at the time, who had mostly never heard him offer such a definitive view on the market before, he correctly called the bottom of the bear market, almost to the day. This was no idle comment either. A few weeks earlier he had, it turns out, suggested to the board of his investment trust, Fidelity Special Values, that it would be a good moment to consider increasing the amount of gearing in the fund to take advantage of an expected upturn in the market.[21] Three years later, in the spring of 2006, having given some public warnings about his feeling that the bull market had largely run its course, Bolton reversed tack, suggesting to the board that it should eliminate all the fund's gearing and take out a put option to protect the value of the fund against a possible general fall in share prices. This again proved to be a timely and profitable call.

INTO THE LIMELIGHT: THE ITV SAGA

Bolton has always taken care to develop and sustain good relationships with financial advisers and the media, recognising that they are the two external groups that have the most influence over the direction of fund flows in the UK. While he responds regularly to requests to give interviews and presentations, it would be wrong to describe him as a publicity-seeker.

---

[21] Bolton made his remarks at a seminar for financial advisers organised by Jupiter Asset Management (at which the author was present). It is not clear whether he realised that his prediction was going to be reported in the media. I suspect not.

Though happy to talk about the markets and his current thinking, it is not his style to gossip about his competitors, or to use the media to talk up the shares in his fund, as some professional investors have been known to do. That kind of approach does not sit easily with his character. When he does talk to outsiders, he tends to err on the side of caution, being measured to the point sometimes of blandness in his comments about companies and their managers.

Those who know him well were therefore surprised to find his name being spread all over the business news pages in the summer of 2003 as the alleged leader of 'a plot' to oust the leaders of the two largest surviving independent television companies, Carlton and Granada. According to the *Sunday Times*, in a front page story in its business section, "the City's most respected fund manager" was canvassing the television industry for candidates to replace both Michael Green, the chairman of Carlton, and Charles Allen, his counterpart at Granada, when the two companies merged. The merger was something that the two companies had announced they were planning to do a few weeks earlier. The paper went on to quote an unnamed City analyst describing Bolton as "the City's quiet assassin".

It was a vivid phrase, one that helped to give the story a striking headline. In reality, Bolton's stance was at that stage merely that of the concerned shareholder. He had been an investor in both Carlton and Granada since at least 2001. This is how he recalls the matter now: "I did not propose the idea of merger between the two companies, but once it had been aired as a possibility, I was definitely in favour. There were some obvious inefficiencies in the existing ITV structure, and I could see that the merger was capable of bringing great benefits, provided that it was structured in the right way." Over a period of weeks he talked to a number of people in the media industry to canvas their views on who should best run ITV if the merger of Carlton and Granada was to go through. He had not at this stage, he says, talked to any other shareholders in the two companies concerned. The story of what the paper chose to call Bolton's "back-room plotting" was, he discovered, leaked to the *Sunday Times* by a senior figure in the media industry, for reasons that remain unknown.

The biggest hurdle to any merger at that stage was whether or not the Competition Commission, to whom the matter had been referred, would allow the two largest ITV companies to put their businesses together. When he raised his concerns with the companies or their advisers, their line, Bolton recalls, was always that raising issues about the structure of the new merged company while the commission was still debating the issue would "rock the boat". It could even, he was told, threaten the chances of a deal taking place. Once the initial story came out, Bolton therefore opted to keep his counsel until the Competition Commission had reached its decision, something he now rather regrets, while continuing to canvas opinion in private. Fidelity put out a carefully worded press release after the *Sunday Times* story, saying that it supported the merger proposal 'in all respects', but pointedly (in its own opinion, at least) saying nothing specific about the management issue.[22]

It was not until the autumn of 2003, when the Commission finally cleared the idea of a merger, that Bolton and his colleagues decided to press the issue of who would run the company in the event of a merger going through. The proposal from the two companies was that the top jobs should be shared between the top executives of each company, with Michael Green, chairman of Carlton, taking the chairman's job in the new company, and Charles Allen of Granada, becoming chief executive. There was a general recognition, says Bolton, that if any changes to the proposed management of the company were going to be made, they would have to be agreed before the listing particulars for the newly merged company were finalised. Time was therefore short. The need for urgency, coupled with the strength of some of the personalities involved, played a part in turning what began as a serious but not terminal point of difference into a headline-grabbing showdown between the two companies and their leading institutional shareholders, all played out in a blaze of media publicity.

---

[22] William Lewis, the editor of the *Sunday Times* business section at the time, disputes that the statement could be read as anything other than a denial that Fidelity was seeking management changes.

Although Bolton was the first person inside Fidelity to express concerns about the management of the merged entity, he was by no means the only player involved. Other fund managers in the Fidelity stable also owned sizeable shareholdings in the two companies, and it quickly became a matter for the company's senior management team as a whole to handle. When Fidelity went to talk to the non-executive directors of the two companies, Bolton was typically accompanied by Simon Fraser, the chief investment officer, and Trelawny Williams, the recently appointed director responsible for corporate governance. In fact, at one meeting that the trio attended, Fraser recalls, Bolton said nothing at all, somewhat scotching the idea that he was the sole driving force behind an activist shareholder plot.

THE BATTLE INTENSIFIES

What is not in dispute is that the non-executive directors of the ITV companies expressed doubt at their meetings with Fidelity whether its reservations were in fact shared by other shareholders. It was only at that point, says Bolton, that he and his colleagues set out to canvas the views of other large institutional shareholders. Fidelity's contacts with several other institutions revealed that there was near-universal support for his views about the undesirability of Green and Allen splitting the top jobs between them. The two men were known not to be huge admirers of each other and could hardly have been more different in personality and behaviour. The proposed board structure looked, as it clearly was, a compromise that owed more to realpolitik than to the best interests of the merged business. Bolton and his Fidelity colleagues thought it imperative that there should be an independent non-executive chairman instead, capable of holding the ring between the two merger partners. This view was relayed back to the two companies, both directly in meetings with the non-executive directors, and indirectly through the companies' banking and broking advisers.

All this while the business sections of the national newspapers, having spotted a good story in the making, continued to give the ITV saga prominent coverage. To Bolton's intense irritation, they continued to present the issue in a highly personalised way, making out that he was using his position as a leading shareholder to pursue a personal vendetta against the top management of the two ITV companies. The 'quiet assassin' epithet, once coined, proved hard to shake off. This was far from fair, though doubtless it suited the other shareholders involved to allow Fidelity to take most of the public heat. Inside Fidelity, it is clear that the issue of how to deal with this unexpected publicity attracted a lot of head-scratching. Making waves in public is most definitely not the house style, though in retrospect it is not easy to see how the publicity that surrounded the ITV story could have done anything but enhance the firm's reputation. Bolton was careful to say throughout that there was nothing personal in his attempts to block the original proposals. If Allen rather than Green had been proposed as chairman, he would still have sought the appointment of an independent chairman from outside the business.

In the end, when it came to a showdown, the ITV companies relented, though only at the last minute. This was virtually inevitable once the boards were confronted with evidence that so many of their largest shareholders were opposed to the original proposed boardroom structure. The board of Granada was the first to blink, deciding that the proposals could not go through as originally planned. Their decision was seen as something of a betrayal at Carlton, which then reluctantly followed suit. The Carlton chairman, Michael Green, was the one who departed, leaving Charles Allen of Granada in place as the chief executive of the newly merged company. Some time later, Sir Peter Burt, the former governor of Bank of Scotland, and a man with a reputation for toughness, accepted the job of ITV chairman and in due course confirmed the appointment of Allen as chief executive. Bolton, who had earlier touted another name as a possible chairman, says he was happy with the choice and remains a shareholder in the new ITV company. Its subsequent performance has, however, been a continued disappointment, implying that his original pressure for change was more than justified.

In hindsight, could the whole messy ITV saga have been avoided with more careful handling on all sides? Given the high stakes involved for those on the company side, arguably not. Bolton's view throughout was that the row would best have been dealt with quietly behind closed doors, as happens, he claims, in a good many other corporate governance cases that never reach the public eye. The ITV saga is interesting mainly because it points to the growing influence that institutional shareholders as a group are now starting to exert on the behaviour of quoted companies, something which they have been criticised for not doing in the past. In an interview with *Real IR* magazine in 2004, Bolton said that Fidelity typically intervenes in some 50 cases a year, of which only a fraction are likely to be reported. While it remains the job of company boards to decide how businesses should be run, he says that Fidelity expects to be consulted about big strategic decisions, such as M&A proposals, or disposals of business, that are likely to rebound on the value of the company's shares.

The irony is that if whoever leaked the original story intended to try and spike Bolton's guns, it probably had the reverse effect: once challenged by the companies to prove his views were widely shared, Fidelity had no option but to join forces with other leading shareholders and insist on a change. In the process, although he found the intense media coverage uncomfortable, and the 'quiet assassin' tag distressing, the episode has served to underline how much influence Bolton now enjoys in the City. "Because his manner is so quiet", says his colleague Simon Fraser, "it is easy for those who don't know Anthony well to underestimate the strength of his feelings. The non-executive directors of the ITV companies may genuinely not have appreciated initially quite how serious his reservations about the proposed management of the merged company were." When it came to a showdown, however, the fact that Bolton was prepared to put his hard-earned reputation on the line over the issue was clearly a decisive factor in persuading Fidelity to press the issue, and the boards of the two companies to back down. The outcome is one more indication of how far the shy and thoughtful 29-year-old recruit of 1979 with a flair for picking stocks has travelled in the ensuing quarter of a century.

ENTERING THE HOME STRAIGHT

Speculation about when Bolton might decide that enough was enough and hand over his remaining fund management responsibilities has been a perennial topic of discussion in the professional community for several years. Given the size of the fund, and its commercial importance not just to Fidelity, but to those who make a living advising clients on where to invest their money, this was hardly a surprise. Most funds in Britain are sold on a commission basis: that is to say, the financial advisers and other professional intermediaries who recommend the fund to their clients are rewarded by being paid commissions by the fund provider. The typical commission on sales of a fund such as Fidelity Special Situations is of the order of 3% of the value of the initial investment. In addition, although this is less widely known, advisers and others who recommend a fund typically also benefit from an annual "renewal commission" for every year that the investor remains in a fund they have recommended. Renewal fees, sometimes also known as "trail commission", is normally paid at the rate of 0.5% of the current value of the fund.

A back of the envelope calculation therefore suggests that at its peak, with assets of more than £6 billion, Fidelity Special Situations was earning advisers and other intermediaries up to £30 million a year for their foresight in having guided their clients to his fund. While it is not part of this book's remit to analyse the rights and wrongs of the commission system, it is evident that these are significant sums of money (and made all the more agreeable for those who benefit by the fact that the trail commissions roll in every year without the need for additional effort on behalf of the advisers). The question of who would replace Bolton as the manager of his UK fund was always therefore going to be one that commanded close attention. For Fidelity's part, the challenge was to find a replacement who could realistically entertain the hope of continuing in Bolton's footsteps without materially damaging either the interests of the investors, who have done so well from his success in running the fund, or Fidelity's own business, for which Special Situations is the largest single source of revenue. The financial stakes surrounding the succession, in other words, could hardly have been higher.

Bolton himself, it is clear, was determined to take a strong lead in the internal debates with his management colleagues about the best way forward. Rather than handing over the entire Special Situations fund to a single successor, the solution that the company eventually came up with was to propose splitting the fund in two with effect from September 2006 and phase in the handover to two new managers over a period of 15 months. Splitting a fund is something that had never been attempted before in the UK. Half of the assets were to remain in the UK Special Situations fund under Bolton's continued management until his final handover in December 2007, while the balance was to be transferred immediately to a new Global Special Situations fund. This would attempt to do on a global scale what Bolton himself has done so successfully in the UK. After months of speculation about who would be chosen to run the new global fund, Fidelity announced that it would be a hitherto largely unknown Finnish employee of Fidelity named Jorma Korhonen. He would work alongside Bolton in setting up the new fund in September 2006 and take over completely in January 2007. The announcement inevitably attracted acres of newsprint in the national and trade press, confirming the extraordinary high profile that the manager of Fidelity Special Situations enjoys within the fund industry.

While it is possible to feel a measure of sympathy for Mr Korhonen, thrust into the shoes of such a successful predecessor in the full glare of the media spotlight, for Bolton himself the transition is a more ambivalent event, as his own account makes clear. His hands on approach to the task of selling the new arrangements to a sometimes sceptical audience bears testimony to his continuing commitment to Fidelity and the interests of investors in his fund. He publicly extolled the virtues of his chosen successor and talked sincerely of the similarities in their approaches. In private he surely would have been less than human if he were not to worry about what effect the handover might have on his legacy. In one of the many newspaper interviews carried out over the summer of 2006, to coincide with the impending splitting of the fund, he confessed to some anxiety also about how his final year in charge of the remaining UK portion of the Special Situations fund might go. Because market headwinds have been so favourable in recent years, with value as a style of investing enjoying an exceptional run, and his favoured midcap sectors of the stock market comfortably outperforming the other sectors of the market, the risk of those trends reversing and damaging the fund's performance during his last 12 months in charge had clearly crossed his mind.

Time will tell whether such anxieties are justified or not.[23] In the event, the proposal to split the fund was approved by the fundholders in September 2006, with more than 95% of those voting in support. While Fidelity had prepared contingency plans for a possible wave of redemptions, it was clear that the majority of Bolton's investors would do what he urged them to do, which was to give Jorma Korhonen, the first of his two chosen successors, a chance to show what he could do with the new Global Special Situations mandate. Going into his final year in charge, the UK fund meanwhile still had a higher proportion of shares amongst the top 100 quoted companies on the London market than for most of its history. Reduced in size by the split to some £3 billion in assets, the fund surrendered its position as the largest equity fund in the UK to one run by Neil Woodford of Invesco Perpetual, another dyed-in-the-wool value investor whom many in the business regard as the man most likely to succeed to Bolton's long held title as the number one fund manager in this country. What was most striking however about the reams of coverage that filled the newspapers for weeks on end was how little new there was to say about his methods. The markets may move on, but the qualities that make a successful fund manager – discipline, hard work, a phlegmatic temperament and that elusive nose for value – change but little.

INTERPRETING THE PERFORMANCE

For those who appreciate the dynamics of the investment business, the message from the performance of Bolton's funds is an unequivocal one.

---

[23] They were, in the sense that neither the global nor the UK fund have performed as well under their new managers as they did in Bolton's hands. He was however able to retire some months before the 2007-09 bear market, during which the UK stock market lost some 50% of its value.

Three things in particular are striking: the consistency of his funds' performance; the fact that Bolton has managed to build a comparable track record in two major markets (the UK and Europe) at the same time; and the fact that he has been able to sustain his track record despite running a fund that has grown so big that it dwarfs almost every other in the retail fund sector. How can this exceptional performance be explained? And what lessons can investors draw from his success?

Bolton would be the first to admit that he has benefited from running in his fund during a period that has mostly been exceptionally favourable to equity investment. The long and powerful bull market that ran from 1982 to 2000, fuelled by strong disinflationary impulses, was without question the best period in which to own shares in the 20th century. Over those 18 years the annualised return from the stock market (11% per annum in real terms) was 50% greater than the long run historical average for equity investment. It was clearly an exceptional time to be a fund manager; and if ever there was a time to set up shop as a stockpicker, the beginning of the 1980s was that time. The bull market created powerful tailwinds for an aggressive risk-seeking fund manager of Bolton's type.

It was also, we can see now, his good fortune to have the chance to join a world class fund management house just at the point it was launching its push into Europe. At the time, as we have seen, there was no guarantee that Fidelity would enjoy the success that it has done subsequently. In 30 years the firm has gone from nowhere to the number one position in the UK unit trust and OEIC business, where it has an 8% market share of retail sales. As events have turned out, there can have been few more congenial or supportive environments in which to pursue a stockpicking career. As a privately owned company whose sole business is fund management, Fidelity has largely been able to avoid the internal battles and multiple changes of ownership that bedevil the lives of fund managers elsewhere.[24]

---

[24] It may be no accident that the American group Capital International, which is widely regarded as one of the more successful modern fund management groups, is also a private company with a strong internal culture and no distractions from the central fund management effort.

By his own admission, the Fidelity way of doing business, with its intensive focus on research-led equity investment, has suited Bolton well. "Investment people are well protected in Fidelity", says Richard Timberlake, Bolton's first boss, who now runs a fund of funds business that brings him into regular contact with all the main fund management groups. "They don't get drawn into the marketing or administration of the business. Most other fund managers spend a huge amount of their time doing marketing, doing their own admin and doing their own client service. If you can separate the three elements, investment, IT/administration, and marketing, and you can find the best team in each area, and rely on the others to do the other bits, you have a much greater chance of creating a good organisation. In recent years Anthony has been strongly supported by good analysts. I think he is good at getting what he wants from them."

But neither the happy circumstance of his time running money coinciding with a glorious bull market, nor the good fortune of landing his job with such a favourable employer, can fully explain Bolton's success in beating the market so consistently over so many different phases in the market cycle. The fact that he continued to outperform the market by the same margin during the savage bear market that succeeded the bullish conditions of the years up to 2000 is testament to the fact that his working methods capture something that other fund managers seem to lack. Although he has had poor patches in relative terms, some lasting 18 months or more, the longer the holding period in his fund, the better and more consistent its performance has been.

HOW OTHERS SEE IT

Canvassing the opinions of those who have worked closely with Bolton over the years produces a number of explanations for what it is that has helped to make his time as a fund manager so successful. Everyone that I have spoken to has talked eloquently about the discipline with which he approaches his job. According to Sally Walden, who worked alongside him for more than twenty years, Bolton manages his time extremely carefully. "He is not the kind of guy who lingers for a chat at the coffee machine. He goes out of his way to make sure that no part of his working day is wasted. While he is never unpleasant to anyone, he has the knack of letting you know, in the most charming way, when he has got what he wants from you."

Drawing on his many years of working with fund managers, Timberlake says that one of the keys to Bolton's success has been his uncanny ability to measure and interpret what the market's expectations for a share are. "The most important thing to understand about Anthony, in my view, is that he is two-brained. Good fund managers are not usually the first class degrees in maths, or someone who is a brilliant accountant or actuary. They usually make poor fund managers. It is far more important to understand crowd psychology, which is a creative skill. A degree in crowd psychology is a far better qualification than being an accountant or an economist. People who are both right and left brained, as Anthony is, are the ones you want. Not only has he got a first class all round brain, but he also understands the market and crowd psychology. He has a creative side that understands other people's behaviour."

Alex Hammond-Chambers, the chairman of the Fidelity Special Values investment trust, agrees. His view is that Bolton has "the most uncanny knack for understanding what the market is discounting in a stock. There aren't many people who can look at a stock and immediately understand what the market's view is. People think they do. You ask 90% of people what the market thought of Vodafone in March 2000 and they would have been wrong. But Anthony has an instinctive understanding of what the share price is telling him the market thinks about a company, and with his perception and experience, he knows whether to agree or not. If he doesn't agree, then that's a buying opportunity."

Simon Fraser, who worked with Bolton for more than 20 years, latterly as Fidelity's Chief Investment Officer, says that his colleague's confidence in buying unloved stocks is underpinned by his acute sense of what the value of a business is, not just to the stock market but to potential trade or private equity investors as well. "One reason that he is happy to buy illiquid stocks that nobody else is prepared to touch", says Fraser, "is that he knows from his innate sense of value that one day someone will come along and bid for them." His success in finding stocks that are later taken over suggests that this is well-founded. In one miraculous year (1999), 30 companies that he owned that year were the subject of takeover bids or some other form of corporate activity. "At the end of the day successful investment is about seeing things more clearly than the rest of the market and acting on them before everyone else has come to the same conclusion. Anthony has the ability to do it, not just to think or talk about it." The most important thing about Bolton, however, says his colleague Sally Walden, is his temperament, which is unshakeably implacable. A good deal of his intelligence, she thinks, is internalised. "He is a very difficult person to read. What he says always sounds very simple, even simplistic. Quite frankly there a lot of fund managers out there who sound a whole lot better when they get up to speak. But none of them has done anything like as well. Anthony is very dispassionate. Whatever happens, he just gets on with the next job on his list. In my view, there is no question that he is a better fund manager today than he was 15 years ago." His colleague Barry Bateman, makes the same assessment. "Aside from his performance, which has obviously been exceptional, the fact that Anthony is such a nice guy, quiet and not in any way a prima donna, has helped to set the tone for the whole investment operation. Let us face it, many so-called 'star' fund managers can be unreasonable and difficult to manage. We haven't had that problem, and in large part that is because Anthony has set such a tremendous example."

THE QUALITIES GREAT INVESTORS NEED

Peter Jeffreys, who worked alongside Bolton in his early days at Fidelity before leaving to co-found Fund Research with Timberlake, says there is no question in his mind that Bolton is one of the few true 'greats' in the UK fund management industry. "There are a number of attributes common to all good fund managers – knowledge, skill, enthusiasm, dedication and 'love of the game', to list only the more obvious ones. Great fund managers, however, have something extra, something less easily definable, which sets them apart from the field." Bolton shares a number of these attributes with Peter Lynch, Fidelity's high profile fund manager in the United States, with whom, says Jeffreys, he can validly be bracketed. "The most important one I would say is that both are their own men. Anyone who has worked with Anthony will know he possesses an independence of mind that is second to none. When researching a company, he will draw on the widest possible range of fact and opinion, but his final analysis will be driven solely by his judgement of a situation, a company's future prospects, or a share's valuation. He will not be influenced by fashion or fad, or the current market view." It may be no accident that, in contrast to many of his colleagues, Bolton likes to draw on other ideas than simply those generated by Fidelity's research machine.

Alex Hammond-Chambers, who carried out his own analysis of Bolton's performance shortly after being appointed the chairman of Fidelity Special Values, says there are many analogies that you can use about good fund managers. "Jimmy Gammell [the founder and guiding light of the Edinburgh investment house Ivory & Sime] always said that the best analogy was sailing; even though you went sailing from point A to point B, you didn't always just go in a straight line. Sometimes you tacked, sometimes you ran, and sometimes you reached. Sometimes, because the winds were very vicious, you had to pull in a reef or two. In other words, you had to adjust your sail and your sailing to the conditions. That's what investment brains do very well, and that's what Anthony does very well. I think he has a very good hand on the tiller."

According to John Chatfeild-Roberts, who runs a successful fund of funds operation for a rival fund management company, Jupiter Asset Management, and has invested in Fidelity Special Situations for many years, Bolton is a rare example of the 'complete' fund manager. The things Chatfeild-Roberts and his team look for when seeking out the best fund managers are "capacity and desire for hard work, the ability to spot opportunities and act on them quickly and decisively, and the imagination to see further ahead than most around you". Bolton has all three in strong measure. "If you see him on the train home, you will find him reading research which, when read, he then deposits in the litter bin before alighting at his station; this is still as true today as it was twenty years ago. Opportunities? Over the years there have been themes that ran through his portfolio. A recent example was the Lloyd's insurance vehicles, which many people didn't believe, or if they did, sold them too soon to reap the full rewards. Imagination? Well you only have to look at the long term holding in Nokia from the early 1990s, when mobile phones were bricks and most people (myself included) swore blind that we would never countenance having such interruptions. What would we all do without them now? Any one of these abilities may make a good fund manager, but to have all three makes a great one."

Chatfeild-Roberts also speculates that there might be something in the fact that Bolton likes to compose music in his spare time. "It has been found that if you play classical music to babies in the womb this stimulates the parts of the brain responsible for both musical ability and mathematical skills. Anecdotal evidence also suggests a strong link between music and maths. In the University of Oxford, maths students approaching their final exams are reported to have a preference for attending Bach recitals. An innate appreciation of pattern in numbers – which might appear in something mundane as company financial statistics – may therefore be something which helps give Anthony an edge." Bolton himself promised that he would spend more time listening to and composing music when he finally retired at the end of 2007.

Hammond-Chambers adds: "It is the amount of thought that goes into the investments Anthony makes and his ability to think differently from the crowd that more than anything else has enabled him to spot value in a stock in a way that others cannot. The thing I noted was how incredibly few failures he has. He doesn't bomb. He doesn't make big mistakes. I think that's in part because he's so value conscious, so many of the investments he makes don't have a huge big downside. He doesn't chase popular stocks. I'm sure he makes mistakes – we all do – but you need to look at his gains/losses ratio. You normally reckon that a very good portfolio manager is going to get perhaps six pluses, two equals and two minuses for every ten stocks he owns. That will certainly be enough to produce good returns. Anthony does better than that, with the emphasis on very low minuses." The figures given earlier, showing how rarely his fund's loss-making months exceed those of the market as a whole, bear out the truth in this observation.

This in turn plays well with those who make their living out of selling funds. Mark Dampier, head of research at Hargreaves Lansdown, a Bristol-based stockbroker that has grown to become the largest player in the fund broking business, says that while Bolton exudes self-confidence, he lacks the arrogance that is so often the downfall of fund managers. "His style of management is difficult to pin down, but his ability to look at stocks in a different way to the market as a whole seems to be his real talent. In other words, he believes in his own valuation techniques, rather than those employed by others." His investment process, finding cheap stocks that the market has overlooked, is not complicated. "While this style can go out of fashion over certain stock market cycles, particularly when we are in recession, he bounces back strongly and makes up for any losses when it does come back into style. Investors have tended to forget that after the stock market crash of 1987, and through the recession of the early 1990s, Anthony's performance was relatively poor. In order to make money with his fund, you have to be patient and hold him through the hard times. He has rewarded you amply if you do this."

HOW THE PRIVATE INVESTOR CAN PROFIT

Bolton has some excellent advice on how his methods can be adapted by private investors to make money out of investing in smaller companies.[25] This can be summarised as follows:

- Know what you own. Think of what you are doing as buying 100% of a private business rather than a small fraction of a public one. Read as much about the company as you can. Do your own research, rather than relying on tips in newspapers or magazines.

- Concentrate on a few stocks that you can follow closely, rather than a lot which you cannot, and avoid areas such as high technology unless you have a specific personal knowledge of the area and know a lot about what the companies are doing.

- You should be able to sum up in a few sentences the reasons that you own each company in which you have shares. The point about sticking to companies in businesses that you know something about is that "the stock market deals in perceptions: if you know the reality is different, then you may be able to use this to your advantage."

- The best companies to own are ones which are, for reasons that you can readily identify, likely to grow consistently over the long term. This may be a niche area of the market, a product for which there is no substitute or an industry which is unregulated. Ideally, the companies should have some sort of unique franchise and be capable of generating cash.

- In the long term, the ability to produce free cash flow is the most attractive attribute that a company can have. It pays to distinguish between companies whose growth is due to temporary circumstances and those which look more durably based.

- When it comes to rating management, look for those managers who patently have their shareholders' interest as their first priority and who are honest with their investors about their successes and failures.

---

[25] It is contained in a small section of *The FT Global Guide to Investing* (FT Pitman, 1995).

2. ANTHONY BOLTON: The professional's professional

- Try to buy shares when the market is depressed or when a stock is going through a temporary hiccup. Don't sell a share just because it has gone up – i.e. do run your profits. Selling too soon is the best way to miss out on some of the most spectacular winners in the stock market.

- Don't waste time on the futile pastime of trying to guess which way the markets as a whole are going to move. Don't expect too much. You will be doing well if your successes outnumber your failures by a ratio of two to one.

- Given the choice, stick to buying companies which are well financed.

- Ignore directors' dealings at your peril, especially if two or more directors are acting the same way and buying or selling shares in their companies in reasonable size.

If all this sounds rather familiar, then remember finally, says Bolton, that "there is little original thought in investment". If the cardinal sin is to follow what the herd is doing, there is still an awful lot of money to be made by following the ideas of those gifted few who do have the happy knack of being able to sort the wheat from the chaff, and can cock a snook at the prevailing wisdom. To do exceptionally well in the stock market, you have to dare to be different.

UPDATE (2012)

Anthony Bolton retired from running his UK Special Situations fund at the end of December 2007, with his reputation and track record firmly intact. A little over two years later he came out of retirement to launch a new China "special situations" fund for Fidelity, based in Hong Kong. Although this new investment trust raised more than £600m at launch its initial performance has so far been disappointing, with the stock price falling some 30% below its issue price at its lowest point. He remains confident of its longer term potential.

3. IAN RUSHBROOK:

Managing risk in style

Were Hollywood to make a film about this country's stock market millionaires, it is unlikely that for all his virtues Anthony Bolton, the understated Englishman, would land a part. It's a fair bet that Central Casting would be more likely to take a look at Ian Rushbrook. Of all the professional investors in this book, he is the one who – on the surface at least – most closely fulfils the popular image of what a stock market impressario should be. If they ever decided to make a film about the life and times of Bernard Baruch, the legendary Wall Street financier, Ian Rushbrook would make a plausible candidate for the title role.

This is a man who, at the age of 58, still drives a silver Porsche around the unforgiving streets of Edinburgh. He likes to live well: two handsome houses, nice pictures, good food and wine. Champagne is a favoured companion. Rushbrook has made a lot of money out of his investment career and, while no spendthrift, is determined to enjoy it. As fund managers go, his background is unconventional. This is someone who flunked his first attempt at a degree by failing to read the examination instructions, who subsidised his time at the next one by playing high stakes poker and who likes nothing better than stirring up trouble and challenging conventional wisdom. His time at Ivory & Sime, once indisputably the premier investment house in Scotland, was marked in equal measure by great triumphs and the most fearsome internal power struggles, in which Rushbrook's rebarbative personality undoubtedly played a part. While his investment prowess has given him the financial independence he always craved, it is a privilege he uses to the full. He is combative, amusing, opinionated and splendidly intolerant of lesser intellects – in short, extremely good company.

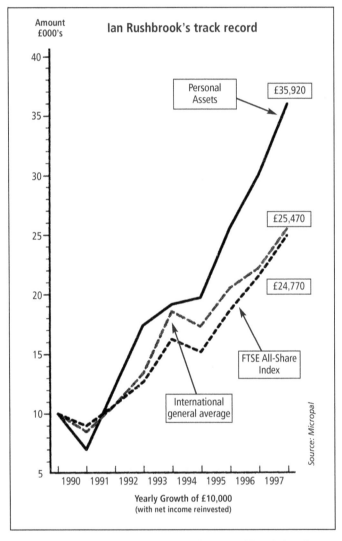

Personal Assets, the exclusive investment trust run by Ian Rushbrook, has done consistently well since he took over as Investment Director in 1990. Note how the rate of growth has continued to outpace the market despite a low turnover rate and a below market degree of risk in the portfolio.

Yet there is also a paradoxical quality about this engaging and unusual character. Ian Rushbrook may be a free spirit, with a great zest for life, but at an age when many successful men are starting to weary of work and head for the golf course, he is also quite astonishingly devoted to his craft, working long hours alone at his desk, perfecting his analytical techniques and pondering the ineffable mysteries of the markets. His conversation bubbles with new and provocative ideas which positively demand to be challenged. Yet he is also, it turns out, a former academic with a First Class degree in physics and a Master's degree in operational research and someone who is never happier than when engaged in the highly disciplined task of constructing complex financial models on his computer or valuing an exotic derivative security.

The same paradoxes apply to Rushbrook's investment style. He is a fund manager who made his name at Ivory & Sime by investing at the higher-risk end of the spectrum – in venture capital, small companies and out of the way oil and technology stocks. Yet he is also now, unquestionably, the most risk-averse of all the professional investors I have talked to. And while he delighted at Ivory & Sime in putting together some of the most Byzantine corporate deals that the Scottish financial establishment has seen, all his efforts now are focused on a single investment trust, Personal Assets, which has the simplest and most straightforward capital structure possible.

In fact, there are few safer havens for a wealthy individual's money than this small and largely unknown general investment trust – not surprisingly, perhaps, since it is where most of Rushbrook's own wealth is now tied up. The objective of the trust is as much about preserving capital as it is about seeking exceptional returns. Unlike most professional investment managers, a good proportion of his own family's money – around £6 million of it – is at stake when he makes decisions. This is a powerful discipline and always a good sign for an outside investor. He, his father and other family trusts between them own 24% of the shares. Ironically, the one regret that he has is that he cannot persuade his son to follow him into the investment business. A determination to do your own thing and resist family pressures seems to run in the family.

TROUBLESOME YOUTH

Ian Rushbrook's father was in the fire service. As Fire Master of East Ham, in London, his area of responsibility included all of docklands. Rushbrook says he had a "very peculiar" childhood: he had tuberculosis of the hip at the age of five, and spent over six years lying on his back encased in plaster in hospital. He still walks with a noticeable limp. His early education was badly disrupted; his first school reports painted a damning picture of a bright but incorrigibly idle child. Later, thanks to his father's efforts, Rushbrook found his way to East Ham Grammar School, where, he says, he spent all his time playing chess. "Perhaps I could have been described as a child prodigy: at the age of 12, I was playing number two board for Essex. However this would belie the sheer effort required to be outstanding at any game. I literally spent all my time playing – I would go to bed at night with *Modern Chess Openings* and get up in the mornings and read some more. I'd play at breaks, at lunch and stay behind to play in school tournaments. In the evenings, I was allowed out to play league chess." Then one day, at the age of 16, he lost a game unexpectedly and impulsively gave chess up, totally and for good.

Precocious, but clearly determined even then to be awkward, Rushbrook next applied his wayward talents to the business of higher education. His original plan, he says, was to go to Cambridge, but the university said it would only take him if he was prepared to spend another year in the sixth form. Deciding that he wasn't, he opted instead to spend a year at the University of Leicester, and then go to Cambridge. "I had a very good year at Leicester. Rather arrogantly, I didn't attend any classes or anything like that. I deemed myself far too intelligent for that." Nemesis struck when it came to the exams. Rushbrook sailed through all the written ones, but when he sent his girlfriend to find out his results, discovered that he had failed the chemistry practical. Having by his own account only turned up "at the last minute", he had failed to read the instructions, overlooked the requirement to clean his equipment and ended up with "pink crystals" instead of white. As he hadn't been to any lectures, the university refused to allow him to resit the practical exam.

Chastened but somehow one suspects not very repentant, Rushbrook retreated to the family home, now back in Edinburgh, where his father had achieved his lifetime ambition of becoming the city's Fire Master. He applied to Edinburgh University and got a First in physics before joining Ferranti, then still a big name in the electronics business. Too proud to take any money from his father, who was deemed too well off for Rushbrook to qualify for a grant, he financed his university years by playing poker (five-card stud) two nights a week in the city's recently opened gaming clubs. He also enjoyed a ferocious reputation among his fellow students as a bridge player.[1]

Interested even then in making money, when Rushbrook joined Ferranti, he declined to work in R&D or on the technical side of the business but started instead as a personal assistant to the marketing director. While taking time off to do a business degree at Cranfield, he hired a couple of people for Ferranti. In the process he discovered what the company's pay policy was. Like many other companies at the time, Ferranti had a paternalistic policy of paying married employees more than those who were single. Rushbrook decided that this was not going to be the place for him.

"When I got married, I thought I would probably have to work a little less hard, and I didn't really want to work for a company that was going to pay me more for working less. So I left and decided to go to the London School of Economics and take an MSc in operational research, which is what particularly interested me." Having completed that, he returned to Edinburgh and took a job as a lecturer at the University. His entry into the investment business came by chance, when he approached Ivory & Sime, then very much one of the hottest names in the Scottish investment business, to try to raise some money to do a PhD in computerised finance. Despite insisting that he knew nothing about economics, accountancy or law, he found himself being offered a job by Jimmy Gammell, a legendary character in the Edinburgh financial community, shortly to take over as

---

[1] When I asked what useful lessons as an investor he had learnt from his poker-playing days, he replied, "Everything. It is all about risk management."

senior partner. Having established that the salary would be twice that of a university lecturer, Rushbrook decided to abandon his PhD there and then and started work the following Monday.

THE EDINBURGH SMARTS

As luck would have it, Rushbrook had come to the right place at the right time. Ivory & Sime had originally been established as a partnership in 1895. Soon afterwards, James Ivory set up the firm's first investment trust, called British Assets, a vehicle established to invest in banks that had gone into liquidation lending to farmers in Australia and New Zealand. None of the farmers could pay their mortgages after a four-year drought. Ivory issued a prospectus setting out the terms on which he proposed to buy the debentures and shares of a dozen liquidating banks, and offered 1.25% commission to anyone who could deliver them to him. "What British Assets did," says Rushbrook, "was apply liquidity to a specialised investment sector. The rains came, the farmers went back into business and British Assets made a fortune. It was a brilliant concept and an excellent early example of specialist investment management."

By the 1960s, when Rushbrook arrived at the firm, James Ivory's son Eric was nearing the end of his time as senior partner. Gammell and his colleagues enjoyed a glowing reputation as sharp and innovative investors. They had a family of investment trusts and a number of other funds which produced some spectacular investment returns, way ahead of most of their main rivals. When Rushbrook pitched up on the doorstep of One Charlotte Square, Ivory & Sime's Edinburgh address, the firm had just taken on its first graduate from outside its traditional breeding ground, the so-called Charlotte Square mafia, a network of Edinburgh families long associated with finance. Jimmy Gammell, with his shrewd financial brain, took the view that finding talented young men with *chutzpah* and setting them to compete with each other was more important than a grounding in the traditional professional qualifications. His new recruit quickly proved to be an inspired choice.

Although he had said his long-term ambition was to run an investment trust, the first job Rushbrook was given was to set up a research department for the firm. Within two years, he had 22 people working for him, researching "every damn thing" they could lay their hands on. It was a very good research department, he says, which came up with lots of excellent recommendations. The only trouble was that none of their brilliant work had "any impact whatsoever" on the investment process of the firm. Having started out in the belief that investment management would be 90% analysis and 10% subjective judgement, Rushbrook quickly discovered that reality was rather different. Ivory & Sime's fund managers simply ignored what their excellent in-house research department was doing and continued to take advice and stock tips from the brokers instead. "The reason being, of course, that fund managers in essence are pursued very vigorously by brokers who make their living from selling them transactions." In any event, most of the large broking firms had analysts who knew a lot more about individual companies than any in-house research department ever could.

The effectiveness of Rushbrook's new department, therefore, he soon concluded, was "absolutely zero". He asked again for a fund to run. The firm gave him the worst one they could find, a "total dog" which went under the name of Scot Income. "I then had the luxury of a 22-man research department to run one relatively small fund for about two years." Not surprisingly, perhaps, it turned out to be the top performing income fund in the UK over that period. Rushbrook was finally on his way as an investment manager. Shortly afterwards the research department was disbanded, and its members given new roles within sector specialist fund management teams.

By 1972, five years after joining, Rushbrook was made a partner of the firm and began to take a bigger role in its investment management business. In a short and frenetic burst of activity, Ivory & Sime overhauled its whole range of funds, setting new objectives for several of its investment trusts (including British Assets), buying a couple of European funds and launching a number of new specialist funds, particularly in oil and gas. This was the period when the first great wave of North Sea oil discoveries was being made, and there was something of a boom in North American exploration as well. Rushbrook ran the oil and gas funds for a couple of years.

Then in 1975, the year that Ivory & Sime incorporated, he was given the task of sorting out Atlantic Assets, an investment trust which had an excellent long-term record but which had got into all sorts of trouble in the property and banking crisis of 1973-74. Gammell had conceived the idea of building a merchant bank controlled by Atlantic Assets. It was an idea that turned out to be ill-conceived. The bank that Atlantic Assets ended up with was called Edward Bates and proved to be a disaster. When Rushbrook took over, the shares in Atlantic Assets were trading at a discount of around 60%, and it was close to breaching its borrowing limits.

One of the first things Rushbrook had to do was to sort out the borrowing problem. One of Atlantic's biggest creditors was a Slater Walker company, Britannia Arrow. The loan note of £5.3 million, which had been issued to acquire 11% of Haw Par (another disastrous Atlantic investment), badly needed redeeming. At the time Britannia Arrow was being run by Jimmy Goldsmith, who had just taken over after Jim Slater's resignation. Goldsmith gave Rushbrook an early insight into how to prioritise his business life. "I appeared at his office and I started on a long spiel about the background and the analysis of the loan note, what sort of price I would be prepared to pay, how he would clearly like to have it redeemed and so on. After a while he just cut me short. 'Just tell me what are you offering, Ian.' I said, 'Well, not a penny more than £4.2 million.' He said, 'Fine.' I put away my pile of analytical sheets and the deal was done. Jimmy took me to a delightful restaurant where we shared half a pound of caviar and drank three bottles of champagne and I learnt something about how life should be lived."

The ten years that followed, from 1975 to 1985, were the ones in which Rushbrook learnt all there was to know about investment management. As well as Atlantic Assets, he soon ended up running another investment trust, which bore the grand title of The Independent Investment Company. This was a company that Maynard Keynes had originally set up in the 1920s with a stockbroker friend, Oswald Falk, and the Scottish financier Carlyle Gifford, to try out some of his investment theories.

Although Keynes enjoyed some spectacular success investing the funds of his Cambridge college, King's, The Independent Investment Company had only mixed fortunes, and eventually became moribund. It was taken over by an industrialist, John Sheffield, as an investment vehicle for his family interests. He brought it eventually to Ivory & Sime in 1969, when it was acquired by Atlantic Assets. In 1980, it was relaunched by Rushbrook as a specialist technology investment trust. In another intensely complicated transaction of the kind which Rushbrook has always relished ("powerful and elegant" in his words), Atlantic Assets invested £541,000 to acquire 29% of Ivory & Sime itself, which then used the cash to fund the purchase of the firm's offices at numbers One and Two, Charlotte Square, Edinburgh.

As a result of these various transactions, Rushbrook found himself in a powerful position of influence at Ivory & Sime, running its two most successful investment trusts and controlling a big chunk of the management company's shares. This position was one that proved to be important when the great management bust-ups started at Ivory & Sime in the early 1980s. Relationships at the top of the firm soured so badly that both the chief executive and Rushbrook himself were asked to leave. This was a unanimous board decision but, characteristically, Rushbrook refused to go.

By now, he had also started to make some real money, thanks in part to his longstanding conviction that investment managers should take the largest possible stake in the funds they are managing.[2] Early on in his career, he borrowed the equivalent of a year's salary (£10,000) to buy a chunk of warrants in Atlantic Assets which grew tenfold before he sold them.[3] When he was put in charge of managing the trust's investments, he acquired a substantial number of shares in the trust. The big discount at which the shares were trading when he first took over effectively gave him a highly geared investment and set him up to make a lot of money if the

---

[2] "It is frankly incredible to me that there are fund managers in Edinburgh who are managing a pool of £400 million and who hold just 2,000 shares in those trusts."

[3] Investment trust warrants are effectively options to buy shares at a predetermined price. The irony is that Rushbrook's warrants, had he hung on to them, would eventually have expired worthless.

trust performed well. In fact, under his management, Atlantic Assets did not just do well, but spectacularly well, clocking up average annual returns of just under 30% over a ten-year period. By the time he cashed in the shares, they were worth well over £1 million.

Rushbrook steered the trust into small company stocks, particularly technology companies; 1983 proved to be his *annus mirabilis*. One of his stocks, an unquoted company called WICAT (the Worldwide Institute of Computer Aided Training) was another 'tenbagger', rising tenfold in little over a year. In the 12-month period to the end of June 1983, the net asset value of The Independent Investment Company was up 125% and that of Atlantic Assets by not much less – 96%. A year later, as is often the way with technology stocks, WICAT then fell out of bed, losing nearly all its gains. Small company stocks started to go off the boil and Atlantic Assets' performance tailed off, too. It ended up being reconstructed yet again in the late 1980s.

In February 1985, Rushbrook carried out what he describes as his best deal. At the time, the UK was in the midst of the miners' strike. The pound was sinking like a stone: at one stage it looked set to drop below $1. Despite considerable internal opposition, he took a huge bet that sterling would recover against the dollar, by selling $153 million one year forward for sterling at $1.07. A year later, when the contract was closed out, the exchange rate was $1.42, which netted a profit of £35 million. The *Scotsman* was moved to comment: "At the time, Mr Rushbrook was privately predicting that by the year end sterling would be back to $1.30. At that point he had either to be an idiot or a genius. With the dollar at $1.45, Mr Rushbrook is certainly no idiot."

In 1990, at the age of 50, tired of the infighting at Ivory & Sime, and keen to return to his first love, which was managing money, Rushbrook resigned as deputy chairman of the company (although he remains a non-executive director) and was appointed investment director of Personal Assets.[4] This was yet another investment trust in the Ivory & Sime stable,

---

[4] Ivory & Sime had floated as a public company in 1985, making millionaires of the executive directors.

and one Rushbrook himself had managed briefly in the early 1980s. It had been created from the surplus assets of Ivory & Sime and was launched alongside the management company in 1983 when Atlantic Assets offered its shares in the two entities to shareholders by way of rights. Unfortunately, its policy of investing in small-growth companies and unquoted venture capital was not a success, and its performance had been distinctly lacklustre. Rushbrook decided to raise his shareholding to 30% and manage the portfolio himself, severing all his other management links with Ivory & Sime.

For the last seven years, therefore, Rushbrook has concentrated on running the trust for his own and shareholders' benefit, while pursuing his lifelong ambition to develop a computer model which can predict future movements in the stock and bond markets. He now works, on his own, in a flat just round the corner behind the Ivory & Sime office in Charlotte Square. He has a board of directors to support him, and Ivory & Sime provides all the administrative backup for the trust. But essentially he is now a one-man band, running what is effectively his own money and that of a few hundred fellow wealthy shareholders in the way that he chooses.

It is, he says, the ideal job for an investment manager. Owning a large proportion of the shares,[5] he is under no pressure to do what almost every other fund manager in the land has to do, which is to appear every month before boards of directors, or trustees, and justify his existence. "The great advantage is that nothing here is forced. I don't have to do anything if I don't want to. In fact the board is quite happy if I do nothing, provided the performance is still there. For somebody running an ordinary trust, it is very embarrassing to have to turn up before the board and say I didn't do anything."

Managers like turning up with a big list of purchases and sales that they can talk about. After all, investment managers get paid very well and it's

---

[5] Personal Assets had issued a number of new shares at a premium to net asset value in the last few years which has effectively reduced the Rushbrook family's interest in the company.

embarrassing to get paid a lot of money to do nothing. The professional investment manager is involved in a lot of activity just trying to prove his worth. It's essential that he is seen to be doing something, or else the directors and trustees start to wonder what the hell they are paying him for.

SEEING THE BIG PICTURE

There is no simple way to categorise Rushbrook's style as an investor. In his time at Ivory & Sime, he emphasises that he has run just about every kind of investment fund there is – large-company stocks, small-company stocks, income and growth funds, oil and gas funds, technology and unquoted stocks. You name it, he has probably done it, and nearly always with great distinction. His interest is in what works. Since taking over at Personal Assets, he has concentrated on managing a diversified portfolio in a way that at least matches the performance of the main market indices, while minimising the risk to shareholders' capital. He quotes with approval what Warren Buffett calls the two great rules of investing: "Rule Number One: don't lose money. Rule Number Two: never forget Rule Number One."

Shareholders in Personal Assets have seen their shares grow at a compound annual return of 23% in the seven years since he took over running the trust. A big chunk of this gain has come from two sources: the elimination of the discount and the success of the initial changes that he made to the bizarre portfolio that he inherited. The trust measures its performance over rolling three-year periods: over the last three years, the net asset value of the trust has grown by 56.9%, comfortably outpacing the comparable rise in the FT All-Share Index of 35.1%.[6] Furthermore, the volatility of the shares has been notably lower than that of most other general investment trusts, underlining Rushbrook's general aversion to risk.

---

[6] The figures are for the three-year period to the end of April 1997, the trust's year end for reporting purposes. Against the Footsie index, the outperformance is less marked, as big companies have generally outperformed their smaller brethren.

Not surprisingly, given this kind of performance, Personal Assets has regularly sold at a small premium to its asset value. Turnover is also low by industry standards. Rushbrook says he is pathologically opposed to paying any money to brokers by way of commission if he can possibly avoid it; he even claims to be the only investment manager in Britain who gets absolutely no calls at all from brokers. They know it will be a waste of their time.

Rushbrook likes to think in big picture terms about the investment cycle. One of the key decisions for an investor is whether to focus on small or large companies. For most of the period that he was running Atlantic Assets, it was a time of high inflation and high interest rates. This is the kind of environment, he points out, that favours smaller companies. It is the big companies who suffer most from inflation. "Small companies have much greater opportunities in time of high inflation. Big companies fail to move their prices rapidly enough. They continue to grow at whatever their historic growth is. They don't adjust for inflation." So, for a decade or more, small companies proved to be the destination of choice.

Contrast that situation with the late 1960s, when Wall Street was led to a new post-war peak by the strength of the so-called 'Nifty Fifty'. These were the big companies of the day – the likes of IBM, Xerox, Polaroid and so on. For a while they were selling on absurdly high multiples, with share prices that were 40 to 80 times the companies' earnings per share, ratings that are normally associated with small-growth stocks. It is true that prices on the stock market discount the future, rather than reflect the past, but the future that these valuation levels were discounting was economic Nirvana, a land where the good times roll forever. In fact, of course, OPEC and all the inflationary horrors of the 1970s lay just around the corner.

Theoretically, these valuations could be justified, says Rushbrook: "If you hold companies growing at 15% with 3% inflation, then you are making a real return of 12%, plus the dividend yield. Their multiples can get very high and they are justifiable mathematically – provided inflation doesn't go up. But once inflation started to rise, as it did in 1972, then the Nifty Fifty, the golden oldies, Vestal Virgins, call them what you will, all collapsed. One saw that if inflation was in double digits, you really want to invest in companies that are growing at 25, 35, 40%. It is the only way you have of making money."

All good things come to an end, however, and the great boom in smaller high technology companies ended, as far as Rushbrook was concerned, in 1983. At that point, he says, "It became totally apparent that the small companies were grossly overvalued and the large companies massively undervalued." Why was it apparent? "Because by then inflation had started to come under control. One knew that it had to start coming down. It was totally unsustainable." The yield at which the US long bond – the benchmark for long-term interest rates – was trading, was unsustainably high. The yield, he notes, was over 14% at the time.

Note that Rushbrook did not have an inside track on what the US Federal Reserve was going to do next in monetary policy (although its chairman, Paul Volcker, had in fact realised the year before that the high interest rate policy he had been using to drive inflation out of the economic system was starting to work too well; the Fed started to ease monetary policy in the middle of 1982). Nor was Rushbrook's policy the result of long and detailed analysis of the monetary aggregates, a pursuit on which he has never wasted much time. His method more akin to the gambler's intuitive feel for a sea change in the odds – what Rushbrook calls "seeing the clarity of what the scenario is. Things just sort of grow on you".

So confident was Rushbrook that inflation had been broken that he went to the board of Atlantic Assets and asked to take out a five-year £100 million loan in order to buy US long bonds. If inflation was indeed coming down, then yields on long bonds would fall sharply, and their price would rise.[7] The board told him to borrow £50 million first and borrow the rest later if the first attempt was successful. "So we bought a long US Treasury

---

[7] One of the golden rules of fixed-interest investment is that a given change in interest rates has a greater proportionate impact on bonds with long maturities than on those with shorter redemption dates. The US long bond is a 30-year government security and is widely regarded as the benchmark indicator of the long-term market interest rate. When yields on fixed-interest securities fall, the price goes up, and vice versa.

and amazingly enough the five-year investment went up something like £13 million in three weeks. I then sold the Treasury, closed down the loan and forgot about it."

However, he had less success in trying to persuade the board to change the investment policy of Atlantic Assets from small companies back to large ones. "It was just patently obvious that this was the right thing to do," he says now. "But when boards have been looking at a decade or more of outstanding performance from a particular category of investment, changing the style or changing the approach is viewed as tinkering with the winning formula. In fact, there is no such thing as a policy for all time. As things change, you must view it in the reality of what might happen in the future."

Ironically, even though Rushbrook did start to shift the portfolios of his trusts towards larger companies in the mid-1980s, he did not always get his stock selection right. He thinks now that the team of analysts he still had then was overstretched. They had difficulty breaking out of their old small company mindset to analyse big companies as well. Whatever the reason, he found he started off by buying the wrong things. He bought IBM for example and it did appallingly – a mistake that he repeated in 1991 when he started to reshape the Personal Assets portfolio. Fed up with being badgered by one of his fellow directors about how badly his IBM shares were doing, he sold them – at which point they promptly rose threefold. Frustrating? "I swore never to allow anyone to influence me ever again on any decision," says Rushbrook, with feeling.

He sees a lot of parallels between the markets in the days of the Nifty Fifty and the markets now. "We are seeing the evolution of another 1972 market where the big companies are once again on very high multiples. It can be justifiable in a low inflation environment, but one always has to worry about inflation." For the moment, the low inflation scenario that sent Wall Street soaring in 1995 and 1996 is still in place, but for how long?

Rushbrook is not alone in seeing the decision by Alan Greenspan, Volcker's successor as chairman of the Federal Reserve, to raise US interest rates unexpectedly in February 1994 as one of the key developments in sustaining the current bull market. "Politicians and central bankers normally raise interest rates after inflation has appeared, not before. If central bankers are prepared to damp inflation before it has emerged – which is what Greenspan did in 1994 – then you have a formula for the long-term development of equities. So although the US market is historically overvalued, it is not necessarily going to retreat from here." In other words, we are approaching, but not yet at, a point where it is time to call a big turn in the investment cycle.[8]

THE RUSHBROOK RATIOS

As I have already mentioned, Rushbrook is fascinated by numbers and spends a lot of time using his background in operational research to construct computer models to analyse securities and test his many theories about investment. Fairly early on in his career, when inflation was high, he discovered that two simple economic ratios, wages as a proportion of sales, and wages as a proportion of pre-tax profits, provided a very good indicator of which companies were going to perform well. These were dubbed the Rushbrook Ratios by a friendly stockbroker. Since then, over the years, he has added hugely to his modelling work, culminating in the development of a model which assesses the fair value of the main markets he follows. These are the stock markets in London and New York, and the main alternative asset classes: gilts, index-linked gilts and Treasury bills. So confident is he now in the power of his algorithms that he has started to provide his shareholders each year with an illustration of what the model is saying about the overall level of the market. (This kind of work is now commonplace at the big broking firms, but Rushbrook is rare among fund managers in doing all the modelling himself.)

---

[8] This conversation was held in March 1997, when the bull market in shares on both sides of the Atlantic still had several more months to run.

The first reference to the model came in the 1992 Annual Report of Personal Assets, although it was not until 1996 that shareholders were shown a graphical picture of what it could do (see following page). What the model does is provide a snapshot at any given point of time of the London financial markets, and the extent to which they have deviated from their 'fair value'. The charts also show how the model's predicted value has shaped up against the model's predictions. The analysis extends to looking at each of the main asset classes – equities, gilts and index-linked gilts – and applying the same valuation methods to each of them. The model is by no means infallible, but its long-run record at forecasting the level of the stock market, when backtested, has been good. It seems particularly good at spotting when markets are overvalued.

This raises an interesting theoretical point, which Rushbrook attempted to address in his 1996 Annual Report. There are, he reminds his investors, two main methods of outperforming the market averages over time. One is through superior stock selection – in other words, picking better individual stocks than the rest of the market. The other is through market timing, which he defines as "being able to value markets more accurately than other investors and knowing when to use liquidity or gearing to improve returns". Neither method is easy, but common sense points to superior stock selection being the less difficult of the two. All logic, says Rushbrook, suggests that market timing is "futile". As he points out, the rapid growth of derivatives markets, where investors can take out insurance against future uncertainty, presupposes that no investor has the ability to predict market movements on "better than a 50-50 basis".

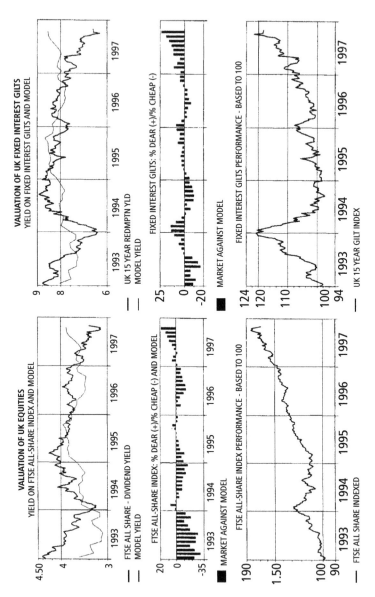

Ian Rushbrook's market models are designed to indicate whether the stock and gilts markets are fairly valued or not. When the theoretical yield suggested by the computer model (the thin line in the top of the panels of the graph) is below the line of the actual market yield, the implication is that the market is undervalued. When the lines are reversed, it suggests the opposite.

And yet, says Rushbrook, this is not quite the end of the story. Efficient Market Theory is flawed in at least one respect, which is its assumption that investors always act rationally. There is clear evidence that share prices and stock market indices are far more volatile in practice than they should be in theory.[9] It follows therefore that "if it is possible to produce reasonable mid-range estimated values for either companies or markets, this irrational volatility of stock prices and indices can be exploited to make profits". In other words, although academic theory suggests that the Rushbrook Ratios and their successors should have no practical value, in practice they can be very useful in helping to determine an investment strategy based on market timing.

One question, says Rushbrook, that he used to find intensely annoying was the one all amateur investors tend to ask first: "What do you think about the market?" The questioner usually means, "Is it going to go up or down?" but begs all sorts of other questions such as: which market, over what time frame? "All one could say truthfully was that in the short term there was a 50-50 chance that the market would go up or down and that in the long term it would be volatile around an 8% growth trend.[10] This left the questioner wondering if I was stupid, incompetent or simply being facetious. Nowadays, if I were asked, I would pull out a series of my charts and bore the questioner for half an hour. However, as you might guess, once you have the answer, nobody asks the question!"

However well it seems to work, Rushbrook stresses that the market models are only a guide to action, not an investment discipline in themselves. For example, although the model was suggesting in the latter half of 1996 that the UK stock market looked cheap, he was not rushing to buy shares.

---

[9] What Rushbrook means by this is that the expected cash flows which a share price is ultimately meant to reflect do not change as violently as the frequent sudden movements in prices imply that they should. The same applies, at an aggregate level, to a stock market index.

[10] 8% approximates the rate at which equities have grown over the very long term.

Instead, because of his concerns about a Labour victory at the forthcoming election, and his worries about the level of the US stock market,[11] he had steadily increased the proportion of cash in Personal Assets portfolio to 25% by the time of election in May 1997, a high figure given his normal predisposition to keep his portfolio fully invested. When the election result was known, however, and the new chancellor, Gordon Brown, announced his surprise decision to give the Bank of England control over the setting of interest rates, Rushbrook quickly reversed tack, buying £2.8 million of bank shares, in the belief that one at least of the threats posed by a Labour government had been neutralised.[12]

However, he has also started an experiment, which is investing in futures in order to try make some money out of the model's predictive power. He bought a put option on a long gilt future in 1996 which produced a profit of 24% by the time it was sold a year later, and another in 1997 which returned an even more impressive 80%. More such experiments are likely to follow. Now that he is confident he has a formulation that works, Rushbrook has proposed to his board a detailed strategy for exploiting its potential as a market timer. Only time will tell if he really has unlocked a new Rosetta Stone of investment: Rushbrook says his head tells him it cannot be possible for a model to formulate a successful market timing strategy, but his stomach still insists that it can.

Meanwhile, he is pressing on with another project, which is to try to devolve a model for analysing companies to the same degree of reliability as he thinks he has now achieved with the market as a whole. This is a

---

[11] One of the specific concerns in early 1997 was that if the US market did show a big correction after its long bull run, the impact would be felt even more markedly in London than in New York. A 20% drop in Wall Street could easily translate into a 35% drop in the London market. The London market traditionally takes a strong lead from what happens on the other side of the Atlantic.

[12] In his annual report, Rushbrook said he still thinks public spending will prove to be an Achilles' heel for the new government, but believes that the change in interest rate policy means that the bill for failing to control spending, if it arises, will no longer be felt by the banks, but by the Labour government itself.

much bigger undertaking. The technique is based on matching pairs of similar individual stocks – say a Tesco and a Sainsbury's – and comparing their financial characteristics, looking for anomalies and areas where improvement could lead to a re-rating of the shares. Ultimately, Rushbrook wants to be able to conduct this kind of exercise across the whole market, but it will take a lot of time to complete the modelling. An earlier attempt to write these programmes was thwarted when Extel, the main provider of company financial statistics, decided to change the way it presented all its data. Rushbrook has now installed a new computer which has the processing power to start the calculations.

THE MAN WITH THE GOLDEN PEN

As should be clear by now, Personal Assets is not like most other investment trusts. For one thing, it is still very small in comparison with many of its brethren.[13] For another, Rushbrook has a large shareholding in the company, and its dispositions reflect his own priorities and circumstances as well as those of its shareholders. Because it is specifically targeted at high net worth individuals, it makes only a modest attempt to market itself and is not out to attract the ordinary unit trust or investment trust saver. Investment strategy is very much in the hands of Rushbrook himself, although the Edinburgh-based directors meet informally at least once a week and the full board once a month.

Among the directors, the one with the greatest input is Robin Angus, who acts as a one day a week consultant to the company. In the Edinburgh investment business, Angus knows fame in his own right, as one of the investment trust gurus at the broking firm of NatWest Securities (still better recalled North of the border as Wood Mackenzie, a broking firm which did much to pioneer high-quality investment research in the 1960s and 1970s). A cerebral figure who looks and dresses the part of a Victorian

---

[13] It was small in 1997, but has since grown to more than £330 million in assets (December 2012).

gentleman, complete with fob and chain, Angus is widely known for his literate and entertaining commentaries on the investment scene. He has the distinction of being one of the few brokers able and willing to publish his research with a title and numerous other references in Latin.[14] His main role at Personal Assets appears to consist of giving advice and acting as a voice of reason when Rushbrook is propounding one of his extravagant ideas.[15] He also writes the trust's quarterly reports to shareholders.

According to Angus, he became friends with Rushbrook in the early 1980s because they discovered they shared a common interest in "thinking the unthinkable" about the realities of the investment business. (They also discovered, more bizarrely, a shared passion for the novels of Herman Hesse.) His quarterly reports offer a valuable and always entertaining insight into the way that he and Rushbrook have developed their ideas. To give a flavour, here is a more or less random sample of some of the homely truths that Angus has offered the shareholders in the past six years. These are not the kind of things, it is safe to say, that you will normally hear from your friendly stockbroker:

• *On why the trust will never invest in emerging markets*

We are ignorant and we're not ashamed to admit it. Ian and I know next to nothing about the Far East, or emerging markets, or property, and we haven't got time to learn. If we tried to make the time to do so we would lose our grip on things we do know something about, which would be foolish.

• *On the dangers of listening to stockbrokers*

Stockbrokers are delightful people who can be the most attentive of friends. In this they are like shopkeepers, who welcome browsers and will gladly pass the time of day with them as long as they are confident that money will eventually tinkle into the tills. But except in rare cases, the

---

[14] *Haec Olim*, a collection of investment trust pieces by Robin Angus, is highly recommended to anyone who is interested in understanding more about the way that investment trusts work.

[15] Angus says of Rushbrook: "The great thing about Ian is that he likes to be challenged. Some of the things he says are complete and utter nonsense."

relationship is a commercial one. Friendships are bought, as are the accompanying invitations to Wimbledon and the Savoy. No orders to buy and sell, and the relationship shrivels.

• *On the greatest secret known to successful investors*

It is said that Albert Einstein, when asked what he believed to have been the single greatest human discovery, replied, "Compound interest." If the story is true, then Einstein was right.

• *On the danger of putting too much reliance on earnings figures*

Given that no stock is ever correctly priced by the market, the price progression of a stock doesn't depend primarily on the earnings it reports, as it would if the stock price were correct. Most analysts and investors worry far too much about what the next quarter's earnings will be, and far too little about whether the company itself is intrinsically cheap or dear, or well managed or badly managed.

• *On the real risk in investment, and why Personal Assets will only exceptionally (as in 1996) take money out of the market and put it into cash*

It is always dangerous to be out of equities, because in the longer term equities always rise. In equity investing, the perceived risk is that your equities may fall in price. The real risk is being out of equities.

• *On why an obsession with short-term performance is a mistake when choosing someone to manage your money*

Point to point comparisons are at best useless and at worst misleading. Who cares which runner has the fastest time over a random hundred yard stretch in the middle of a marathon? No one. But a runner who treats a marathon as a series of hundred-yard sprints will be certain to lose, because a marathon isn't run that way.

Looking through the Personal Assets portfolios themselves, what is most striking is the catholic range of its investments. The board says it dislikes investment theories and investment styles and seeks to be "prudent and flexible and to use our common sense". Its objective is to achieve as high a total return as possible "given our dislike of risk significantly greater than that of investing in the FTSE All-Share Index". The portfolio is built around a number of core blue chip holdings in the UK and US markets, together with some medium-sized companies such as Airtours and Scottish Television, and topped up with what looks at first sight like a strange mix of oddballs.[16]

In early 1997, for example, no less than 6% of the portfolio consisted of an obscure warrant in Investors Capital, a Scottish investment trust which Rushbrook decided, after careful analysis, had been seriously mispriced by the market. This large and, on the face of it, risky investment is explained by the fact that the warrant was issued by an Ivory & Sime trust, and turns out (much laughter from Rushbrook at this point in his narrative) to have been devised by Rushbrook and Angus themselves, in their capacity as consultants to Ivory & Sime. His deadpan comment on this is: "Although the market does not leave money lying around on the table very often, it does occasionally get things wrong and if you just now and then spot something that's not right, it can help."

Also in the portfolio is the put option on the long gilt future which was Rushbrook's first big play using his market model: a small Scottish computer maintenance company which dates back to the portfolio of venture capital issues that Rushbrook inherited when he took over Personal Assets;[17] and an obscure investment trust which turns out to be the rump of another, only marginally less obscure, investment trust called London American Ventures. When Rushbrook says that his approach is a catholic one, this is saying no more than the truth. This is not a portfolio, one suspects, which would win any prizes from a pension fund consultant, as it defies easy characterisation. There are only 30 to 35 securities in it, compared to the 100 to 200 stocks that you will find in an average investment trust portfolio.

One of the amusing things about Robin Angus's quarterly reports to the shareholders of Personal Assets is how little space is devoted to the changes

---

[16] Appendix 2 gives details of the Personal Assets portfolio at 30 April 1997.

[17] Rushbrook has gradually disposed of nearly all the unlisted securities he inherited and says that he does not intend to buy any more in future, since the search for good ones "absorbs more time and effort than it is worth".

in the portfolio. This is for the simple reason that Rushbrook really does try to keep buying and selling to a minimum; often there is next to nothing to tell. In the first quarterly of all, for example, all that Angus had to report was a single purchase of 70,000 shares in Bass and the sale of a tiny scrip issue for £2084. When he and Rushbrook reviewed the quarter's investment performance, "what struck us chiefly was how little we'd actually done". Over half of a subsequent quarterly report was given over to defending this policy of "masterly inactivity" against a journalist who had dared to query whether either of the two men could justify their salaries from the trust, given how little they appeared to have done during the period.

While it might seem trivial, this point is actually fundamental to the trust's success, and to Rushbrook's whole philosophy of investment. When I asked what he had read which had particularly influenced him, the first thing he mentioned was an article by Charles Ellis, of Greenwich Associates, a leading American investment management consulting firm. It is called 'The Loser's Game'. This is an elegant and coherent explanation of the reasons why most professional fund managers do less well than the market averages, and why they bear out the dictum that "too much investment activity is death to performance."[18]

There are, says Ellis, essentially two reasons. One is that every buy or sell decision involves investors in transaction costs. The more you buy and sell, the higher these costs are, and the more they damage your performance. The second reason is that most investors try to do too much and invest beyond their level of competence. It is their mistakes that kill their performance, as much as their successes which make it. There is a parallel with tennis, where the experts play one type of game – in which the outcome is determined by playing for a position in which a winning shot can be played (a Winner's Game); and where the amateurs play another – in which the winner is usually the player who makes the least number of mistakes (a Loser's Game).

---

[18] The piece is reprinted, for those who are interested, in *Classics*, an anthology of investment writing, published by Dow Jones-Irwin (1989).

Investment, Ellis argued, has become a Loser's Game. The reason is that the market, which was once dominated by private investors, is now dominated by professionally run investment institutions instead. By definition, these professional managers can no longer outperform each other because they *are* the market. In such a climate, says Ellis, the fund manager does best to adopt a Loser's Game strategy. That means making fewer but better investment decisions; spending more time on working out when to sell (and a bit less on when and what to buy); and accepting that not everyone can be a winner. Few fund managers have taken this message to heart, but Rushbrook has accepted the insight and based his whole investment philosophy around it.

Among a number of other things which have made an impact on his thinking as an investor, says Rushbrook, is a speech that Charlie Munger, Warren Buffett's longstanding associate, gave to a group of students in the United States. It is a highly entertaining account of all the "worldly wisdom" about life and business which students ought to know but never seem to be taught. Munger's theme is that anyone who wants to succeed needs to draw on multiple "mental models" and intellectual disciplines, rather than rely on one simplistic approach. "To the man with only a hammer, every problem seems like a nail" is how he puts it.

But Munger's verdict on the business of professional investment is not dissimilar to that of Charles Ellis: "To me," he says, "it is obvious that the winner has to bet very selectively", just like a professional punter on the horses. There are not many cases where you are likely to know enough about a business or an industry to see an outstanding bet when it comes along. So when it does, you should "load up" on it. Like nearly every professional investor I have met, Rushbrook is fascinated by Buffett and his extraordinary success. One of his theories, as we will see in a moment, is that Buffett in practice applies hardly any of the value investing criteria which he says he does. What Buffett is scrupulous about however is (i) investing only within his own very narrow circle of competence; and (ii) making big bets when he does decide to commit his capital.

When it comes to picking individual stocks, what distinguishes Rushbrook from most of the other investors in this book is that he places little credence on visiting or talking to companies, although he might go to a presentation if a company is in Edinburgh. The reason is that he is, at heart, more interested in "the financial dynamics" of a share than in its business. Ask him why he bought a share and he will tend to say simply, "it looked cheap", or it was "obviously undervalued". Thus, he bought shares in Bass and Scottish & Newcastle in 1994 because they looked "significantly undervalued", and BT in 1996 for a similar reason. BT has a powerful franchise and is an "outstanding company financially", with everything being masked by the enormous redundancy payments it has paid out while halving its workforce since privatisation. Its shares were pushed down by exaggerated fears about the likely impact of the windfall profits tax if Labour were to win the 1997 election. This is the kind of market overreaction where those with decent memories and a sense of where the true value lies can always hope to profit.

One of Rushbrook's biggest successes has been buying fund management companies, which he correctly saw, in 1992, as offering a geared play on the rising equity market. Mercury Asset Management, which has risen three and a half fold since he bought it, has done best of the lot, but he also bought Edinburgh Fund Managers, Henderson and M&G. In conversation, however, it becomes apparent that despite his predilection for financial analysis he is also influenced by the calibre of managers he has met over the years. Thus he bought Airtours at its flotation because he knew and was impressed by its managing director, David Crossland. GEC shares he also bought because, apart from the fact that they seemed cheap, he admired Lord Weinstock, "the most intelligent man I have ever met".

Rentokil is a different story. This is one of those rare companies that seems to have become a permanent growth stock, clocking up, under its chief executive Sir Clive Thompson, 20% plus increases in earnings per share year in year out. It took a long time, says Rushbrook, for him to work out why it could still be attractive to buy a company of this sort, despite the fact that it is not sold on a high price/earnings ratio, a very high price to book value and had a low dividend yield. It was only when he came to realise that one of the keys to successful investing was to turn the traditional criteria adopted by value investors upside down that the explanation began to present itself.

The three main things which value investors look for, says Rushbrook, are a low price/earnings ratio, a low ratio of share price to book value, and a high dividend yield. Yet all three value criteria, he thinks, are flawed and on occasions downright misleading. Needless to say, he has a set of equations to prove his argument which are too complex to reproduce here. His point, in essence, is that the traditional value criteria are usually better indicators of a poor business than they are of a cheap stock. Price/earnings ratios in particular often tell you more about the quality of a company than they do about its attractions as an investment. At the same time, it is a simple mathematical observation that the best businesses enjoy a high return on equity. As such, they will tend to have a high, rather than a low, price to book value. And in these cases, the investor will always do better to see his money reinvested in the business, where it can accumulate at a high compound rate of return free of capital gains tax, rather than having it paid out each year in taxable dividends.

This is one of the insights that Rushbrook thinks Warren Buffett has been so clever to see. Overall, however, he says that what pleases him most about the performance of Personal Assets since he took charge of the portfolio is not his successes, but the fact that he has managed to avoid making many mistakes. The one that sticks out in his portfolio is Redland, the tiles and buildings material company, which he inherited when he took over in 1990, but which has simply never performed. "It was always cheap and got cheaper, and then the results moved to justify the cheapness" is how he explains it! He is hoping his new company valuation model will prevent him picking another dog like this one again, but for the moment he keeps it around "as a reminder of how stupid you can be".[19]

---

[19] Not that stupid. Redland has since been taken over, allowing Rushbrook to exit from the position with some dignity intact.

As far as selling shares is concerned, Rushbrook advises against selling too early: "When a stock has gone up, it continues to go up well beyond any rational level, so it makes no sense at all in getting out too early, since it is often going to go much higher. There is no doubt that the one real inefficiency which exists in the market-place is the undue volatility in the stocks. They go up too far and they come down far too far as well."

Although he is adamant that it is wrong to waste time on short-term movements in share prices (merely "corks bobbing on the water" in his dismissive phrase), Rushbrook insists on updating the prices of all the individual shares in his portfolio himself each morning. This he does by calling up a phone line share price service, which is customised to his needs, and punching in the opening prices on his computer keyboard. "It is important to get a feel for what the prices are," he says. Through his computer, he has access to a wide range of data and information services which he brings up and displays on a large screen in the corner of his office. He also uses a combined phone/fax machine, and a scanner for transferring interesting documents into his computer. The basement room where he works is in fact more like a lair than an office. It is small and quite dark, with very few of the trappings of a business about it. When visiting, you would hardly think that this is where the business of a £40 million publicly quoted investment trust was being carried out. Rushbrook spent most of the hours I talked to him leaning back, with his feet on the desk in front of him, the very picture of someone who is at ease with himself and his situation in life.

Turning to the wider investment scene, and the choice open to ordinary investors, he is not a fan of unit trusts, which, he says, are rarely run for the investors, but rather for the benefit of the fund management company. "The talent in a unit trust group is not usually applied to running the funds; it is applied to expanding the unit trust group. Where investment trusts are run by merchant banks, you will usually find that the best trainees gravitate to corporate finance and the less successful end up on the investment side." Investment trusts, if run by independent investment management firms, provide a much cleaner and attractive vehicle for most investors. Their running costs tend to be lower, and they have the flexibility to borrow. His advice to ordinary investors with no particular skills to bring to bear on their task is to spread their money across five or six of the better known investment trusts, including two to three of the general diversified ones. Both he and Robin Angus are fans of the Alliance Trust in Dundee, for example, which boasts some of the lowest costs of any collective investment fund.

"For a private investor to be his own investment manager is virtually impossible unless he is a really talented investment hobbyist. I think he should simply abandon any idea of running his own portfolio unless he has a lot of time on his hands, and has some real understanding of the investment management process." The markets are broadly efficient, and getting more so, but equities still offer a very good long rate of return, and the way to own them is through a diversified fund, "at the lowest cost possible with the best investment manager you can find". Avoid managers with only a few years' experience, however, he says. Investment management is extraordinarily difficult to do well. After 30 years, Rushbrook doubts whether he himself is more than two-thirds of the way towards mastering it.

UPDATE (2012)

Ian Rushbbrook died in October 2008, ironically only a matter of weeks after the collapse of Lehman Brothers triggered the global financial crisis that he and his colleagues had been predicting so confidently for many months. More than a year before the bursting of the credit bubble he told the annual meeting of Personal Assets: "Is the financial world sleepwalking into disaster? No. It's worse than that. It's walking into the disaster, wide awake." He correctly identified the explosion of sub-prime mortgage lending in the United States as the catalyst which would eventually bring the world's financial system to a shuddering halt. He was, said his obituary in the Scotsman *newspaper, a rare example of "men who passed away in the hour of their greatest triumph." Personal Assets meanwhile continues to go from strength to strength, with Robin Angus now a full-time employee and Troy Asset Management the Investment Adviser.*

4. NILS TAUBE:

Thinking globally and having fun

Now that the City has become a much more professional place, where hours are long and the pressure relentless, it is easy to lose sight of the fact that investing can – and should – be fun as well as lucrative. One man who has never lost sight of this objective is Nils Taube, who has been in the investment business for just a few months short of half a century but shows no sign of losing either momentum or a sense of fulfilment in what he does. In fact, Taube says he has never enjoyed investment management as much as he does now, and it is impossible, talking to such a relaxed and entertaining fanatic, not to believe that this is indeed the case.

Taube was originally a successful stockbroker, rising from office boy to become senior partner in 1975 of one of the City's older broking firms, called Kitcat & Aitken. In 1982, shortly after Big Bang swept away the old divide between brokers and jobbers and ended the practice of fixed commissions, Jacob Rothschild (now Lord Rothschild) made an offer to buy 30% of the equity in the firm. Following this agreement, Taube moved across to become a director of RIT and Northern Investments, chaired by Lord Rothschild, where he took on responsibility for institutional fund management. It was the beginning of a second career as a fund manager which has prospered ever since, through all the many twists and turns in the subsequent history of the businesses associated with the Jacob

Rothschild name.[1] In 1997, he and his three colleagues, John Hodson, Cato Stonex and John Haynes, were managing or providing investment advice to unit trusts, investment trusts and life funds worth a total of some $2.5 billion. These included a number of unit trusts and insurance funds run by the newly merged St James's Place Capital/J. Rothschild Assurance group and two trusts in Lord Rothschild's personally owned investment business.[2]

Taube is a prosperous and comfortable man, of mixed Estonian and English descent, who can claim one of the best and most consistent records in the fund management business. His funds include a unit trust which he has been running, in one capacity or another, and with extraordinarily successful results, since 1969. The St James's Place Greater European Progressive Trust, as it is now known, started life as the suggestion of a lawyer friend of Taube's who had become bored with the hassle of doing all the tax paperwork on his shareholdings. This trust, which has followed Taube from his first career in stockbroking, when it was known as Bishopsgate Progressive Trust, to his subsequent home with Jacob Rothschild, has clocked up a remarkable record; it has done the best of all his funds, although his international fund is not far behind.

---

[1] Lord Rothschild decided to set up his own financial services business after severing his links with N.M. Rothschild, the Rothschild family's investment bank, which is run by his cousin, Sir Evelyn de Rothschild. He later also started a new life assurance business, J. Rothschild Assurance, in partnership with Sir Mark Weinberg. In May 1997, this was merged with St James's Place Capital. Lord Rothschild ended his direct involvement with both companies at this point, but retains his own investment group.

[2] Following the merger of St James's Place Capital and J. Rothschild Assurance, Taube and his colleagues now operate as an independent fund management company, Taube Hodson Stonex Partners, providing investment advice and running their various funds on a contract basis.

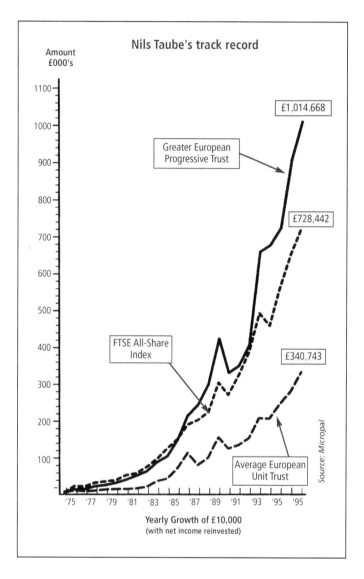

Nils Taube's track record

Amount
£000's

£1,014.668

Greater European
Progressive Trust

£728,442

FTSE All-Share
Index

£340,743

Average European
Unit Trust

Source: Micropal

Yearly Growth of £10,000
(with net income reinvested)

Nils Taube has been managing unit trusts longer than anyone else in the UK. The power of compound interest has helped to produce spectacular returns for anyone who bought his Greater European Progressive unit trust when it started life in 1969, but his record of sustained outperformance across a range of managed funds is still remarkable.

The units started life at the equivalent of 10 pence each. By the middle of 1997, the accumulation units (which make no income distributions to unitholders, but reinvest the money as capital) were priced at more than 800 pence. In other words, the value has grown more than eightyfold over a period of 28 years, equivalent to a cumulative annual return of 16.8% per annum. The ordinary units, which pay out income but do not reinvest capital, have grown fiftyfold over the same period, a compound annual return of 14.8%. This compares with the UK All-Share Index's return of just over 10% in the same period – proof, if proof is needed, that professional investors, like cognac, can also mature well with the passage of time. The fund has maintained an edge of around 4% per annum over the market for most of its life.

It is an impressive track record for a fund with no gearing, and one, notes Taube, which would look more impressive still if you had started buying the units in 1974, at the bottom of the bear market, when the price had fallen to just 5 pence. In its time, the fund has changed its name, as well as its ownership, but essentially it is a vehicle through which Taube can apply his analytical skills and years of experience to picking stocks. As its name applies, the trust's main working canvas is now Europe, although for a while in the 1970s, while exchange controls were in force, and the dollar premium was still a factor, most of its assets were concentrated in the UK.

After such a long time in the business Taube is fabulously well connected, and knows all the most important players around. He is a non-executive director of George Soros's Quantum Fund, for example, and moves easily in central banking and government circles which helps to keep him well informed. The name of Rothschild is still a powerful draw and opens doors that might otherwise remain shut. When thinking about buying American banking stocks, it helps to be able to call on the advice of a former chairman of the Federal Reserve. Paul Volcker happened to be passing for a visit a few years ago when Taube was debating the merits of buying Citicorp, the largest of all the American banks, and convinced him that there was no need to worry about its ability to trade through the difficulties it was facing at the time.

But connections alone are not in themselves enough. Taube was one of the early pioneers of serious investment research in this country, and in his funds has repeatedly demonstrated how handsomely serious analysis can pay off. He was one of the founders of the Society of Investment Analysts in the 1950s: "At the time I was poor," he recalls, "and did not have any money to invest, but it became clear to me that you could make money by understanding about things that were not generally understood." His forte has always been spotting price anomalies and looking for hidden value with an international, rather than a purely domestic, perspective. In the last few years, he has again been a pioneer in looking at stocks on a pan-European basis, taking companies in the same industry in different countries and finding opportunities to exploit the valuation differentials between the various markets.

A ROOM WITH A VIEW

On the day that Gordon Brown, the Labour Chancellor, was presenting his first Budget, I spent three hours talking to Taube about his philosophy and investment experiences. It was potentially quite a big day for anyone in the investment business, but you would hardly have guessed it from his demeanour, which is that of a benign and wealthy uncle, comfortable, humorous and wise. His eyes laugh a lot behind his spectacles, and he is full of amusing anecdotes. While we were chatting amiably in a basement meeting room, his three colleagues were upstairs in the large first floor room where the four of them work together, watching Mr Brown on television. "Remember the golden rule that the way the markets react in the two days before and after the Budget," Taube says, "is almost invariably in inverse proportion to its quality."[3]

---

[3] In which case the verdict of history on Brown's Budget may be less favourable than the initial positive reaction it received from the press and markets.

The four men sit at a cluster of desks in a spacious corner room, overlooking St James's Place on two sides. They each have a screen, and the desks are piled with bits of paper, newspapers, circulars, listing particulars and so on – all the usual paraphernalia of the business. In the corner is a bookcase with yet more circulars piled on top. This, says Taube, rolling his eyes in mock horror, is his weekend's reading material; he once estimated that he works his way through more than a hundred circulars each weekend and an equal number of annual reports, looking for the spark of a new idea. Amidst this cheerful clutter, which is faintly reminiscent of a college common room, a huge painting hangs rather incongruously on the wall. The working style is informal and collegiate. Taube is the first to emphasise that the performance of his funds is a joint effort. He has worked with John Hodson, who is 20 years his junior, off and on for 15 years; and with Cato Stonex, who is another generation younger still, since 1989. At different times, he has had successful partnerships with other colleagues, among them Nicholas Roditi, who now works for George Soros and whose exceptional skills as a trader have earned him a fortune. The practice of working opposite other like-minded and intelligent minds clearly suits his temperament, although it can be emotionally precarious, too. Working so closely every day with someone is very much like having a family. "We have a very strict rule that we live in glass houses and no stones should be thrown. You could destroy someone with five chosen words." While the four of them have different areas of expertise, in practice they pool their ideas and spread them across their various funds and clients.

Apart from meetings which take them out of the office, Taube and his colleagues sit and bounce ideas off each other, pausing only to watch the prices flickering on their screens. There are echoes here, perhaps deliberate, of the way that the famous partners' room Morgan Grenfell used to operate, and some firms such as the redoubtable Cazenove still do. Taube is one of the survivors of the old City, a man who reached the top of his profession in the days before deregulation. While most of the other leading brokers of the pre-Big Bang era cashed in their chips when their firms were sold to outsiders, Taube is unusual in having opted to carry on. The reason is simply that he finds fund management so much more enjoyable than stockbroking, and relishes the fun of it all.

Has he any plans to retire after such a long time (50 years) in the business? "Not yet." Is it still fun? "Absolutely, absolutely," he replies, bouncing up and down in his chair, as if to prove the point. When he does finally retire, he plans to sell his share of the business to his colleagues at net asset value, not at a premium. Nothing else would occur to him. When he was made senior partner at Kitcat & Aitken, his first decision was to cut his share of the profits to 10%, even though it meant a drop in his income. This is the spirit of the old partnership system writ large. It is a far cry from the "give me £1 million or I'll move to another fund management house" attitude of the younger, more mercenary breed of City fund manager.[4]

INTERNATIONAL PLAGIARISM

Taube has coined the phrase "international plagiarism" to describe one of the themes that has run through his investment philosophy from his earliest days as a stockbroker. What he means by this is that if you know what is happening in business elsewhere in the world, there is a fair bet that, if it works, something similar will happen over here before too long. Like all the great investment insights, this one is deceptively simple. But when he first started trying to apply it more than 40 years ago as a young broker, it was little short of revolutionary. Even now, many professional fund managers remain stubbornly parochial in their approach to security analysis.

One of his earliest, and most successful, discoveries was the UK supermarket. In the mid-1950s, supermarkets had developed in the United States, but nothing had happened over here, except that Express Dairies

---

[4] Taube told me he was offered a partnership in one of the big merchant banks in the early 1960s, but refused it, "not because I didn't want it, but because I felt I had an obligation to stay and look after a firm which had taken a poor boy off the street." Sadly his plans for a harmonious retirement did not work out how he hoped they would.

had started a self-service set up and Tesco had started as well. "It seemed obvious to me," says Taube, "that the concept would travel. With Express Dairies it never did happen, because they made a fool of themselves and gave it up. But with Tesco, it was different, and the value you could buy at that stage was tremendous." Anyone who bought the shares in those days would have seen the shares grow something like 500 times since – all this from spotting a social trend which, although novel to most people in this country at the time, had proved to work in the United States.

"The basic idea," says Taube, "is that good ideas eventually travel. You could foresee what would happen simply in terms of: 'Now I have seen the future and I know it works.'" He has been playing variants on this simple concept ever since. A lot of his investments in Europe, for example, derive from the same kind of thinking. One of his biggest recent investments has been in Coca-Cola Amatil, a company which is listed in Australia but which owns bottling rights to Coke, not just in Australia and New Zealand, but in Indonesia, the Philippines and large parts of Eastern Europe as well. Of all the products of Capitalism which the newly liberated people of Eastern Europe might choose to buy, the one which looks a racing certainty to do well is Coke.

Such thinking has caused the shares of Coca-Cola itself to soar in the last few years. But it is typical that Taube should choose to invest in the trend by a more roundabout route. Coca-Cola has a 40% shareholding in Coca-Cola Amatil. Many investors are wary of investing in companies where effective or majority control rests with a single large shareholder. But Taube is not so concerned, provided there are reasons for thinking that the interests of the larger shareholder are aligned with those of the rest. He believes this is the case with Coca-Cola, whose aim is to support the creation of viable bottling companies with its own high standards, not to stifle shareholder returns. Large or majority shareholdings rule out the prospect of an unsolicited takeover, but the presence of a well-run company as a shareholder with a shared objective in growing value is compensation, he believes, for the loss of the potential takeover premium. As a route into emerging markets, in particular, it has obvious attractions when compared with buying direct holdings in local companies, which are often less well attuned to the needs of Western shareholders. Coca-Cola Amatil has served Taube well: the shares have risen from A$2.64 in 1989 to A$13.45 in 1997.

OIL AND TOBACCO

The first time that Taube realised the value of analysis came only months after he joined the firm of Kitcat & Aitken. The firm was one of two in London which had the bulk of the market in American, Canadian and (to a lesser extent) Australian shares. When his mother escaped from Estonia after the Russians moved in, her son went too, eventually arriving in the UK and becoming a British subject. Originally he was interested in science, and spent a couple of years at night school, but the studying, he says, "interfered with my deb dancing", and the chance of a degree began to seem fairly remote. By 1948, even then a convinced Capitalist, he had begun to feel that there might after all be some future in a financial career. "It is easy to forget that between '45 and '47 one began to think that the whole of Europe would become more and more socialist and left wing, so you might as well know about physics and chemistry as about finance."

As an eager young office boy, Taube spent his spare time reading all the back copies of Moody's in the office. "I read what happened in the Slump. I read the history and said to myself: 'What would I have done in 1929? What would I have done in 1932?'" Within months of starting, he had his first analytical success at Kitcat which set him irreversibly down the path of what we now call 'fundamental research'. Because of the threat of a Labour government, the firm was interested in finding companies with large overseas earnings. However, until the passage of the 1948 Companies Act, which paved the way for the first consolidated group accounts to appear, there was no way of breaking down how much sales and profit came from overseas.

Taube started to look closely at BAT, the tobacco group, which had a large American subsidiary called Brown and Williamson. It didn't publish separate earnings figures, but he managed to get hold of an American advertising magazine called *Printer's Ink* which showed exactly how many cigarettes each of the tobacco brands was selling. By taking a line through the sales figures for the leading American companies, which did publish their earnings figures, and applying a similar weighting to BAT's market position, he was able to make a reasonable guess at how much money Brown and Williamson was making. It turned out to be a lot – something like 50% or more of BAT's total earnings – which made the shares look highly attractive to a British investor.

"People were paying a 36% premium for the dollar and here was something that was at least half and probably three-quarters a dollar earner, available at a very low multiple of earnings and a huge yield basis. I wrote a circular describing what BAT did," says Taube, "and we immediately got orders for millions of shares, at a time when commission was at 1.25% for the first £2500 and then five-eighths of 1% for the rest." The firm made something approaching £100,000 in commission, and the young recruit's salary was put up: from £400 to a princely £500 a year! None of the big London firms had a research department at that stage, and the success of the BAT coup ensured that Kitcats began to think "maybe it was a good idea to let someone loose doing that sort of thing".

Five years later, Taube had another big coup, this time with BP, then still known as the Anglo-Iranian Oil Company. It had just suffered the indignity of having its refinery in Abadan seized by the populist Persian leader, Dr Mossadeq. It meant that all the oil that BP produced in Kuwait and Iran had to be sent at huge cost to its refineries in Europe before being shipped out to its customers in the Far East. BP decided to build a refinery in Aden. "It sounds a crazy idea now, but it was quite a bright idea at the time," says Taube. Pouring over the numbers, he worked out that the decision was worth at least £2 or £3 a tonne to BP, and that all the benefit would flow straight through the company's bottom line. His note to clients resulted in the shares jumping 25% in a single day. Nowadays, when all the leading broking firms have specialist oil and gas analysts, and companies such as BP employ full-time in-house investor relations executives, such glaring anomalies could not exist. But in those days, information was much scarcer and attitudes were very different.

"Actually my bosses didn't believe what I had written," Taube recalls, "so they sent me to the treasurer of BP and showed him the papers and he looked at me and said, 'Of course I cannot comment on them.' But I asked him if he thought the figures were rubbish and he said, 'No.' So it began to work that way." It was around this time that the Society of Investment Analysts was born. The technical sophistication of investment analysis is light years forward from where it was in the 1950s, but the basic principles – "you have to find out what is happening in other countries and assume that ideas travel" – have remained the same. What Anthony Bolton calls his "industry arbitrage" approach is based on similar thinking. The remarkable thing about Taube is not that he is still so committed to the "journey of discovery" that led him into investment analysis in the first place, but that 40 years on he is still showing most of his younger rivals a clean pair of heels.

LATERAL THINKING

Even when he was still a stockbroker, Taube was aware that the broker's traditional method of managing money for individual clients was unsatisfactory, not least because it made no economic sense to make separate decisions for each individual investor. That was how the unit trust which survives today as the Progressive Greater European fund started life. (It was originally called the Bishopsgate Progressive Unit Trust, but that had to be changed when the fraudster Robert Maxwell acquired an investment trust with a similar name.) In fact, Taube says he hated a lot of what being a stockbroker was about. The money was good. He was earning £250,000 a year by 1972, the equivalent of £1.5 million today (although even then broking was "nothing like the fantastic business it is today"). "But the reason I didn't like broking was that it was essentially selling ideas to other people rather than doing things yourself. I found it somewhat humiliating to have thought out something in great detail and then finding that people rather dismissed it."

So, I suggested, it was more the fascination of doing the analysis than the money which motivated him. "Yes, it is the analysis that excites me. Also I suppose a form of vanity. Trying to do things that other people aren't doing." His family in Estonia had been quite rich before the Russian Revolution, but there was certainly no great tradition of money-making in his family. "My father was very bright with this sort of thing, but I am not conscious of him ever having done any work." The one thing he knew for certain from an early age, says Taube, was that he was a Capitalist at heart. To make money from the stock market, as with any other activity, it helps to set out with an unshaking faith in the wisdom and necessity of what you are doing.

When Taube talks about the value of plagiarism as an investor, he means it quite often in a literal sense. There are plenty of occasions, he says, when all you have to do is borrow somebody else's ideas and then apply them with profitable advantage yourself. He gives the example of insurance company shares. He made a lot of money – up to a hundred times his original money in some cases – by buying the shares of German life insurance companies in the late 1960s and early 1970s. This success was almost entirely down to the work of an American friend and professional colleague called Shelby Cullom Davis. Taube met him through the Society of Investment Analysts. He was the president of the American society and also the man who, as they say, "wrote the book" about how to value life insurance shares. He was the first analyst to explain in detail why the way in which life insurance companies traditionally reported their earnings (charging the full cost of selling a policy to profits in the first year) had the effect of masking the real, or underlying, value of their business. He "completely changed the valuation of insurance shares and I think left a billion dollars", says Taube. Before Shelby Davis, the traditional way to value an insurance company was on a dividend yield basis. His innovation was to add back the cost of accruing each new policy and depreciate it over a period of years, recognising that the acquisition cost was akin to an investment of capital, not an annual expense. Valuing the companies in this way gave a truer insight into their economic value, and in time led to a fundamental re-rating of their shares by the market. Applying the same analytical principles to German and English insurance company shares reaped Taube handsome rewards.

What qualities then does Taube think it takes to become a successful investor? Top of his list is "curiosity about everything and anything". Without an ineffable zeal for discovery, any amount of technical analytical skills counts for little. Investing professionally, he believes, is not, and never can be, a nine-to-five job: it has to be totally absorbing. A reputation for being one of the market's "top guns" is also a help. "If the market knows that you are one of the better guns, they are more likely to call you before they call anyone else. Better still, when you own something, is to be early on the list of those who get a call when something goes wrong, as it often does. This is where the quality of your connections can really make a difference." Other important qualities are a willingness to be opportunistic (a word that comes up again and again in conversation with Taube) and the ability to see the bigger picture that lies behind the endless "noise" created by the torrent of daily news and information which floods across the trading floors of the main brokerages and fund management houses around the City.

His own experience cautions him, he says, against trying to predict where the market is going to go. "I have always believed in looking at companies and industries rather than saying the Japanese market is about to go up, or the Spanish market will go down. I have accepted the fact that prediction is futile as far as markets are concerned. There are simply too many different things that affect them." As a result, he said once, "People always ask me what I think of the market. But I argue it does not matter much what I think. It does not go up or down because of my views."[5] He admires those, such as Soros, who are prepared to try to call the turns in the market, and back their judgement with huge bets. But, in his own experience, there have been only a handful of occasions since World War II when it has been important to take notice of the overall level of the market: 1973-74 was obviously one. Another was in 1987, when the

---

[5] Interview in *Money Observer*, January 1995.

market became seriously overheated and most of the traditional valuation indicators, such as dividend yield, went off the scale of historical experience.

When the market crashed dramatically in October of that year, it came as no surprise to him, although it proved not to have permanent long-term effects. Taube had increased his liquidity in the months leading up to the crash. The company also took a big bet on the futures market that the stock market was going to fall. For a while this left him heavily out of the money, and exposed to ribbing from his fellow directors, but proved to be the right thing to have done. By the end of the year he had covered his short position and was once again fully invested, taking advantage of the much cheaper prices now on offer, regretting only that he had not had the courage of his friend George Soros and taken an even bigger position. The great secret of Soros's success, he believes, has been his continued willingness to take big positions, betting the firm on his judgements about the markets, long after he has proved his ability to outmanoeuvre everyone else. It is common for Soros to lose tens of millions of dollars in a morning; yet, says Taube, he always remains as cool as a daisy.

MANAGEMENT MATTERS

Sometimes Taube will make an investment solely on the strength of a change in the management of a company. One recent example is Great Universal Stores, the retail and mail order business which was built up over many years by Sir Isaac Wolfson, and which boasts an almost unrivalled record in consistent dividend growth over a period of more than 40 years. Since Sir Isaac's retirement and death, the company has been run in a much more conservative way, unwilling or unable to catch up with the changing dynamics of the retail business. But all that changed, in Taube's view, a couple of years ago, when the company appointed a new chairman from a different branch of the Wolfson family. David Wolfson (Lord Wolfson of Sunningdale) had been Mrs Thatcher's chief of staff in Downing Street for several years before becoming chairman of Next, the

High Street fashion chain, and presiding over its remarkable recovery from near bankruptcy in the early 1990s. "The company was getting very sclerotic," says Taube. "David Wolfson is a very capable businessman and retailer, and we invested solely on the basis of the regard we have for him and his business acumen."

It has been a similar story at Cable & Wireless, once a government-owned telecommunications company, which after a bright start as a privatised company has struggled to make further headway as an international telecommunications operator. In 1996, it became embroiled in a bizarre internal power struggle which ended, unusually, with both the main combatants, the chairman and the chief executive, being asked to leave the company at virtually the same time, leaving behind a boardroom that looked like the last act of *Hamlet*, with the bodies of protagonists all around. Taube says he had little admiration for the previous management's decisions, but has a high regard for the man, Richard Brown, who was brought in to clear up the mess. "He is doing very much what we hoped he would do," says Taube. This is to use the company's shareholding in the Hong Kong Telephone Company as a lever with which to gain access to the enormous potential of the mainland Chinese telecommunications market. The key point is that the investment was based "very much on the management issue". Taube bought the shares for 450 to 500 pence.

Most managers, in Britain and abroad, are "really quite competent and intelligent", Taube reckons, but how important those qualities are to investors depends on what business they are in. Traditional cyclical industries are a case in point. "I mean, you might be a brilliant manager in a ready-mix concrete business, but if a huge slump comes along, what the hell can you do about it? That is one of the reasons why I don't invest in the ready-mix concrete business. All right, you might have three or four good years; but there are too many other things to decide. I don't really like the steel business for the same reason. You are flotsam on a big pool. If the steel business is so awful that everyone thinks it is going broke, you might play a game of buying it for the recovery, but then you just make another mistake and decide to sell it at the wrong time." Taube says his own preference is for undervalued growth companies, where the growth potential is not recognised, or, failing that, for companies where strong growth is the exception but where there is an underlying pattern of stability in the earnings. That way, provided there is reasonably intelligent management in place, you don't have to worry too much about things going too badly wrong. "But if you have the sort of manager who has done brilliantly well in Beechams or Coca-Cola taking on a steel company, well, he simply couldn't do it."[6]

KEEPING IT SIMPLE

Looking through the lists of shares in Taube's portfolio, what stands out is that they tend to be shaped around a handful of relatively simple investment themes. These are his ideas of the moment, and they tend to dominate what he owns: not for him the elaborate modern business of constructing "optimised" portfolios with the help of a computerised model. At 31 May 1997, for example, the year-end of his Greater European fund, the portfolio had plenty of European bank shares, reflecting his biggest current theme – the inevitable restructuring and consolidation of the financial industry across Europe in the run up to the introduction of a single currency. Despite widespread scepticism in Britain, Taube says he has no doubt that monetary union will happen, and says everyone will be "very surprised" at the extent to which Britain will be a participant in the process. He also had a number of holdings in German and Italian insurance companies, where he expects widespread consolidation to take place, and in Peugeot, Fiat and other European car manufacturers. The theme here, apart from the necessary requirement that the shares look cheap, is that, as internal trade barriers come down, and foreign competition intensifies, Europe will no longer be able to support having five or six independent national manufacturers, each with a 10% share of the market. The United States has long got by with just "two and a half to three" big manufacturers (General Motors, Ford and the now successful,

---

[6] Warren Buffett has a famous aphorism on similar lines: "When a management with a reputation for brilliance tackles a business with a reputation for bad economics, it is the reputation of the business that remains intact."

but previously periodically near-bankrupt, Chrysler), and that is the kind of structure at which Europe must eventually arrive. But haven't people been predicting this for years, I asked, without it coming to pass? Taube smiles and replies: "Shake the tree long enough and you will be surprised what falls out."[7]

When Taube has a good idea, he likes to back it in more than one way. As an opportunist, quite how long he runs with an idea depends on how events fall out. If the story seems to be a valid one, he may add more stocks of the same type. If, on the other hand, it turns out that the original thesis was flawed, he will just as quickly change his mind, dump the shares and try something else. Some ideas he likes enough to let run for some time. On other occasions, he takes his profit when he thinks the price has risen high enough, and tries something else instead. Later, as with, say, his holdings in IFI (the holding company for Fiat and other Agnelli-controlled companies in Italy), he may come back to a company for a second or third bite of the cherry. On the relatively rare occasions when the overall level of the market is important, he will happily move heavily into cash. His holdings show that he is, as he says himself, an out and out opportunist, an analyst of value who also accepts the inherent unpredictably of the markets and has the ability to swim with the ebb and flow.

The phrase that kept coming into my mind, listening as Taube talked about his triumphs and disasters over the years, was the one that someone once applied to another consummate investor, Keynes. Like Keynes, Taube has a 'liquid mind', one that can range widely and shift gears, so to speak, in order to keep pace with the changing course of events. ("When the facts change, I change my mind. What do you do?" Keynes memorably retorted when accused of inconsistency.)

Another striking feature of Taube's conversation is the facility with which he uses numbers to support his recollections. Like many great investors, while the detailed reasons why he bought or sold something may have long since been forgotten, the price at which he bought and sold his past investments is the one thing which never seems to go. But his view is that while numeracy is important in analysing investments, it is far from the

---

[7] Appendix 3 gives details of Taube's portfolio at 31 May 1997.

only necessary quality. Mathematically, he says, he is "aware of the rule of 72, but that doesn't mean I am a great genius at numbers".

When analysing companies, Taube prefers to focus on cash flow multiples rather than on conventional price/earnings ratios, and finds enterprise value divided by pre-tax and pre-interest cash flow another helpful measure. Unlike Colin McLean, whose analysis produces pages of detailed numbers, Taube has reached a stage where he is happy to work with broader strokes, relying on the quality of his ideas and his years of experience to pick up pricing anomalies. The key point, and the one which McLean also makes, is that the numbers shape decisions, but never define them. As in other walks of life, the important thing is to be roughly right rather than precisely wrong.

In addition to unbridled curiosity, the other quality an investor needs, he thinks, is the ability to listen well. When he was an investment analyst, Taube used to take pleasure in talking to different managers of a company – the chairman, finance director and so on – and putting the various bits of information they gave him together to form a more rounded picture, rather like filling in a jigsaw. Quite often, it enabled him to surprise the company by telling them what the margins of a product were without having been formally told. Having a good memory, remembering what had been said before and extrapolating from it to the present is another invaluable technique for investors, he says. The more you know about a company, and the more you can surprise the management with your knowledge, the more information they are likely to give you.

THE NEXT MARKET CORRECTION

Given his track record in calling the big stock market corrections of the past, does Taube think that current valuations are getting dangerously high? His answer (in July 1997) was that we are approaching a stage where euphoria in the US market is once again starting to match the level it reached in 1987, shortly before the market crash of that year. He points out that the main market indices have risen something like eight times in the last 15 years. This is a compound rate of return of 14% per annum, something which with inflation at 4% simply cannot be sustained forever. If his Greater European fund were to grow at the same rate of growth it has done in the 28 years that he has been running it, it would not be long before it would be bigger than the GDP of several countries. The mathematics, Taube concludes, are inexorable: "There is no way that anyone who buys my funds can expect to do as well in the next twenty-eight years as they have done in the previous 28." A fall in the rate of return from the stock market is therefore inevitable at some stage: the only question is how it is achieved – in one big crash or more gradually over time. How does he think it will play out? "Like it has always played out before," says Taube. "Greed overtakes sense and things go too far and some unexpected thing happens. It could be a war, it could be anything. You never know." What worries him is that even sophisticated private investors have become so used to living in a bull market that they have started to take returns of 20% a year as the norm. With low inflation, that is simply not a sustainable long-term rate of return, and investors will have to learn to live with nominal returns which are lower. Money illusion is a dangerous phenomenon, and one that may itself contribute to the development of a climate of excessive expectations and the froth at the top of a market cycle.

Like a number of UK-based investors, Taube's recent performance has been held back in the previous 18 months by his underestimating the continued strength of the US stock market, but that does little to change his view that the market is getting dangerously high. "It would be foolish to say that the American market will break in the next three months. It may do. It may not. But the valuations have become so high that it is unreasonable to expect it to go on for much longer." He mentioned a report that Tobin's q ratio, a measure of the stock market's value relative to the replacement costs of the country's productive assets, had reached an all-time high of four times in the United States.[8] In his view, about the only thing that is keeping the US market going now is the market's own

---

[8] The q ratio is named after Professor James Tobin, one of America's many Nobel Prize winners in Economics.

momentum. "There are a lot of players who come into the market who only believe in momentum and of course as soon as there is a stumble and momentum tilts the other way, they will have exactly the same feelings about the downside as the upside." At the time of our most recent conversations, with the Dow Jones Index heading towards a record level of 8000, Taube had been selling what he called "a modicum of S&P shorts" (i.e. futures contracts which will pay out only if the main US market index, the S&P 500, falls). "They are costing us a fortune, but it is still an anaesthetic that I think we need." The US market, in other words, is in his view ripe for a correction.

The best warning sign that markets are set to fall is usually an upward movement in interest rates, Taube says, and a consequent widening of the gap between yields on government bonds and equities. At the time of writing, this particular warning signal had not yet started to sound. The yield ratio between bonds and equities had not entered a danger zone.[9] "In 1987, you had a six- to eight-month warning signal from the bond market, and it is normal to expect an advance warning of about that time. That is not there yet today," he says. Whereas in 1987 bond prices fell steadily for most of the year, while share prices continued to go up sending the yield ratio to near record levels, in 1997 the stock market has been very strong, but medium and long bond yields have if anything been trending lower. So the yield ratio is still not greatly out of line with its normal trading parameters.

The UK market is "in some ways not dissimilar", but with the intriguing added factor of a new Labour government that is keen to establish its centrist credentials. "The main thing you can say about the UK is that we have got, for I suppose the first time in my lifetime, a market where fear of socialism is totally absent. When Margaret Beckett [the Cabinet minister for trade and industry in Tony Blair's new government] makes speeches saying that she doesn't mind utilities making money, these are strange times. But at the same time the Conservatives are behaving so

---

[9] The yield ratio measures the relationship between the yields on medium- or long-term government bonds and the dividend yield of the stock market as a whole. Thus if gilts are yielding 8% and the stock market is yielding 4%, the yield ratio is 2.0. In the UK, the ratio tends to fluctuate in a range from 2.0 to 2.5. In 1987, the ratio touched 3.0, a height it had only reached once before, in 1972.

irrationally, quarrelling with each other, that it is just possible that the Labour Party will be able to keep the central ground and keep the middle classes happy." With the pound too high, the other important determinant of how well the UK performs is going to be how quickly Britain is able to enter the single currency, something which Taube, with his pan-European perspective, regards as essential.

COMPANIES IN THE SPOTLIGHT

Most of the time, however, the general level of the market, says Taube, can be safely left to take care of itself. With companies, the story is different. On the assumption that a company is being run properly, he says, looking at the comparative value of stocks on a worldwide basis creates "a kind of osmotic pressure between countries which causes valuation anomalies to converge over time". Rank Xerox was an early example where he made a lot of money. John Davies, then head of Rank, managed to persuade Xerox to set up a 50-50 joint venture to market its then revolutionary photocopying technology. He set up a company structure that gave a small and otherwise little-known company called A. Kershaw an indirect holding of 10% in the new joint venture. For a while, because the market failed to understand this complex structure, it meant that by buying Kershaw shares, you could effectively buy 10% of Rank Xerox for £1 million. This was at a time when the parent company, Xerox, was valued in its own market at $1 billion. When the joint venture was eventually unwound many years later, the Rank Xerox business was valued at £1 billion, giving shareholders in Kershaw a hundred-fold return on the original cost 30 years before. Some time afterwards, Taube also unearthed the fact that you could buy shares in Rembrandt, the penultimate holding company for Rothmans, at a price which valued it at no more than a single year's cashflow. That investment, too, has since performed spectacularly, rising by "something like a thousandfold", Taube reckons, although "like an idiot", he says, he sold out well before the full value had been realised.

With the professionalisation of the investment analysis business over the last 40 years, it is becoming more difficult to make such huge returns "because there are so many people around looking for the needles in the haystack. If you are the only one looking for the needle, there is a fair chance you will find it first, but if you set a thousand men on the job, then the odds on being the first to find the needle are clearly not so good." Perhaps, says Taube, on reflection, he should not have been so keen to educate the competition, which is what the Society of Investment Analysts he founded helped to do. At this point I mentioned something which Warren Buffett once said to me: that although the methods he was using were hardly mysterious – "the secrets have been out for years" – their manifest superiority was not in itself enough to prompt more of his competitors to adopt a similar approach. "That's absolutely correct", Taube agreed. "I think that the element of disbelief and fear and greed hasn't really changed. Most investors still refuse to see things even when they are staring them in the face." He mentioned two topical examples: (1) the Japanese stock market, which despite falling 60% since 1989 and offering "tremendous value", was still widely shunned by many investors who thought it was finished; (2) bank shares, which in the UK and the United States have had a spectacular run since the 1990-91 recession. What has been overlooked, Taube reckons, are the remarkable anomalies in the way the banks are rated between and within different national markets. For example, Citicorp, the largest American bank, has gone up nearly fifteen times in value in the last seven years. Having been valued at just 2-3% of its total assets at one time, the company's shares are now valued at 30% of total assets. Yet, across the Atlantic you could still buy BNP, the French bank, at 3-4% of total assets, most of the German banks at 10 or 12% on the same measure and Italian banks at 4% or less. Some of the UK bank shares have followed the US example, and appreciated strongly, but here too the valuation differences are enormous: Lloyds/TSB sells at 23% of total assets, Barclays at 13% and NatWest at 7.5%.

It is absurd, says Taube, to have this huge range of pricing discrepancy. "The prices are telling you that Lloyds is successful, but is it three times more valuable as another bank which is doing exactly the same thing but marginally less successfully?" Taube has been loading up on UK and European banks for some time. "The market's assumption was that Barclays or NatWest cannot get sensible management in. But sooner or later this is going to have to change. In fact this has already begun. The one thing you never want to buy is something because you think a takeover is about to happen. It really is an asinine reason for buying, because maybe NatWest will be taken over, but it is much more likely that they are going to sort themselves out." The point he is making is that such anomalies are unsustainable in the medium to longer term; to that extent Taube is an old-fashioned value investor. If things get so bad that a takeover does happen, the chances are that the new owners will find they have even greater scope to improve margins and returns than anyone dreamed possible beforehand. This is what happened to the Midland Bank in the 1980s. "They were so miserable that they just couldn't sort themselves out. They had to be taken over. When the Hong Kong & Shanghai Bank took them over, I just couldn't believe what they were able to do with it. We had sackfuls of Midland, but again I sold much too early." The original Rothschild formula for making money was based on the premise that it was never wrong to sell too early, but this helpful advice clearly still rankles with professionals when they miss out on an extended run in something they have bought and sold.

Rather like Michael Hart, Taube says that he didn't really begin to realise how good he was at managing money until he started running unit trusts and discovered from the performance tables that he was doing better than most other people. Until then, running his broker funds, he had always assumed that everyone else was doing better than he was. He draws an analogy with another activity where performance is not always readily comparable. "If you wanted to make love to a woman," he says, "she's not going to tell you you're better than the others. She might even keep quiet." It was quite a shock when he found out that the average level of performance was so low when what he was doing seemed so simple that "a blind fool could have done it".

One thing Taube has never forgotten from his days as a stockbroker is the need to have a healthy scepticism about the realities of business compared with the way that it is presented by those in it. In the days before the Big Bang, anyone who was a partner in one of the big broking firms that dominated the gilts business was more or less guaranteed a good living, as commissions were so high. Some firms made millions of pounds in a matter of months. One broking acquaintance told Taube that his firm made more money in the great bear market of 1974 than in the previous year – despite the fact that the rest of the City imagined the firm was bleeding to death. The only problem with the system as it stood was that partners had to finance the business themselves. The Stock Exchange insisted on unlimited liability so that a partner's assets were effectively tied up in the business as capital. Taube reckoned he needed to make £250,000 a year simply in order to pay the taxman, educate three children and put cash back into the firm. It was a great business while it lasted, in other words, but not quite as lucrative as it was made out to be. Taube says: "I lived largely on what I made in the market myself." As a fund manager, not only is the work more fun, but the rewards are more readily realisable as well.

As will be apparent by now, working on such a broad international basis means that Taube also likes to cast his net wide in the search for ideas. Companies are one source of ideas, and so too are broking analysts. He and his three colleagues don't talk to brokers so much, except for a dozen or so whom they use as what he calls "bird dogs" in their own organisations. "If you have got big companies such as Morgan Stanley, I cannot easily find out which of their individual analysts are good or bad. Sometimes I find out because of what they write, but it is useful to have people inside the organisation who can say, 'Fred here has got a good idea. Can I bring him round?' Then we can judge whether Fred has got a good idea or not ourselves. That is the value of a good broker; plus the fact that some are good at executing business, especially on the selling side. If a share hasn't been successful, I don't feel obliged to go to the person who put us in. All our unsuccessful ideas go to one or two brokers who we know are particularly good at selling shares." He mentions Cazenove in this context, for their unrivalled placing power, and Henderson Crosthwaite. The important thing about brokers, he says, is that "they should be people whom one feels comfortable with". For international stocks, the need to have good relationships is even more important, especially in Japan where outsiders are "paddling in the dark".

Unlike, say, an Anthony Bolton, who is looking for a fairly rapid return on his investment, Taube is prepared to be more patient if he has to be.

He too likes to build up relatively large holdings of shares about which he has strong convictions, and will happily sit with 5, 8 or even 10% of the shares in a particular company he likes. His turnover is not particularly high by industry standards, he reckons, but this too he points out is an area where fund managers are often capable of deluding themselves. "On the whole our turnover is motivated by something not going well. If something doesn't do too well, we'll cut it rather than keep it. Our turnover is governed more by fear than by greed. When something goes well, we are likely to let it run." Taube has no more time for efficient markets, or academic theory, than any of the other investors in this book. Despite his analytical background, he says he finds it impossible to read most of the material produced by financial economists, as it is so complicated and "articles written by two people I naturally suspect anyway".

Overall, he likens the idea of finding new investment ideas to fishing. "I am not a fisherman, but I imagine fishing is a bit like what we do. You sit by a pool and when you think there may be something there, you get your fly over the water and you fish for it. But the main thing is that when you see something, you must have a sense of proportions in your head." This turns out to be a key point in his approach, and one which prompts a sudden display of apparently meaningless waving of the hands. "How do you see a group of figures going from one to a hundred million. How do you visualise it?" he asks. "I see it as a sort of path which goes like this [his hands weave in and out, like a child describing the movement of a fish]. I have done it all my life. I can always tell exactly where everything is in relation to each other. From one to a hundred is like this, to a thousand goes like this, to ten thousand goes like this. It is a sort of repeating path. I can see it all before me. I have got the comparison between values and capitalisations in my mind all the time. If it deviates, it strikes me straight away."

His mind operates with a kind of early warning system that alerts him when something looks out of line with the value that he is mentally carrying in his head. Like an experienced chess player, whose deep memory carries thousands of positions which he recognises the moment they come up, Taube hears the alarm bells ring when something departs from its normal trading range. He gives the example of IFI, the Italian holding company, controlled by the Agnelli family, which owns Fiat. "I hadn't looked at it for years, having made lots of money out of it 12 years ago. I felt negative on Fiat. I think I sold IFI in 1986 for L30,000 or L33,000. Then suddenly I saw it at L11,000 and I said: 'Well, they must have split the shares, or something.' But they hadn't. So I went back and asked, 'What is the asset value now?', and they said, 'It is L45,000 before tax.' So I said, 'You mean it is at 25% of book value?' They said, 'Yes'. So I said, 'Well, if what they have got isn't so bad, I might as well buy it at a third of what we sold it for 10 years ago.'" The shares have since gone from L11,000 to L22,000. It was simply a case, concludes Taube, of reading a lot and waiting "to suddenly click the connection".

CONCLUSION

Not all professional investors are people one would necessarily choose to spend one's time with. Investment can be a dull subject in the wrong hands. Nils Taube is an exception, a man whose mind is a ferment of new ideas. He is as far removed from the technocratic approach to investment as it is possible to be, a stylist in the mould of a David Gower or Tom Graveney, rather than a Geoffrey Boycott. He is not, by some accounts, the easiest man to work alongside. What excites him is the pursuit of new ideas and the discovery of something different. His method, he says, relies on "a lot of reading and a lot of talking", which is why he operates best when he can bounce ideas off a like-minded colleague. He works on a five-year time horizon, but is prepared to change tack quickly if need be. His view is that to be a successful investor requires "a mixture of steadfastness and just a dash of cowardice as well. To be totally stubborn is dangerous."

UPDATE (2012)

Nils Taube died suddenly the way he wanted, at his desk in his office in March 2008. By then he was widely feted as one of the longest serving and most brilliant investors of his generation. Two years before his death, aged 77 he founded a new firm, Nils Taube Investments, having parted company from his colleagues at Taube Hodson Stonex shortly before.

5. COLIN MCLEAN:

Seeking the truth behind the numbers

If you were asked to go and find some entrepreneurial talent in the investment business, it is a fair bet that one of the last places you would want to look is in the actuarial department of a Scottish life insurance company. There may be more conservative business institutions than a Scottish insurance company, but there are certainly not many – just as there are few more conservative professions than actuaries. A career spent calculating the odds of people dying before their time is not, by and large, a natural testbed for budding entrepreneurs.

Yet, remarkably, Colin McLean emerged from just such a background to become one of Britain's most successful specialist fund managers. At the age of 37, with three children to provide for, he left his job running the European operation of one of the world's best known specialist fund management companies, Templeton, to launch his own uncertain business. For two years he survived without a salary, drawing on the capital that had been earmarked for his pension fund, and relying on consultancy income to keep him afloat while he tried to establish a foothold in the lucrative business of managing other people's money, and recruit a team to help him do so.

Twenty years on, McLean has secured his reputation as a successful boutique fund manager, with more than £700 million of investor funds under management. The risk that he took in starting his own company,

Scottish Value Management (since renamed SVM Asset Management), has turned out, he recalls, to be a great investment. "I effectively funded it myself, which involved raiding my own pension fund, so I was investing pretty much all of what I had. I suppose it might have been easier if there had been any tradition or experience in my family of establishing businesses, but there wasn't. On the other hand, I knew there was a lot of interest in what we were proposing to do among the investment institutions, so we had reasonable encouragement from an early stage that there was going to be a role for the company."

In the twenty years since the company started, the amount of money under management has risen from £30 million at the end of the first year to £200 million two years later and around £700 million at the last count. McLean and his team now run a number of different investment funds, including two investment trusts and open-ended equivalents. His two best known vehicles are the SVM UK Growth Fund and the SVM Global Fund (formerly the Scottish Value Trust). In its early days SVM Global Fund set out to buy shares in poorly performing investment trusts and act as a catalyst to bring about improvements in performance, for example by engineering a takeover and ousting the incumbent management group. Today it is run as a more conventional global fund of funds with nearly 50 different closed and open-ended funds in its portfolio. McLean's business has had its ups and downs, losing two of its investment managers to a rival firm and suffering another setback in 2012 with the sudden resignation of his co-founder, Donald Roberston. Such incidents are a reminder that investment management is first and foremost a people business. Personal issues can threaten even the most successful firms, as a number of hedge funds have discovered in recent years. It can be trying to strike the balance between the needs of the business and the demands of the investment process.

VALUE INVESTING WITH A TWIST

The investment philosophy that runs through all these different activities is the same. As the company's origins suggest, Colin McLean is, by experience and instinct, a 'value investor'. That is to say, he works on the basis that shares have an intrinsic value which is often at odds with the price at which the shares are trading on the stock market. His belief, like that of all value investors, is that if you buy a share which you believe is trading at less than its intrinsic value, the share price will eventually rise to reflect that higher value. It may take a few months, or it may take several years, but the 'valuation gap' will eventually disappear. The first essential skill of a value investor is therefore to identify undervalued shares.

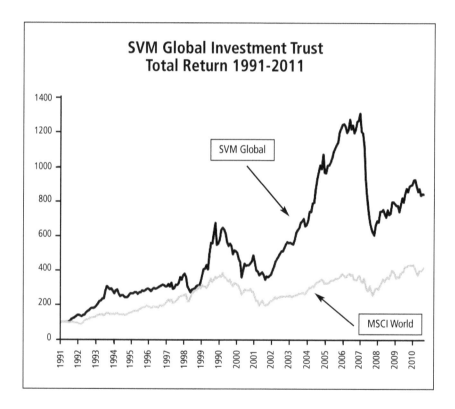

Colin McLean had been racking up good performance figures for some time before he started his own fund management business. The SVM Global Fund (formerly Scottish Value Trust), launched in 1992, continued that trend for many years before suffering badly in the 2008 financial crisis and again in 2012.

This is what Colin McLean sets out to do. However, he differs from other, more conventional, value investors in a number of ways. For a start, his valuation techniques are more sophisticated than most. They rely on a highly developed method of financial analysis which clearly owes a lot to his professional training. While actuaries may not be natural entrepreneurs, they do tend to love numbers with a passion and intensity that is beyond the ken of most ordinary investors. The credo of SVM is built around the belief that they can get more out of company financial statistics than their rivals. As McLean's colleague Neil Veitch puts it: "Our value added is valuation."

Second, McLean has a conviction that identifying undervalued shares is not enough. The investment portfolio needs to be actively managed as well if it is to produce superior results. In particular, that means identifying the catalyst which is going to cause the stock market to recognise the intrinsic value of the shares. There has to be a change in something for the value to be realised. It may be a change in management at a specific company. It may be a change in market sentiment towards that company. Or, it may be a new trend in an industry. There are lots of possibilities. What McLean recognises is that professional investors do not have to sit back and wait passively for others to see the value which is there. It is part of their responsibility to go out, if necessary, and help to engineer that change. How you manage your share portfolio, he says, is in some ways more important than picking the right shares in the first place.

Third, McLean has based his investment career on the need to be disciplined but open-minded in approaching the stock market. His rigorous method of financial analysis provides the discipline. He will not invest in a share where he has not analysed and fully understood its financial characteristics. But the ideas themselves come from a wide variety of sources – from quantitative methods, stockbrokers, newspapers, conversations with other investors, and from his own contacts and experience. He is as happy to invest in a casino business as he is an aerospace company. The only restriction he imposes on himself is that he has to be comfortable that he understands the dynamics of the business in which he is investing. This, ironically, he finds, is one of the hardest constraints of all to overcome.

A MINIMALIST BUSINESS

Although he did his actuarial training in Glasgow, McLean plies his trade today in Edinburgh's New Town, the heart of the Scottish capital's financial quarter. His office is on the sixth floor of a ten-year-old office block in Castle Street. From the balcony, and through the floor-to-ceiling windows, there are extensive views across Edinburgh (at least when the rain ceases and the mist lifts). To the north lies the Firth of Forth, to the south the brooding dark stone bulk of Edinburgh Castle and Arthur's Seat. Immediately below is the bustle of Princes Street, Edinburgh's main shopping thoroughfare. Charlotte Square, traditional home of Scotland's investment elite, is just around the corner.

McLean works in a single open-plan office, surrounded by two dozen staff. He is a quiet, undemonstrative man, solidly built with a ready smile and a soft voice that betrays none of the hard edges of a classical Glaswegian burr. This may be deceptive: the one word that rivals use most often about McLean is 'tough'. He is not afraid to confront vested interests or to court unpopularity if need be. His colleagues sit at clusters of desks, all within easy talking distance. When McLean set up on his own, he had just two colleagues. One was Donald Robertson, formerly of Ivory & Sime, responsible for looking after the investment trust portfolio. The second was his wife, Margaret Lawson, an investment manager in her own right, whom he met while at university. (This is no longer unusual in an industry which in little more than one generation has ceased to be an all-male preserve and now attracts many of the brightest female graduates.) She juggles her time between looking after their five children and helping to research and make investment decisions in her specialist areas of media, leisure and retail. Since then he has recruited a number of other investment managers to support the team. The senior three, Neil Veitch, Hugh Cuthbert and James Cooke, are in their mid-thirties and cast in his own mould of acute numeracy.

Fund management is a business that relies on a flow of good information, but McLean's office policy is to keep paperwork, and all the other extraneous trappings of a business, to a minimum. When SVM was set up, he had the very clear idea that he wanted to set up a specialist boutique which sold 'pure' fund management skills, without the burden of a large administrative or marketing apparatus on top. The way the office is set up reflects this minimalist approach. The library, for example, barely fills one corner of the office. It has annual reports and documentary material about SVM, but little else – unusual when he started, more common now in the digital age. The brokers' circulars and other clutter which you still find in many fund managers' offices are not much in evidence. Administrative work is either carried out by one of McLean's administrative assistants or contracted out elsewhere. At first, to encourage the spirit of informality, there were no formal investment meetings at all. Now there are weekly investment meetings, where the fund managers swap ideas about individual stocks and the information they have picked up at company meetings. Little time is wasted on the macro-economic climate. The setup is simple, tidy and efficient, as befits a specialist fund management business, run by a tidy and efficient mind. All the extraneous paraphernalia has been pared away deliberately, one might say, leaving only the intellectual capital on view.

WORKING WITH NUMBERS

I have mentioned already that McLean is obsessed with numbers, and so he is. This is the man to visit if you want a tutorial on detailed company analysis. His business is founded on a commitment to understanding the financial characteristics of business. Over the past twenty years, he and his team of six fund managers have refined and developed their own computerised model of investment appraisal. This they use for two purposes: (1) to 'screen' the available universe of quoted companies looking for those that are likely to meet their investment criteria; and (2) to build a detailed financial profile of any potential investment they are considering. This is no more than many of today's fund managers do. But McLean and his colleagues claim, with justification, to have been earlier into it and to do it better than most.

Their basic working canvas is the UK and Europe, where they routinely screen basic financial data on 3800 companies. A typical filtering exercise might go as follows. They start with a database search to find all the companies that meet the following criteria:

- a market capitalisation of £100 million or more

- positive cash flow (both before and after capital expenditure)

- six years of positive sales per share growth

- a return on capital in excess of 10%.

This might typically winnow the list of potential candidates down to a hundred. Of these, say, two-thirds will be ruled out on other grounds. McLean's team then sit down to work their way through the names that remain in much more detail. If they are lucky, they will end up with three or four specific investment ideas, which they will then go off to research further, through online searches, brokers' reports and so on. It sounds a laborious process, but sophisticated terminals with real time data means that the screening process can be completed in a matter of minutes. When he first started analysing companies, it would have taken weeks of concentrated effort.

The data for the screening exercises comes from established sources of online information, mainly Reuters and Bloomberg. This is commercial information that is available to any fund manager or private investor who can afford it. On its own, therefore, it confers no appreciable competitive advantage. What matters is what you do with the data. This is what adds the value. Data needs to be combined with external information to gain insight. The methodology McLean and his colleagues use is very much their own creation, and has been refined over the years.

Unlike conventional investment analysis, which focuses on accounting data and market-derived ratios such as price/earnings ratios, dividend yields and price to book value, McLean's team have developed their own, more sophisticated, discipline. Because of differences in accounting standards, says McLean, the traditional US techniques of value investing, pioneered by Ben Graham and refined by Sir John Templeton and others, do not translate all that well to the UK. "I realised that while value investing was a good approach and a sensible way of looking at investment, the actual tools you need to make it work in the UK were slightly different from the traditional ones."

Whereas traditional security analysis is based on accounting ratios, McLean's is based on a search for what is now more widely known as economic value.[1] The principle is to focus more on the cash generated over time by a business than on the short-term trend in reported profits. It also involves looking first at the value of a business as a whole, and only secondarily at how it has been financed – how much by debt, and how much by equity. A typical report on a company will run to six or eight pages of data, and be classified under a number of different headings: key performance ratios; cash flow and liquidity; balance sheet analysis; and investment considerations. McLean emphasises that while each company is analysed in broadly the same way, the numbers are only the raw material which precedes a decision. They do not make the decision for him.

The figures provide a historic snapshot of what a company has done, based on accounting data which inevitably soon gets out of date. It is not a forecast of what it will do in the future. The historical perspective is vital, however. McLean says that until you are sure you know where the value of the shares has come from in the past, you cannot begin to make a reasonable assessment of its future prospects. His golden rule is that he will not make an investment in a share until he has first analysed and understood its past performance to a high level of detail.

His faith in value investing goes back to his early days working in the investment department of his insurance company employer. "I recognised then that the UK market was not an efficient one, and that there were many anomalies. There were even quite persistent patterns to these mispricings. Small companies, service sectors, companies with substantial cash or debt, and neglected or low profile businesses were the areas where many bargains were to be found."

Beyond this, too, there were also what he calls "more subtle inefficiencies". Like today, many businesses, especially the capital-intensive ones, were not maintaining their "productive capacity and earnings base". In the

---

[1] Strictly speaking, McLean follows a methodology similar to that known as Economic Value Added, or EVA©, which was pioneered by a firm of US consultants, Stern Stewart.

1970s, inflation was the enemy. It allowed many companies to go on reporting increases in sales and profitability but masked their inability to replace their capital assets in real terms. Industries such as tankers and chemicals bore the brunt of the inflationary impact and suffered a prolonged period of gradual decline.

Today, says McLean, increased competition, regulation and over-distribution via dividends and share buybacks may be concealing similar problems in companies such as GlaxoSmithKline and BP. They may be making money today, but their long-term profitability is threatened if they cannot also invest enough to sustain their competitive position. He tends to avoid them: he is scornful of 'value investors' who buy shares in companies just because the dividend yield is high. They overlook the fact that the company may simply be distributing too much capital to shareholders. The number of companies who were forced into cutting their dividend or launching rescue rights issues after the credit crisis hit in 2008 shows how widespread the problem had become, not just in banking but in other parts of the economy as well.

The broad theme of a distrust of manufacturing was a big influence on the shape of his portfolios in his first decade as a fund manager. His portfolios at the time tended to be dominated by companies in the financial sector, in services and in specialist areas such as energy and transport. It also tended to push him away from many of the largest capitalisation stocks in the Footsie (FTSE 100) index in the direction of midcap companies. Since then many of the manufacturing companies that failed to impress him, such as Pilkington and Blue Circle Cement have disappeared, and those that have survived, such as Weir Group, are better managed and more able to compete successfully abroad. While still disliking many of the largest companies in the FTSE 100 index, today his portfolios have a greater sprinkling of stocks further down the capitalisation scale, both in the FTSE 100 and the FTSE 250 indices. After the growth stock bonanza of the 1990s, growth has much become harder to find in the last decade. Like Jim Slater, he has found it worthwhile to pay up for the relatively smaller number of companies such as ARM and Burberry which can demonstrate genuine top line sales growth.

As is obvious, McLean has no time for the theory that financial markets are efficient, in the sense that financial academics construe the term. It is palpably not the case, he says, that share prices accurately reflect all the publicly available information about a company's value and prospects. "We do not need long-term studies to tell us what is plainly obvious from examination of any individual day's trading: much of what happens in the stock market does not make a lot of sense." Each day there are companies whose share price falls by 25% or more; "Yet even though this may be triggered by profit warnings or dividend cuts, there is rarely any evidence that true underlying worth in a substantial business can change to this extent in a matter of hours." In March 2009, the shares of HSBC, fell 19% in value in a single day, cutting the market value of the company by £14 billion. And that was the third largest quoted company on the London stock market at the time! Later in the same month, the shares recorded daily gains of 14% and 12%. The volatility of leading shares has continued to increase in recent years.

SIX KEY RATIOS

McLean says there is no "black box", or mechanistic mathematical formula, for finding a good share. Despite his fascination with financial analysis, he likens his attitude more to that of a potential trade investor. What interests him are a company's profit margins, its growth potential and the value of its business franchise, not simply the financial characteristics of its shares. He likes to spend a fair amount of time looking at the prices at which unquoted businesses are sold, for example. Such 'trade prices' provide a valuable reality check on the value of companies seen through the often distorted lens of the stock market.

His system of financial analysis is designed to capture the characteristics that most interest him about a business. His objective is to find fundamentally sound businesses which are growing consistently and have the capacity to sustain their competitive position. Specifically, he looks for companies where the profit margins are on an upward trend and which generate enough cash flow to "maintain their enterprises and renew their productive capacity". In other words, he mostly wants companies which can fund their growth from retained profits, not through outside finance.

He and his team put particular emphasis on six ratios in their investment appraisal work.

1. SALES PER SHARE GROWTH

This is a measure of how fast the turnover of a business has been growing. McLean is interested in companies which have demonstrated positive sales per share growth in the past and have the potential to increase sales in a sustainable and readily comprehensible manner in the future. The reason for making this a per share, rather than an absolute, measure is to screen out companies which merely go out and buy turnover with shareholders' money, which is often a zero sum, or losing, proposition. What matters most to investors is the amount of genuine sales growth which they are buying for each £1 that they invest. Unless it is rising over time, the company is unlikely to do well enough to merit purchase. What matters is real sales growth (over and above inflation), not just the headline figure.

2. CASH FLOW

There are a number of different ways of measuring cash flow, and McLean looks at at least three – operating cash flow, cash flow net of the depreciation figure and cash flow net of all capital expenditure. His essential requirement for a good investment is a company that is capable of generating 'free cash flow' – i.e. each year's activities leave it with more cash in the bank than it started with, after it has met all its costs and financed both its working capital and the amount of capital expenditure it needs to sustain its operating capability. A good business, as Warren Buffett and others have pointed out, will tend to generate free, or surplus, cash flow over time, even if it has to invest heavily to achieve that growth. This must show up in the numbers sooner or later.

3. OPERATING MARGIN

Profit is an essential requirement for a successful long-term investment, but McLean differs from most conventional analysis in making operating profit – that is profit before interest and taxation – rather than net profit (or 'earnings') his key measure of profitability. He prefers to analyse the ratio of a company's operating profit to its share price, rather than a conventional price/earnings ratio. The reason is that accounting measures of bottom line earnings are notoriously easy to manipulate. Although UK accounting standards have been tightened up in recent years, too much discretionary judgement is still involved to make earnings numbers reliable.

In McLean's view, operating profit is "a much more reliable measure of how much money a business is making, and a truer reflection on how well the management is performing". McLean typically looks for a company with operating margins (operating profit as a percentage of sales) of at least 10%, or at least the potential to reach that kind of margin quickly. The operating profit is also measured against other companies in the same sector and adjusted for the state of the economic cycle. As a rule of thumb, an average company will be valued by the stock market in terms of market capitalisation plus net debt (enterprise value) at around ten times its operating profit. A low ratio of enterprise value to operating profit can indicate a business that would be attractive to a trade buyer.

4. RETURN ON CAPITAL EMPLOYED

Using conventional accounting data, this is a figure that is also notoriously capable of manipulation. Return on capital can be defined in several ways: a common one is operating profit before interest costs as a percentage of total capital employed in a business. Both the earnings figure and the value of capital employed (effectively, a company's debt plus its shareholders' funds) can diverge markedly from the true figure. Company reported results, unless adjusted, can be highly misleading. McLean makes various adjustments to the basic accounting formulation to provide a more accurate picture of the return a company is making on the money it has invested in the business. This includes adding back the value of any purchased goodwill that has been written off and adjusting for assets that have been leased rather than purchased. He uses operating profit as the numerator, rather than net profit. On his definitions, a company will normally need to demonstrate it is capable of a double-digit return on capital – and ideally a figure in the mid teens – to meet his quality threshold.

5. TAX CHARGE

The tax charge is one of the most easily manipulated lines in a company's accounts. Companies with an unusually low tax charge are, ironically, suspect. It is a signal that a company is capital-intensive, or hooked on acquisitions, or simply partial to creative accounting. Actual tax paid is normally a more reliable measure of how well a business is doing. HMRC is not known for letting companies get away with paying less tax than they should be. Good businesses tend to pay at or near a full tax charge. Unless there is some good reason for it, therefore, McLean is wary of companies that consistently show a low tax charge.

6. ECONOMIC VALUE

This is the final piece of the jigsaw, where all the variables come together. The basic principle is to assess the economic value of a business and compare it with the market value, as determined by the stock market. The objective is to find a business whose shares are selling at a price which values it at less than its economic value, having made allowance for the shape of its balance sheet (the amount of debt a company has borrowed to finance its activities affects both the value and the riskiness of its shares). McLean's primary objective is to invest in businesses with favourable economic characteristics, not in companies where most of the value derives from the management's skill at financial engineering.

Where many value investors have gone wrong in recent years, he believes, is in concentrating too much on how a company's market valuation, its dividend yield, price–earnings ratio and so on compares with that of other companies and other sectors. What ultimately matters to an investor is the absolute value of the business; and "the key to any business is real sales growth and a predictable margin pattern on that turnover". Once you have those two elements, it is possible to arrive at "a realistic picture of fundamental worth". Adjust for the net cash or net debt in the business, and you arrive at an estimate of true worth which is directly comparable to the stock market capitalisation.

As a quick guide to a share's attractiveness, one of McLean tricks is to divide the price to sales ratio by ten times the operating margin. If the resulting number is more than one, it makes the shares look expensive. If less than one, then they are prima facie offering good value[2]. This ratio – which McLean calls "an overvalued/undervalued index" – is then factored in with all the other detailed analysis to give an overall assessment of the attractiveness of the shares as an investment. Effectively, he is comparing the price an investor is paying for today's profit margin with the potential margin that could be achieved in future. For completeness sake, a typical company report will also list all the main conventional valuation measures – the price to book ratio, return on net assets, cash flow multiples and so on.

Implicit in McLean's methods is that he has a target price for shares that he decides to buy. Typically he is looking for capital appreciation of around 30% from the current level. But being a cautious Scot, he also looks hard at potential investments from a risk perspective – in other words, at what could go wrong. The system he has developed looks for warning signs, such as overgearing or overtrading, which indicate that a business may be at risk of financial meltdown. The tools here include such widely used credit measures as z scores, and others which are SVM's own creations. Although the company does its own modelling, he also checks his models against those of a number of commercial services such as the Quest service offered by stockbroker Collins Stewart. All in all, there is not much left to chance on the numbers side.

A good example of how the system can save money came in 2007 when the drinks company C&C Group, in which McLean had had a sizeable

---

[2] Note that the "price" used in this calculation is the enterprise value per share, not just the equity price.

holding, shot above his target price, reflecting strong growth and high margins in its Magners cider business. The company's growth and profitability had reached levels that had begun to attract competition from major brewers. His analysis had already alerted McLean to the risks in the company and he managed to sell out relatively early on, before the bulk of the damage was done. Thirty years of experience, he says, have demonstrated that outperformance as an investor depends as much on avoiding mistakes as it does on picking winners.

In his first few years SVM would occasionally go 'short' of shares that looked badly overvalued on their methods. (Shorting shares is a way of looking to profit from a share falling in value.) Finding that his analysis was throwing up more and more examples of overvalued companies, McLean has since expanded his use of shorting. In the 1990s he launched a hedge fund to capitalise on these opportunities, and the introduction of a new set of European fund regulations, known as UCITS III (now IV), has made it possible for his mainstream funds to use the same techniques. His funds have made money from short positions in companies with weak business models, including Royal Bank of Scotland, Railtrack and British Energy. One of his issues with many of the largest UK quoted companies is the lack of effective alignment between company performance and executive remuneration. He believes the wrong incentives can lead a company into a strategy that destroys shareholder value. This is something from which investors with shorting in their armoury should, he believes, take advantage.

THE OTHER SIDE OF VALUE INVESTING

Good investment does not stop with the discovery of an undervalued business. There are three other essential components to being a successful investor, says McLean. One is the necessary mental discipline to act on your beliefs. By definition, a value investor tends to be a contrarian: he has seen something which the rest of the market has not. "Building up a stake in a neglected and unpopular company can be very lonely. I think that it is very important for a value investor to have the right psychological disposition to take a contrarian stance and hold shares for longer periods, if necessary." A "dispassionate attitude" is essential to exploit the market's extremes of sentiment. The way that SVM is organised is designed to create the conditions in which objective decisions can be taken. There are few committees or board meetings.

Another necessary consequence of a value investing approach is the knowledge that you have to be patient. It can take years to happen. As McLean's colleague Neil Veitch, who runs a UK fund for SVM, says: "To benefit from any price anomaly, there as to be a dynamic that releases the hidden value and leads to a re-rating of the company's shares." This remains a key element in the firm's approach today. A rerating can take several forms. If the undervaluation is the result of a violent swing in stock market sentiment, then they expect the pricing anomaly to 'self-correct' once the basic facts and fundamentals have come to be more rationally assessed. "If, on the other hand, the mispricing results from a misconception about a particular industry, then a takeover by a rival company in the industry – who can see the misvaluation most easily – will often be the mechanism that releases the value. If the problem is simply poor management of a solid business franchise, then new management – or again a takeover – can be "the value catalyst." Finally the company can deal with the problem itself, by buying back its shares or paying a special dividend.

LOOKING FOR CATALYSTS

McLean spends a lot of time looking for these catalysts, or surprises. "I am trying to spot earnings surprises, balance sheet surprises and corporate restructurings before they happen," he says. Sometimes these will be company specific, but quite often there are quite long-running industry themes that investors can follow. Government legislation, game-changing new technologies and shifts in consumer habits and tastes can all change the dynamics of whole market sectors. One early example was the widespread restructuring in the brewing industry that followed the government's Beer Orders in 1989, which effectively required brewers to choose between brewing and owning pubs. "Since then," says McLean "we have seen the same thing in insurance, at Lloyd's of London and also in buses and ports. The common theme in a lot of these situations is that of costs being taken out and margins improving as more turnover is put into the hands of better management."

"More recently, we think that increased cost pressures and regulation in the finance sector will drive further consolidation of exchanges, broker-dealers and fund managers. We expect continuing consolidation amongst junior oil producers as the oil majors need to replace their reserves. My strongest current theme is the increasing dominance of online businesses. This is not only hitting retailers and the press, but many other services such as recruitment, advertising and book publishing. This explains my cautious stance on sectors such as media, although I also believe there will be winners such as Pearson, which is establishing a strong global position in online education."

One interesting aspect of this focus on catalysts, McLean observes, is that the benefits can be felt equally by the second or third most profitable company in a sector. In fact, there is often as much money to be made by investing in a company which is third or fourth in its sector as there is in buying the market leader. "We like to buy companies with a solid intrinsic franchise, but if there is a franchise that is not earning the right margins for the industry, but where we can see the means by which that improvement will happen, we will also invest there." A good example of this kind of opportunity was Asda, the supermarket chain, which for several years had been earning subnormal profit margins, but where there was clear scope for new management to come in and make a big difference. Buying in after the arrival of Archie Norman as the new chief executive in 1992 proved to be one of McLean's best investments, even though the business (subsequently sold to the US retailing giant Wal-Mart) still lags behind the two market leaders, Tesco and Sainsbury's.

One of his worst, ironically, was Kwik Save, a company whose profit margins were the highest in its sector, and which was making a return on capital of 40% at its peak. Such abnormal returns invariably tend to attract more intense competition. It happened, for example, to PV Crystalox, a pioneer in solar cells, as its high returns attracted competition, leading to oversupply and a margin collapse. Similarly, Man Group, the hedge fund manager, is now seeing risks to its high margins as its once dominant position in the industry is challenged by new entrants. It is often easier, in other words, for a moderate company to improve its margins than it is for an exceptional one to sustain them. You don't have to buy just the best managed company in every field.

The bus company Stagecoach is another example of a company where the market was slow to do its analytical homework and realise the true value of the shares. The deregulation and privatisation of the industry in the 1980s transformed what had become a very mature industry, one in which the number of passengers had been falling steadily for many years. "The point which was missed," says McLean, "is that the need to restructure an industry suffering from overcapacity presents an ideal opportunity for aggressive operators to expand their businesses, deriving strong profits growth from cost-cutting measures. To a value investor, profits progression within a core franchise is a far more predictable and therefore attractive proposition than a growth story involving the risks of creating a new customer base."

When Stagecoach went on a buying spree, lapping up scores of other privatised bus companies, and risking a succession of references to the Monopolies and Mergers Commission, it did not need more people to use buses in order to make money. Simply raising the efficiency of the acquired businesses to its own standard was enough to generate substantial future profits growth. Yet the market as a whole remained transfixed by the lack of demand growth and the risk of rejection by the competition authorities. This created the buying opportunity.

Another example from McLean's 2011 portfolio is information services group Experian. Although in the FTSE 100, the company was overlooked by many institutional investors as it was demerged from retailer GUS with little fanfare. Experian provides credit information to organisations and individuals, and was initially allocated to the unpopular financial sector.

"Often businesses that arrive on the stockmarket by demerger get much less investor attention and research coverage", says McLean. "A value investor has a much greater chance of finding undervaluation where published research is limited. And the process of initiating research as more analysts start to follow a company can be a good catalyst to recognise value."

In 2006, when Experian was separately quoted for the first time, the City had little understanding of credit services. Analysts had no similar listed companies with which to make peer group comparisons. The listing in London did not help; Experian is one of the three largest American credit agencies and has strong growth potential in Brazil and other markets. The market viewed the company as a risky financial business, rather than a high growth information provider in the services sector. McLean noted that the return on capital exceeded 20%, and also saw the attractions of Experian's strong free cash flow. As a technology-driven business, additional sales required relatively little new investment. The company was in a strong position to fund its growth internally, without new debt or equity issue, thereby meeting McLean's value benchmarks.

"Remarkably," says McLean, "now, even after five years and good share price performance, Experian still meets our criteria. Operating profit margin exceeds 20% and should expand. More City analysts now research the company, but many see the shares as expensive. They focus too much on stockmarket measures like price earnings ratio, and not enough on Experian's business model, which can deliver growth with strong cash flow."

GROWTH IS VALUE, VALUE IS GROWTH

While it is customary to treat value and growth investing as two separate disciplines, McLean thinks that this is a false dichotomy. As a value investor he may be looking for bargains, but the companies which provide the best value, he points out, are often also companies which are growing fast. It is important, however, to know where a company's growth is coming from. "We like businesses where the physical volume of sales is growing, and prices are stable rather than going up too much. We don't like to see growth in turnover coming from price inflation rather than real [i.e. inflation-adjusted] volume. We feel much more comfortable with something that is progressing from a sub-normal margin to a normal one, as was the case with Asda, than say Tesco, which now has the top margins in the industry but which we suspect can only go down from there."

Assessing management is a key part of investing, but McLean cautions against being too hung up on believing you have to be in regular contact with a company's management in order to succeed. "We're trying to see if the stock market has put the right price on a business. We are not experts in the business itself. There's not too much point in going round the business all the time. One of the things I learnt from John Templeton was that managers generally know their own business better than you ever can. They'll always be able to give you very smart answers which you can't readily assess. In trying to value a business as an investment, you don't have to understand how they actually run it or deal with technical issues."

On the other hand, there are occasionally opportunities to be found when management is prone to behaving in an unconventional manner. The stock market's judgements tend to be conventional ones, so anyone who fails to 'fit the mould' is suspect in their eyes. "It is very difficult for the stock market to appreciate that someone like Sir Brian Souter of Stagecoach could be a successful manager, because he doesn't dress the same way as they do in the City. What they failed to appreciate is that his business is not about pushing paper and presenting to clients. It's more to do with dealing with blue-collar workers and understanding the dynamics of the bus business, which is what he is very good at."

What are the bad signs to watch out for in management? Ironically, says McLean, it worries him when management spends too much time following the ups and downs of its own company share price, rather than getting on with running the business. Another danger signal is when companies grow by repeatedly issuing new shares to make acquisitions at a discount to the current price. "A company that is intent on issuing paper at a discount on the pretext of buying a business is not going to release that value for you." All this tends to show, he means, is that management is more interested in size and ideas for aggrandisement than it is in making money for the shareholders.

PORTFOLIO CONSIDERATIONS

A look through the portfolios of McLean's main investment funds reveals that he is highly selective in his choice of shares. Unlike most mainstream fund managers, he makes no attempt to invest in all the main sectors of the economy – a bank, a metal-basher, an oil company, a food retailer and so on. He only picks shares that meet his demanding criteria, and as a result his portfolios often look unbalanced, with 30% or 40% of the value in a single sector, such as financials or transport. The FTSE All-Share Index, he notes, is classified into six main sectors: basic materials and oil; general industrial; consumer goods; services; utilities; and financials. "Of these, we may be in three at one time. Generally it won't be less than three, but it won't often be much more either." He emphasises that this is not because of any rooted objection to any of these sectors. It is more a question of competence and style. McLean doesn't invest in biotechnology shares, for example, because he knows he will never be able to understand what they are doing. Non-life insurers are something he doesn't know how to value properly either. His analytical methods, however sophisticated they may seem, simply don't work well with them. There are lessons for ordinary investors here. One is that you don't need to invest in the whole market to do better than average. But the second is that you are more likely to do well if you stick to those things that you are sure you understand properly.

There is also an important point in this about diversification. McLean says his aim is to reduce risk not through diversification, the classical way for investment managers, but through "intensive research". He believes that "real risk lies within companies, and needs to be dealt with in the analytical process". There is a lot more to risk than volatility, the measure on which finance theory concentrates. In any event, stock market risk usually diminishes with the passage of time. Unlike the Michael Hart approach, his is more of a variant of Mark Twain's famous advice on risk management "Put all your eggs in one basket – and then watch that basket very carefully!"

McLean says his ideas come from a wide variety of sources, and not just from crunching numbers. His screening system, although sophisticated, would not have thrown up the names of some of his biggest early winners, such as Stagecoach and Asda. The sources include stockbrokers, newspapers, online searches and companies' own investor presentations. He spends a fair amount of time talking to other professional investors, too. He was a particular admirer of Martyn Arbib, now retired, and the team he recruited at Perpetual (now Invesco Perpetual). Terry Smith, a City analyst who hit the headlines after he exposed the deceptive accounting practices of some highflying companies in the 1980s, and went on to become chairman of Tullett Prebon and Collins Stewart, is another he admires. Other investors whose views he follows are fellow contrarians such as Hugh Hendry, the manager of Eclectica Fund, and Christopher Mills of J O Hambro. Alan Brown, Chief Investment Officer of Schroders for several years, he says, is particularly good at spotting secular trends.

It is noticeable how many of his most successful investments have been in companies where he has some specialist knowledge, or relevant experience, to bear. He has made a lot of money out of investing in other fund management companies, for example, Perpetual, Mercury Asset Management and Aberdeen Asset Management. His biggest single success in 1996 was Cairn Energy, a tiny oil exploration company which shot up 260% in a year on the strength of a single successful discovery in Bangladesh. The company is run by Bill Gammell, a former Scottish international rugby player, with good contacts in the Edinburgh financial community. Stagecoach, another of McLean's big successes, also started life in Scotland, this time in Perth. More recently Weir Group has served him well. Becoming aware of these situations early enough to catch the first wave of interest reflects the strength of his Scottish connections.

McLean cautions against spending too much time worrying about the overall level of the market. When I asked him (in 1998) whether he thought the great bull market of the previous 15 years was running out of steam, he politely ducked the question. "I don't really think in those terms. The bull market has not been a homogenous or monolithic thing. The index is made up of a lot of stocks which each go through their own cycles. They don't all move in line. If you were a holder of smaller companies, for example, you would probably feel that the last three years have felt more like a bear market than a bull market." This proved to be a perceptive comment. Smaller company shares were about to embark on an extended period of outperformance, while the market itself came to be dominated by the extraordinary rise in value of TMT stocks (telecoms, media and technology) as the internet bubble built to its climax in 2000. Only then did the bull market finally expire.

"The great thing to remember is that there are always opportunities around. You have to remember that the market averages are just that – averages. And unless you want average performance, there is not much point focusing on them. It is better to look at the individual cycles and patterns within each individual company which don't all follow the same trend. The other thing about being in or out of the market is that a lot of the overall market's performance comes in fairly compact periods, often when it is least expected – just before or after an election, for example. You can spend a lot of time and waste a lot of transaction costs trying to nip in and out to get the timing right. A more consistent way to make money is to buy individual stocks and not try to guess the market's timing."

McLean, as should be clear by now, prefers to think in terms of general investment themes rather than worry about the direction of the overall economy. One of the themes that coloured his thinking for some time, as noted earlier, was the long-run competitive threat to Britain's manufacturing industry. Of greater concern to McLean in 2011 was the UK retailing sector, where a number of well-known names either disappeared, or looked set to do so in the not too distant future. The sector was suffering overcapacity, with too much high street space, and was being attacked by new online competition. The gap between the winners and losers in retailing had widened sharply as a result.

Note how this ties in with his focus on margins and turnover growth as the two key drivers behind the performance of stock market successes. Increasing competition from overseas and a shortage of pricing freedom are not a strong platform on which to build. As noted earlier, many of these manufacturing companies have since disappeared. Those that have survived, such as Rexam, Croda International, Rolls-Royce and IMI, are consequently better placed than they were in the 1990s.

McLean was also one of the first to voice concerns about the bank sector in 2007, highlighting the over-expansion, increased leverage and ratcheting up of risk-taking that had become commonplace in the industry, felled by low interest rates and a benign regulatory regime. His concerns were flagged in a number of speeches and articles at the time. Today, he still believes there are few banks that offer value to investors, even after refinancing. "I expect further capital raising and more downsizing," he says, "which will constrain dividend returns for investors." He remains suspicious of banks' reported asset values, despite the apparent cheapness of many bank shares.

BEHAVIOURAL FACTORS

What other lessons can investors learn from McLean? While there are many different ways of making money out of the stock market, he says one thing is common to them all. That is to be comfortable with what you are doing. "It is important to understand your own fortitude and zone of comfort. The worst thing is to be intrinsically uncomfortable. It means you are likely to jump and make the wrong decision and be panicked out of something for no good reason. You will never hold a strong position in something when you will be the first out of it."

A corollary for any value investor is the ability to react coolly to events such as disappointing newspaper headlines. "Remember that events are by definition in the public consciousness, and if you react to what is in the newspapers, you are probably going to be doing the same thing at the same time as everyone else. If it initiates the same activity as others, then you're not applying any superior knowledge." This idea, that investors are competing with a lot of other highly knowledgeable and successful investors, and that if they react the same way as everyone else, they will achieve only average results, is the core of common sense that underlies the otherwise flawed principle of efficient markets. Disproving the principle is difficult, but McLean knows from experience that the inefficiencies are there. What takes skill is spotting them before the rest of the world also finds out.

To that end McLean has spent a good deal of time over the past decade in studying and seeking to apply the findings of a now popular school of thought that goes under the broad heading of 'behavioural finance'. The core insight behind this way of thinking about the stock market is that the behaviour of many market participants, far from being coldly rational and self-interested, as classical economic theory suggests, is in fact driven by a wide range of emotional and sociological impulses that can, in extreme cases, fly completely in the face of logic or reason. Studies by academics such as Kahneman, Tversky and Shiller have highlighted a range of human biases in decision-making about money that in turn help to shape the often erratic and confusing patterns which share prices follow. Phenomena such as "overconfidence", "anchoring" and "confirmation bias" all help to give markets their distinctive character. Herding behaviour contributes to the well documented fact that shares prices are far more volatile in practice than underlying change in company fundamentals can justify.

Understanding that these biases exist and learning how to exploit them for profit, in McLean's view, is an essential part of the professional investor's toolkit. As he put it in a seminar in 2011: "Like many investors, I once focused entirely on fundamental analysis. But increasingly it became clear to me this did not explain all that goes on in the market... These patterns show that the market is not always very effective at price formation. I believe that the psychological traits identified by behavioural finance can tell us a lot about what is going on." Conventional numerical analysis carried out by stockbroking analysts frequently misses simple changes in the underlying economics of companies being analysed. It also suffers from an in-built bias towards optimism. In one recent survey published in the *Wall Street Journal*, not one of the 1485 stocks in the S&P 1500 index was rated by the consensus as a sell! [3]

---

[3] *Wall Street Journal*, MarketWatch, 7 September 2011.

How can investors deal with these problems? One obvious way is to embark on the same study of behavioural finance that McLean himself has done. Being aware of your own biases is a valuable starting point, for example in countering the well-established finding that investors confronted with evidence that fails to confirm their own beliefs tend to become more rather than less certain of their ground. He suggests recording all investment decisions in a daily journal. "This allows a re-appraisal and being in black and white, is much more convincing. From this individuals should aim to build their own checklists for investing that essentially comprise previous errors and what has been learned from them. I find rules helpful. For example, when faced with a decision that must be made, but with uncertainty over the timing or process, I often close one third or one half of the position. This immediately reduces emotion, but also starts the process of recognising that confidence should be reduced."

Even the most skilful company analysts, in other words, need to recognise that there is much more to successful investment than simply interpreting a company's figures correctly, essential though that discipline is. Many models that are used by professional investors to try to understand the dynamics of a particular security are over-complicated, providing too much spurious information. After more than twenty years of working with the numbers, McLean still concludes that all the best investors ultimately rely for success on intuition as well as analytical prowess. That makes sense, since if number-crunching was all that was needed to succeed, the business of making investments would be much easier – and much less interesting – than it is.

6. MICHAEL HART:

Accumulating the singles

Although professional investment managers come in all shapes and sizes, essentially they fall into two camps. There are the 'go-go boys', who promise glittering returns on a short- to medium-term horizon, but who frequently burn out along the way, victims of their own overarching energy and ambition. And then there are the 'steady-as-you-go brigade', who are in it for a longer haul and who, far from burning out, frequently end up married to their jobs, enslaved by the intellectual fascination of following the workings of the market on a daily basis.

Of the few who can claim a genuinely outstanding record in either category, those in the first camp tend to be ones with brilliance, naked ambition and a passion to get rich. Those in the second category may be just as determined to get what they want, but are more circumspect in how they go about it. Their passion is less for the material rewards of success and more for the addictive qualities of what Maynard Keynes, himself a lifelong addict of the stock market, once shrewdly called "the game of investment".[1]

---

[1] The full quotation from Keynes, in all its orotund glory, is: "The game of professional investment is intolerably boring and exacting to anyone who is entirely exempt from the gambling instinct: whilst he who has it must pay to this propensity the appropriate toll."

There is no doubt into which category you would put Michael Hart, long-serving manager of Foreign & Colonial Investment Trust, Britain's oldest (founded in 1868) and most consistently successful investment trust. This is a man who started out in professional life training to be a chartered secretary and to some extent still speaks the part. This is no 'gunslinger', as the hotshot money men on Wall Street in the 1960s were known. His tone is measured and polite, his language punctuated by splendid verbal anachronisms. Michael Hart inhabits a world where men are invariably 'chaps', and he himself is an 'old fogey'. 'Crikey' is one of his favourite words. It is no surprise to find that he is also a stalwart of English village cricket, a bowler who for more than 50 years has harboured the forlorn ambition to come in higher than number 11 in the order.

Yet this quiet and deceptively ordinary figure has one of the sharpest investment minds and best long-term track records of anyone in the UK fund management business. By the time of his retirement in 1997, Hart had managed the investments of the Foreign & Colonial Investment Trust for 28 years. Few, if any, other professional fund managers can claim such a long and uninterrupted period of tenure. The average unit trust manager, for example, is in charge of his fund for barely two years before moving (or being moved) on.

In his time, Hart has witnessed scores of investment fads come and go, and lived through two major stock market crashes, two Middle East wars and a revolution in investment management practice and techniques. The City itself has been transformed by deregulation and the pace of events from being a cosy, clubby village largely run for the benefit of its working inhabitants, to being a much tougher, more businesslike, less congenial place. Yet few UK investment managers stand in such secure regard amongst their peers.

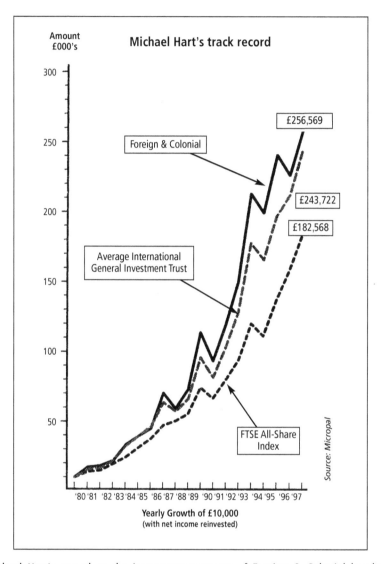

Amount £000's

Michael Hart's track record

£256,569

Foreign & Colonial

£243,722

£182,568

Average International
General Investment Trust

FTSE All-Share
Index

Source: Micropal

'80 '81 '82 '83 '84 '85 '86 '87 '88 '89 '90 '91 '92 '93 '94 '95 '96 '97

Yearly Growth of £10,000
(with net income reinvested)

Michael Hart's record as the investment manager of Foreign & Colonial has been consistently good. The 1980s were probably his best years. With a large and well diversified portfolio of UK and overseas shares, the trust will never outperform the market by far, but its distinctive style gives it a consistent edge.

Over the course of his long career, the assets of the trust Hart manages have grown consistently by an average of 20% a year. Despite a relatively poor year in 1996, and the general widening of investment trust discounts since early 1995, if you had invested £100 in Foreign & Colonial when he first took over as manager of its investments, and reinvested the dividends, you would today have a sum of £3761. This is £3000 more than you would have had if you had invested the money in a typical bank or building society deposit account, and approximately 35% more than if you had put your money in the average unit or investment trust.

On a total return basis, counting dividend income as well as capital gains, I calculate that Foreign & Colonial shares have outperformed the market as a whole by between 1 and 2% a year, depending on precisely how you do the sums and which period you look at. It may not sound like much, but compounded over such a long period, such small edges in performance are all you need in the stock market to harvest substantial gains in wealth. In fact, Hart has outperformed the market in 15 years out of the last 25. His 20% compound return over a period of nearly 30 years is superior to most general diversified unit and investment trusts over the same time frame.

Apart from his track record, what marks Michael Hart out from the pack is his reputation for personal integrity. It is not just his methods and his language which are slightly old-fashioned. Walk around the City, and you soon discover that everyone in the upper echelons of the old financial Establishment, at least, describes Michael Hart in the same terms. "A gentleman, who always plays it straight." "As honest as you will find." "A fantastically consistent record," and so on. Although younger colleagues at Foreign & Colonial have long teased him about his old-fashioned methods, his reputation for combining consistent performance with the highest personal standards is secure.

THE BEST OF TIMES, THE WORST OF TIMES

Michael Hart's misfortune or opportunity, depending on your point of view, is to have been in charge of a large investment fund through one of the most volatile economic periods in living memory. When he first took over running Foreign & Colonial in 1969, inflation was 4.5% and interest rates around 8%. As he approached his retirement from day-to-day management of the fund, the figures on the surface were much the same: inflation at 3%, gilts yielding 7.5%.

Yet between these two dates, the world lived through its most traumatic economic crisis since the 1930s. At one stage during the rock bottom years of the 1970s, inflation in the UK reached 27%; interest rates soared well into double figures; and the stock market fell to its lowest level, adjusted for inflation, for more than 60 years.[2] OPEC came and went. Paul Volcker launched his ferocious assault on inflation in the United States. The Third World went bust. The City itself was turned upside down by the Big Bang.

For once, the metaphor of a rollercoaster that commentators so freely apply to the stock market is not exaggerated[3]. "As I pull myself out from my bed at six of a morning," Hart told one interviewer a few years ago, "I often consider my good fortune in that in all my years as a manager I have only had to deal with such day-to-day matters as the banking crisis of 1974, Black Monday of 1987, the invasion of Kuwait and the Soviet coup of 1991".[4] To keep your head – and your track record – through a period of such profound change is something that distinguishes the true professional investor from the many who have prospered only when times are good.

---

[2] I have taken these figures from BZW's annual Equity-Gilt Study, a mine of useful information about historical trends in the financial markets.

[3] It is a matter of opinion whether the stock market is more remarkable for its volatility, or for the fact that it consistently produced positive real returns over long periods of time.

[4] Quoted in Neil McKendrick, *The Birth of Foreign & Colonial, The World's First Investment Trust*. Privately published monograph.

One of Hart's secrets is that his investment philosophy has remained remarkably consistent through all this turbulence. Like all investment trust managers, he is bound by the stated policy objectives of the trust which can only be changed with the consent of the shareholders. The objectives of Foreign & Colonial are (1) to secure medium- to long-term growth in it shareholders' capital; and (2) to produce regular increases in dividend that exceed the rate of inflation. Note that this is cast, unfashionably, in general rather than specific terms: there is no 'benchmark' index to beat. Managers of Foreign & Colonial have always enjoyed a fair degree of flexibility in what they do.

The bedrock of the trust's policy remains, as it has been since the very beginning, to hold a broadly diversified portfolio of securities in the UK and the other major international markets. The original deed setting up the trust in 1868 emphasised the explicit objective of giving the investor 'of moderate means' the same advantage as 'the large Capitalist' in diminishing the risk of investment by spreading its capital over a number of different stocks. Originally, in keeping with the orthodoxy of the day, the portfolio consisted mainly of government bonds, but over time the bonds have given way first to debentures, then to preference shares and, most recently, since World War I, to equities. Inevitably they now dominate the portfolio.

Such a broadly diversified international portfolio is never going to produce spectacular results, but, within the constraints, Hart has always been given a fair degree of latitude by his board to go out and seek an extra edge in performance. This he has done in three main ways: by borrowing money to enhance his returns, by taking bets on currency movements and by trying to pick the shares that will over time outperform the market as a whole. Thanks to a pioneering low-cost savings scheme which Michael Hart was responsible for introducing in 1984, around 100,000 investors now hold shares in the trust, which has around £2300 million in assets.

Foreign & Colonial owes its longevity to a curious paradox which also underlies Michael Hart's performance. It is a conservative institution which has nevertheless always taken pride in its willingness to experiment with new techniques, new markets and new investment instruments. In its early days, the trust was the first to give ordinary investors an opportunity to invest heavily in overseas issues. The three largest holdings in its original portfolio were Spanish, Italian and Peruvian government bonds, demonstrating that the modern fashion for investing in emerging markets is, like most investment ideas, hardly a new one.[5] A sizeable chunk of the capital of those who grew rich from the success of Victorian Britain went on to finance the development of the developing economies of their day. As its name suggests, Foreign & Colonial was one of the channels through which the money reached its destination.

Ever since, it has continued to manage investors' money in a distinctive way. In the early 1960s, for example, it was one of the first UK investment institutions to invest heavily in the Japanese stock market, a trend that Hart was quick to extend when he took over the fund. As a result, it caught most of the great 20-year bull market in Japanese shares. Hart and his colleagues also took the trust into Brazil in 1972, long before that was fashionable elsewhere. Not all the innovations by Foreign & Colonial Management, the management company which employs Hart and runs the trust on shareholders' behalf, have been so successful. An attempt to launch a guaranteed-income stock market product, using modern derivative instruments, for example, was initially a very public and rather humiliating flop. In its rush to transform itself from a pure investment trust to an all-singing, all-dancing investment management company, Foreign & Colonial has, in the eyes of some purists, sacrificed a bit of investment quality to quantity. If Michael Hart harbours any feelings that the commercialism of the marketing department has run a little ahead of itself (which I suspect), he is far too loyal to say so.

---

[5] And some things never change; when the Spanish government defaulted on its obligations in 1873, it cast a cloud over the creditworthiness of Mediterranean governments which survives to this day.

NEW BUILDING, OLD HABITS

Michael Hart works in the corner of a large open-plan office on the eighth floor of Exchange House, a modern glass-fronted office tower which overlooks the railway tracks as they run into Liverpool Street station.[6] Foreign & Colonial moved to this new building in 1989. Before that, Hart had been in a succession of different offices, starting in a building in Gresham Street, where the clerks still sat on high stools in a single room and filled in ledgers by hand. His desk today is a standard production-line piece of office furniture, cluttered up with files and bits of paper, plus the inevitable computer screen and broker reports. It is hard not to imagine that the earlier offices, however cramped and inefficient, had more character.

There is nothing to distinguish his desk from the scores of others in the room, no outward sign that this is a man with overall responsibility for a portfolio worth more than £2000 million. Hart is a tall, lean man with a disconcerting flop of hair that bounces up and down as he paces around the office with long strides. His day starts on an early morning train from Audley End in Essex. During the hour-long journey, he reads the papers, scribbling scores of notes and underlining things in the margins of his *Financial Times*. Although he knows that newspapers give only a partial picture of events, his aim is to get a feel for the way the world is moving. He also finds that they are a good way to trigger off a new idea. Some of his younger colleagues, he says, find this rather an old-fashioned habit.

Once at Exchange House, the first task of the day is to walk around the office, catching up on overnight developments. Then, at 8.45 a.m., comes the daily UK meeting to review company announcements and other likely developments. Then it is back to his desk to read more papers and look through the day's crop of brokers' circulars, followed by more walkabouts

---

[6] I have used the present tense because, at the time of writing, Michael Hart was still managing the investments of the trust on a day-to-day basis. He handed over this responsibility to his successor, Jeremy Tigue, on 1 July 1997, and remains a director of the company.

in the office and perhaps a presentation by a company. Lunch is usually a business meeting, followed by more meetings, and phone calls to return from journalists and brokers. He reads a lot of brokers' circulars, not so much for the recommendations as for the information that is in them. Although it is fashionable to rubbish the calibre of brokers' investment analysis, Hart says that the broking firms still have some of the best analysts around.

"Then when I have a few moments, I like to look through the F&C portfolio, just go through it and see if I can think of anything bright to do." Once a month, Hart has to write a report for the board meeting, which "forces me" to think about the asset allocation and gearing in more detail. Finally, every day he looks at his currency positions (which he logs on a pad on his desk) and the extent to which they match the geographical mix of the trust's assets. Allowing the two to get out of line, in the hope that the currencies will move in a favourable direction, is one of the ways that Hart can vary the currency exposure of his portfolio.

Newspapers play a surprisingly large part in his daily work. Apart from his daily reading on the train, his desk drawers in the office are full of fading newspaper cuttings, some dating back 40 years and more. These he keeps deliberately to remind him of the fickle nature of markets and the "madness of crowds". One of his favourites is a front-page story from the *Daily Mail* (7 December 1973), headlined: 'The day the City lost its head.' Another he has kept, again from the *Daily Mail*, is a column by its then City editor, Sir Patrick Sergeant, in October 1981. The headline this time: 'The great bear market looks a big dipper.' Hart finds that newspaper headlines are a useful way of measuring where the market's mood is – by and large, the bleaker the better, since bouts of investor pessimism are usually pointers to buying opportunities ahead. The ability to go against the herd is one of the defining characteristics of all great investors and is central to Michael Hart's methods.

Another cutting in his drawer recounts the DTI inspectors' official verdict on the collapse of Rolls-Royce, the aero-engine manufacturer which was brought to its knees in 1971 by a fatal combination of overborrowing and inattentive management. It remains one of the few companies ever to have been nationalised by a Conservative government. Hart, I notice, has underlined one sentence which resonates to this day: 'A hundredweight of ill-assorted facts is no substitute for a screening process which obliges the directors to talk about the most important issues – very different from the issues they would like to talk about.'[7] Hart has heard all the excuses in the world over the years.

SHOPPING IN THE BARGAIN BASEMENT

Also in the drawer is a single sheet of paper headed 'Bargain Basement?' This is a list of blue-chip shares that Michael Hart sat down and typed out one day close to the bottom of the 1974-75 bear market. While all around were despairing that share prices would never recover, he was one of the few to realise that many of Britain's biggest companies were trading at prices that offered exceptional value to anyone who could lift their head above the prevailing climate of gloom and despair, and dare to predict that the good times would return, as they always do. Royal Insurance, for example, had a dividend yield of 11.6%; GKN was yielding 10.8% and trading at four times its earnings; Bass Charrington, the brewer, was on a yield of 9% and a p/e ratio of 5.8. Even the mighty Marks & Spencer, Britain's leading High Street retailer, was yielding 7.1%. (By contrast, in today's buoyant stock market, any blue-chip share that yields more than 7% is usually regarded as too good to be true; the implication tends to be either that its dividend is unsustainable or that the company has real problems which may require new management or a takeover to sort out. The average Footsie stock in mid-1997 was yielding 3.5% and was trading on a p/e ratio of 18.)

---

[7] *Financial Times*, 22 August 1974.

It is easy to spot the bargains now with the benefit of hindsight, but the key test of the best investors is that they have the courage to act on their convictions while all around are losing theirs. As the scribbled notes on his Bargain Basement scrap of paper make clear, Hart decided to take the plunge and buy £600,000 worth of shares (the equivalent of at least £3 million today) in seven of these companies: Royal Insurance, Bass, Allied Breweries, Great Universal Stores, the Prudential, BATs and Redland. Within a year the market had doubled, and the 'Bargain Basement' shares were up sharply. This was in some ways the turning point in Hart's career, proving convincingly for the first time that a policy of buying into depressed markets in the face of conventional wisdom could pay big dividends. Another great success from that time was his purchase of a chunk of shares in Lord Weinstock's electronics business, GEC. Within six years his £300,000 investment was worth £3m.

A company that Hart also picked up early was BTR, the conglomerate which under Sir Owen Green specialised in turning round dirty, boring, capital-intensive businesses that nobody else wanted. Like Weinstock, Green's success was rooted in an almost obsessively tight regime of financial controls. Hart was impressed with these and also by Green's absurd enthusiasm for his latest product – which was rubber dog bowls. Most of all, however, what he liked about BTR was that Green always delivered on his promises. A reputation for delivering on promises remains one of the key criteria he applies to all the managements he has backed. (Such loyalty can also be costly. BTR is still one of the biggest holdings in Foreign & Colonial's portfolio, despite Sir Owen having long since retired and his successors having failed to do anything for shareholders. Hart thinks now he should have sold more of the shares when Sir Owen left.)

In picking shares, as in all his investment habits, Hart is stubborn about refusing to be categorised in his methods. His style has always been about more than pure stockpicking. Most of his holdings, however, he says, are in growth stocks, companies which are growing faster than the average for their industry. He will also look at cyclical shares as well, if the value seems to be there. The turnover rate in his portfolio is relatively low in comparison with his peers. His average holding period is around five years, meaning that on average around 20% of his portfolio changes from year to year. A fair number of his shares including BATs, Allied Colloids and BTR, he has held for more than 15 years.

Such patience can generate large capital gains. Looking through his portfolio in early 1997 produced this list of shares that were showing the biggest capital gains: Robert Fleming, the merchant bank, a very long-term holding, is now valued at 25 times its book value; Swire Pacific at 14 times its cost; Glaxo at ten times; Automatic Data Processing also at ten times; Legal & General at nine times; and Home Depot, Abbott Laboratories and First Data all at eight times. The trust itself, in the years he has managed it, has grown from £118 million to £2300 million or an increase of 19.5 times. The share price meanwhile has risen twentyfold. The fact that this is a larger increase than that achieved by any of the trust's current holdings (with the exception of Robert Fleming) merely demonstrates that the process of refreshing the portfolio is a continuous one.

What Hart likes to do is to trim or add to his holdings if the price has moved in or out of a range he considers as fair value. But essentially he is a long-term investor, who likes to stick to his choices. What he most hates doing is "chasing shares" just because they are popular. Growth is fine, he says but he wants to buy it at a bargain price. That is one reason why Foreign & Colonial has always tended to do best after a period when share prices have been falling.

ACCIDENTAL BEGINNINGS

One of the ironies of Michael Hart's career is that he stumbled into investment management largely by accident. The son of a policeman, and having left school at the age of 15, his original aim following National Service was to become a company secretary. He answered an advertisement for a job in the accounts office of an investment trust company, which turned out to be Foreign & Colonial. Having successfully transferred to the company secretary's department, he started to do some investment analysis and dealing. After work he was also "flogging himself to death" studying for a part-time degree in economics, money and banking at the London School of Economics (LSE).

Since this was the 1960s, student revolution was in the air, but it is hard to think of less promising revolutionary material. "I was too damn busy to have any time for that" is all that Michael Hart says on the subject now. He does recall, however, making the great mistake of asking one of his lecturers which books he should read to get through his next exam and receiving a diatribe on how, 'we're not trying to teach parrots, we're trying to educate' – a distinction to which the City, in its result-oriented way, has rarely given much credence.

Although it had long regarded itself as the fund of socialist economic thinking, the LSE nevertheless provided the young student of Capitalism with some invaluable insights, even if the mainstream economic teaching of the day rapidly proved to be outmoded by the events he was having to interpret in his day job. "We were," recalls Hart, "indoctrinated with Keynesian policies. We thought that everything was possible and that governments could control things. It turned out of course that they couldn't." The basic disciplines of economics and banking have stood him in good stead, however: "My wife says that I tend to think in columns and there is an element of truth in that. It does make you a fairly logical thinker." At the same time, a grounding in economic and political history gave him a valuable perspective on change, including the insight that "extraordinary things" can and do happen.

His big break came in 1969 when two of the investment trust's star fund managers, Tom Griffin and Richard Thornton, abruptly announced one day that they were leaving to set up their own investment management company. The chairman of Foreign & Colonial asked Michael Hart if he wanted their job, offering him the chance to think about it overnight. Hart accepted on the spot. Typically, his own interpretation is that the chairman must have been "a pretty desperate man", having suddenly lost his two best investment managers and facing the possible meltdown of his venerable organisation. He supposed that the chairman had watched him "beavering away at night school" and noticed the work he had done in the investment area. The fact that the previous chairman had also taken a liking to him, to the extent of lending him his house in Ireland for a honeymoon, may have been a factor, too.

Looking back, what Michael Hart recalls most now about his early years is how amateurish the process of managing investments was by modern standards. There was very little serious investment research of the kind that is commonplace now. Broking firms such as Wood Mackenzie were only just starting to introduce the new methods of analysis and research that had been pioneered in the US. Shares were mostly valued on a yield basis, if not on more subjective criteria. Most fund managers' ideas came from "the City grapevine" and from brokers coming to call. "There was certainly a feeling," says Hart, "that it wasn't done to bypass the broker and go to the company direct." Making regular visits to companies, or having them into the office, to find out what they were doing was one of the innovations that he introduced at Foreign & Colonial soon after he took over responsibility for its investments. Another was to introduce a central dealing desk, so that fund managers did not do their own buying and selling of shares.

Yet another innovation was introducing the practice of keeping and updating regular notes on companies' performance – standard practice for any fund manager today, but something new in those much more relaxed times. Hart developed the Churchillian habit of setting out the arguments for a share on one side of a piece of paper, with a few key numbers, a list of the main bull and bear points, and a brief investment conclusion – a simple but effective habit which can readily be copied by ordinary investors. For example, Appendix 5 shows how he assessed the prospects for Rentokil in 1982. As the years have passed, of course, he has developed a formidable body of detailed knowledge about companies and their strengths and weaknesses. A lot of hard work, and a generation of experience, lies behind the diffident exterior.

Inevitably, his attitudes have started to change. "As one gets older, one's not so quick or so adventurous. Like everything else there is a time when you are in your prime. In some ways some of my best successes came from an almost naive optimism. That and persevering even though it seemed the wrong thing to do at the time." The history of Foreign & Colonial, he goes on, "has always been influential with me, in the sense of a need to try new things, to be adventurous. That's a good background to operate against." Is it so different now, I wondered? "The individual managers don't have the freedom that they used to, but I still think it is a fascinating game. You're looking at so many things. The old joke is that it beats working for a living. And I think that is true."

COMETH THE HOUR

Of all that Hart has done to deliver returns to his investors, the single most important thing has, ironically, not involved buying or selling a single share. If investment trusts still traded at the discount they did at their nadir in the 1970s, investors would be at least 20% worse off than they are now. When he took over, investment trusts were in a period of decline, tarnished in part by the reputation of unscrupulous operators such as the infamous Denys Lowson and more generally dismissed as lightweight backwaters in the City. Their boards, Hart concedes, were mostly stuffed with "admirals, generals and other sorts of people with little financial knowledge". The companies themselves made little effort to educate their shareholders, let alone the wider world, about what they were doing. Some constructed a complex web of interlocking shareholdings that served to disguise how much money was being creamed off by directors for their own benefit.

Not surprisingly, in the circumstances, many investment trusts traded at large discounts to their stated asset value.[8] Private shareholders started to desert in favour of unit trusts, which were much more heavily promoted

---

[8] Unlike unit trusts, investment trusts are publicly quoted companies. Investors buy shares in the company rather than holding a direct interest in the assets which it manages. There is no guarantee that the combined value of the shares in issue will equal the value of the assets. When the value of the shares exceeds the net asset value of the company, it is said to trade at a premium. When it is the other way round, the shares are said to trade at a discount. Historically, investment trusts have tended to trade at a discount, which on occasion (such as the 1970s) can reach as much as 30% or more.

by brokers and also had the advantage of being able to sell directly to the public through advertisements in the newspapers. For a while, the obituarists were out in force, predicting the demise of the whole investment trust sector.

One of Hart's achievements is to have played such a big part in making investment trusts a popular and respectable investment vehicle once more. For a period in 1995 and 1996, the shares of Foreign & Colonial even traded at a premium to asset value, the first time that a general investment trust of its kind had done so since 1972. Since then, discounts on all investment trusts have started to widen sharply again and the need for the industry to find a new cheer leader has re-emerged. Nobody was in the least surprised when Hart was named in mid-1997 as the new Director General of the Association of Investment Trusts, the industry trade association. The job gave him a second chance to address the discount issue, this time on a sector-wide basis.[9]

TRIED AND TESTED IS BEST

What is the secret of his success as an investor? Michael Hart himself has no doubt that the answer lies in a sound, tried and trusted general philosophy, coupled with a willingness to experiment and take risks within that disciplined framework. The best analogy may be with a top-class golfer: a consistent and repeatable swing is needed, but shots also must be able to be matched to the circumstances of each hole. Michael Hart has honed the principles adopted by the original Foreign & Colonial trusts to focus on three central themes:

- a broadly diversified international portfolio of equities;
- a shrewd and timely use of currency borrowings to leverage higher returns for the fund;
- a willingness to invest in markets when they are falling.

---

[9] Alas, however, the opportunity proved to be short-lived. Within a few weeks, Michael Hart announced his retirement on the grounds of ill health.

Of these, it is the last with which he will always be most closely associated. Market timing is the hardest thing of all to get right in investment, but Hart is one of the few who can demonstrate that he has a discipline which has worked over a long period of time. He never expects to catch the absolute tops and bottoms of the market cycle but he says the important thing is to be in a position to catch most of the trend. Another key characteristic of his style has been to do almost everything in a gradual, incremental way rather than in one big burst: if something works, he will do a bit more of it, and then a bit more again. The policy, in his words, is one of "accumulating the singles, rather than hitting sixes". After a period of months, it often turns out that this 'nibbling away' process has produced quite a big shift in his portfolio.

"The trust has been successful by using certain methods which continue to deliver," is how Hart summarises the philosophy. "It certainly hasn't been whizzkid stuff, but using common sense and adjusting, adjusting, adjusting [the phrase crops up time and time again in every conversation] and doing a tremendous amount of homework." Hart notes how a few years ago a leading firm of stockbrokers carried out a review of F&C's record. Their aim was to try to identify exactly what had contributed to its successful performance.

Was it primarily the result of making the right asset allocation decision – i.e. successfully weighting the portfolio towards the best performing type of asset each year (equities, bonds, property, etc.)? Or was it more down to its ability to pick the best individual stocks within his chosen countries and sectors? "They came to the conclusion," says Hart with evident satisfaction, "that sometimes it was this and sometimes it was that. A lot of people out there don't believe that way of running a portfolio is possible, but it does work with us." Such resistance to being pigeonholed is anathema to the new breed of performance consultants who increasingly influence where new pension fund business is allocated, but the board of Foreign & Colonial has by and large remained true to their last, preferring to stick to a method that they know works rather than switching to something new which just happens to be the fashion of the day.

Hart himself calls it a case of "using all the weapons in the investment manager's armoury". He insists that he, like the trust itself, is fundamentally conservative by temperament. That is why diversification plays such a prominent part in the way he invests: Foreign & Colonial, he points out, were spreading their investments across a wide range of countries, industries and types of security decades before Professor Harry Markowitz won the Nobel Prize for demonstrating mathematically that investing in assets with sufficiently different characteristics can reduce the volatility of an investment portfolio without damaging the returns.[10] Although the investment trust has grown in size from just over £100 million in 1970 to £2300 million by mid-1997 the number of stocks has remained broadly constant at between 250 to 300. These investments are spread around more than 30 countries. Around 30% is currently in the UK, down from its peak of nearly 60% in the 1970s, when exchange controls were still in force.

But this fundamental commitment to diversification does not preclude Michael Hart from taking apparently risky bets on where the markets might be heading at any one time, and borrowing to enhance the returns. The key to this seeming paradox lies in the fact that to a professional investment manager risk does not mean the same thing as the term is understood by managers in industry and many leading professions. For the latter, doing something unconventional is a risk; for a successful professional investor, who is primarily rewarded for doing better than the average, the equation is reversed. It is impossible to do your job well – and just as difficult to justify your large salary – unless you do something different from the consensus. That means there is no escape from forming and backing your own judgement.

---

[10] Markowitz is the architect of what is now known as Modern Portfolio Theory. His seminal article on the subject was first published in 1953, but it is only in the last 20 years that its influence has become widely felt in the professional investment business. What Markowitz demonstrated mathematically was that by investing in a number of securities whose prices move in an uncorrelated way, a portfolio manager can reduce the volatility of his portfolio without sacrificing any of the expected return. He also showed that the benefits of diversification diminished rapidly beyond a certain level: most of the benefits of diversification in a given market can be captured with around 20 to 30 securities.

"No other trust has as consistent a record as we do over the years," Hart says. "The gearing has helped, but the main thing has been trying to manage the investments in a professional way, and trying to take advantage of the excesses of gloom and euphoria that you get in stock markets from time to time. During these difficult periods, we will tend to buy into the falling market. Now a lot of people think that is ridiculous, and that you should aim to buy when you are at the bottom of the market. But we think that is impossible. So we just nibble away very cautiously into these down periods, knowing – you remember Dick Barton, Special Agent? – that no matter how difficult the situation appears to be, in a tight corner there is always somehow a way out.[11] As a result, in every bear market I have experienced we have come out of it stronger than we have gone in. In the 1987 crash, we were absolutely terrified, but we tried to keep our nerve and bought into it, and we came out of that situation very well. You underperform for a time, but you come out of in far better shape. Some people's nerves could not stand it. I am very fortunate. I have got a very understanding board of directors."

When I ask him what qualities are needed in a successful investor, he says that "keeping cool in difficult circumstances" is high on the list. This has certainly helped him. "When I was young, I was a pretty nervous sort of chap really. Over the years I have got to be calmer. I tend not to get excited about things and in a way I suppose that can make one appear quite a cool customer."

Given this philosophy, it is no surprise to find that F&C did so well in all the main financial dramas – the 1987 stock market crash, the Gulf War in 1991 and the sterling crisis of 1992. During the October 1987 crash, when the market fell by a quarter in less than a week, Hart coolly persuaded his colleagues to go out and borrow more money in order to buy shares as the market continued to fall. That proved to be the right thing to do; the combination of being a buyer of stock and increasing gearing rapidly carried the trust to the top of its peer group table. In 1992, the year when

---

[11] For readers whose memories are not as long as Michael Hart's, Dick Barton was the fictional hero of a BBC radio drama which was popular immediately after World War II!

speculators such as George Soros buffeted Europe's Exchange Rate Mechanism into near submission, Michael Hart again did well. He started "nibbling away" at the UK market as it began to weaken in the spring, and continued to buy throughout the turbulent few weeks which followed John Major's election success in May. When the UK was finally bounced out of the ERM in September 1992, the pound suffered an immediate depreciation and the stock market quickly took off, rising 33% over the next year. Boosted by the gains on its successful bet against sterling, Foreign & Colonial shares again comfortably outperformed the market. The trust's net asset value rose by 49% during that same 12-month period.

Hart cheerfully admits to making plenty of mistakes; in fact, in many ways, he seems happier confessing to the things he has got wrong than he does to celebrating the things that he got right. This attitude rather confirms the theory of Victor Niederhoffer, a well-known trader in New York, that successful investors invariably learn more from their mistakes than they do from their successes.[12] Having made a lot of money out of the Japanese stock market's one big rise in the 1980s, for example, Hart confesses that he started to buy back in too early, following its headlong fall in the early 1990s. In 1992, he largely misread the dollar and again in 1996 failed to appreciate how strong sterling was going to be. This last misjudgement was a contributing factor in making his last full year as manager of the trust one of his least successful.

On the stocks side, few investments can have been as spectacularly unsuccessful as Hart's investment in Eurotunnel, the company which built and runs the Channel Tunnel – a triumph in engineering terms but an unmitigated disaster for shareholders. Pressed for an explanation, Michael Hart just laughs and shrugs his shoulders, as if to marvel at his own folly. The lifting of exchange controls in 1979 by the newly elected Thatcher government opened up the possibility of the trust borrowing in overseas

---

[12] "During the ten years that I traded for George Soros," says Niederhoffer, "I never heard him speak once about a winning trade. To hear him talk, you'd think he had had nothing but losers. Conversely, listening to the biggest losers, you'd think they had had nothing but winners" (*The Education of a Speculator*, John Wiley, 1997).

currencies, making a turn by exploiting the different interest rates across international markets and hoping for capital appreciation on top. That strategy has also produced some spectacular reverses, including a loss of £19 million in one year. Fortunately it was soon gained back again. Overall, betting on currencies has served Foreign & Colonial well. Hart reckons that this policy earned shareholders a profit of £100 million or so in the years since 1979. "I am certainly not saying that we are geniuses," he told me, "or that we are particularly brilliant at what we do. Most of what we do is just the application of common sense and watching trends. But it seems to work, which is what matters."

This rather appealing sense of diffidence characterises all of Michael Hart's utterances. It probably dates back to his early years as a manager finding his feet in a business where trial and error was very much the order of the day. When he started, his first problem was how to generate enough income to pay the dividend, and he was quite happy to cut some corners to get that. Once he had a bedrock of high yielding UK stocks to secure the dividend, he and his colleagues decided to go "hell for leather" for capital appreciation wherever they could find it. "It was only after two or three years that one of the analysts pointed out to us how well we are doing. As far as we were concerned, we were just making a lot of mistakes. But this chap pointed out that we were doing better than all the others. That's still my feeling about it. I am just amazed how successful one has been when one sees all the mistakes one has made. I know I have made every mistake in the book."

Despite such disarming modesty, what makes Michael Hart's performance record stand out from the pack is, first, that he has achieved such a consistent level of performance over such a long period of time; and, second, that he has done so while competing for results on a global scale. While other fund managers increasingly specialise in just one or two areas, from the beginning Hart has been in charge of an internationally diversified portfolio where he is not only having to choose which stocks to buy but also which countries to invest in and which currencies to play. With hundreds of variables to worry about, the opportunities for error are also of a magnitude higher than those faced by less ambitious investors.

True, he has always had other managers working with him, and increasingly, many of them are specialists in particular regions. They are needed, not least, to feed the growing appetite for new specialist investment trusts for regions such as Europe, North America and the Far East. But he alone has had to answer to the board for the overall shape and performance of the trust over more than a quarter of a century. Competition having increased dramatically in the last few years, outperformance is certainly no easier. In many ways, the wonder is not that he has done so well, but that he has not done worse. I asked him what is the most important thing he has learnt which he didn't know at the outset. His reply was: "How difficult it all is. A bull market may make it appear easier, but investment is never easy."

Unlike many so-called 'value' investors who largely ignore movements in the broad economic picture in favour of detailed stock selection, Hart sees his job as looking at both 'top-down' and 'bottom-up' indicators. Judging the next move in interest rates and currencies goes hand in hand with finding the right stocks. He says he believes in market timing, but "it is extremely difficult to get it right. I believe in doing things gradually in the belief that I am near the bottom or near the top." He does not think the markets are efficient: "In the short term, markets are dominated by market makers and traders and they have very short memories." Even top quality stocks such as Glaxo, he points out, now regularly move 10 to 15% within a matter of days. "Is that efficiency? Is that summing up precisely all the knowledge available at the time? I don't believe it."

Historical perspective is very important therefore. A few years ago, the investment community was suddenly swept by a wave of concerns that we might be heading for another 1930s-style Depression. Proponents of the Krondatieff wave, named after a Russian agricultural economist who noted that big world slumps tended to happen every 60 years, were full of talk about a coming crash. Hart was quick to nail that one. "No, I think Krondatieff is something which is always brought out in time of difficulty. I have had him thrown at me a number of occasions over the years, so that I am now rather blasé about it. Obviously a rerun of '29 to '33, if it were to happen, would be incredibly difficult, but 1933 was followed by quite a good time. The overall market didn't recover till 1954, but an awful lot of industrial stocks did do well. So one hopes that one's portfolio would not be too much of a disaster. The first thing I would do is neutralise my gearing. But I do know that I am a dangerous optimist, so you have to tread carefully here."

He does not buy the argument, also much debated in the early 1990s, that in a climate of low inflation and falling interest rates, gilts are more attractive than equities. "Over a 120-year period, the statistics show that equities have been better investments than bonds in periods of high inflation, and even better in periods of low inflation. The only time they have underperformed was in depressions. I personally argue that things are nowhere near as bad as that." He worries, however, that the Germans might be making the same mistake as the Japanese, "keeping the screws on their economy for too long".

On the other hand, the longer-term outlook is more encouraging. "It is incredibly exciting that China may develop tremendously in the next 20 years, the way the rest of Asia is beginning to. Eastern Germany will eventually pick up. Maybe in 20 years Russia will get going. So there are great opportunities. With the information explosion, I am sure that this is going to lead to a lot of new products and developments. It is very exciting. Lots of opportunities for equities."

This is how he summed up the prospects for the markets for me as he approached his retirement from day-to-day management of the trust. The UK "has had a good revival, but it is important to remember that some overseas countries give greater long-term potential, especially if the UK makes a mess of Europe". The United States: "Long term, you must not be out of this market. A rich country, large markets, great companies and technology." On Japan: "Still a great country with innovative people. The market has had a long setback, but it will recover." Emerging markets: "Long term very exciting as they reap the benefits of democracy, private enterprise and new technology." Did the man not describe himself as a "dangerous optimist"?

CONVERSING WITH PENGUINS

Apart from the stock markets, Michael Hart's other main passions are the very English pursuits of travel, gardening and cricket. In the course of his career, he reckons to have visited most countries where there is a stock market. In 1996, he and his wife spent Christmas on a cruise ship to the Antarctic, which is one of the few places left in the world where you can legitimately go if you want to get away from the market. Hart started playing club cricket when he was 14 and did not finally call it a day until he was 56, because that was the same age at which his father had stopped playing. One of the nicest complements he was paid, he says, was being told: "Old Hart, he just plays cricket for relaxation." And that was it. "One liked to win but one didn't get over-excited if someone dropped a catch when you were bowling." Bowling was his strength. He started as "a fast bowler, then medium pace, then slow with a fast one slipped in", and kept going until the end.

This has distinct parallels with his record as an investor. There is something very English in the way that Michael Hart tells his story. It is probably safe to say that his way of managing money is on the way out. Yet his record is genuinely remarkable, and there is much that investors can learn from his career – not least that you don't need formidable academic qualifications to succeed. Patience, humility and the application of hard work and common sense are just as valuable starting points. Many of the disciplines that modern fund managers apply routinely today are things that Hart had to work out for himself as he went along. He has shown particular imagination and innovation in finding new ways to put the flexibility of the investment trust structure to profitable use.

Another obvious lesson is that investment, properly defined, is a long-term business: if you get the basics right, and stick to one well-thought-out approach, however simple, the results will tend to follow. Most investors are in too much of a hurry to get results. They chop and change, desperately looking for the quick fix when they would do better to sit back and let the marvel of compound interest work for them. It does not take long for transaction costs, the cost of buying and selling shares, to eat into any investor's performance record.

A third moral is that diversification can pay: it allows you to make a hatful of mistakes and still outperform the pack, provided you have the patience to wait for results. In fact, all you need to succeed as an investor, Hart believes, is a strike rate of 60% or so to come out well ahead in the medium to long term. And you don't have to be absolutely right in picking the time to buy – going slowly and building up your bets is a profitable route, too. Another key lesson is to avoid becoming a slave to fashion: just because everybody else loves a share, it does not mean you have to buy it. Chasing fashion is the hardest thing for all investors to avoid, yet it is the key to long-term success. Where do most people go wrong? I asked Michael Hart. "Impatience and running with the crowd," was his reply. And the qualities it takes to be a successful investor? "Not to be of too excitable a disposition."

UPDATE (2012)

Michael Hart retired from Foreign & Colonial shortly after the publication of the first edition of Money Makers.

7. JOHN CARRINGTON:

Profiting from prejudice

Not all professional investors enjoy the limelight as much as a Mark Mobius or a Warren Buffett. Many are much happier going about their business in private, shunning the public stage in favour of a life in less exposed circumstances. One investment manager who has done just that with great success over the years is a man whose personality is as large as his public profile is low. John Carrington is a name that is largely unknown outside the ranks of the professional fund management business: yet his record managing money over the last 25 years is just as good as most of his better-known contemporaries. The fund management company that he started in 1970, Carrington Pembroke, has deliberately remained as a boutique operation, shunning the rapid expansion of its larger brethren. It rarely advertises and relies mainly on word of mouth from its clients to win new business.

Carrington, who is now in his 50s, sold his business to the Dutch bank ABN Amro in 1996. For most of its life the firm has had just four fund managers, three of whom, Carrington himself, George Luckraft and Nigel Thomas, are still with the firm and share the clients among them.[1] The three have all been running their funds for many years. In other words, this is a small but stable and successful operation, run in a very distinctive style. Its track record underlines how important continuity is in successful investment management. An investment of £10,000 in Carrington's UK Growth Fund, launched in 1986, would have been worth £59,124 by 31

---

[1] Update (2012): Thomas and Luckraft continue to manage their funds, which are now part of the AXA Framlington group, having been sold on by ABN Amro in one of many ownership changes that has characterised the fund management business in recent years. John Carrington has retired from active fund management.

December 1997, against £41,840 if invested in the FT All-Share Index. This represents a compound rate of return of 17.5% against 13.9% for the market and 12.1% for the average equity growth unit trust. His private client portfolios have also prospered.

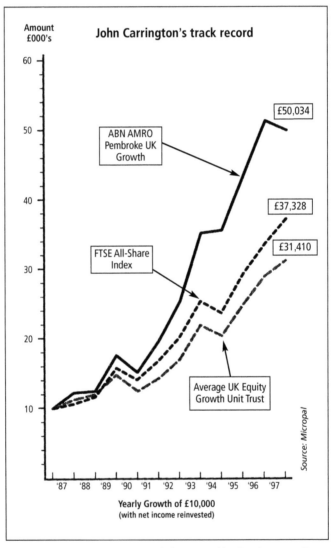

John Carrington's distinctive investment style has served his loyal private clients well over many years. The Pembroke UK Growth Fund, one of his firm's unit trusts, has done particularly well since its launch in 1986.

JD *How did you get into the investment business?*

JC I was a financial journalist. After my first job in Turkey, which was in the salt mines of market research, I came back to work in an advertising agency. I really didn't believe my life was to be spent assessing housewife preference for the colour of soft toilet tissue. When I had been in Turkey, working for the Economist Intelligence Unit, I had also done a bit of stringing for the *Guardian*, so printing ink was in my veins, but I also realised that journalism was only an extension of my education and that I'd need to be out of it by the time I was 30. After a short stint at the *Sheffield Telegraph*, I went to *The Times*. By that time I had managed to pay off my debts, and I wondered what to specialise in. I asked myself what I was interested in and there were two things: foreign affairs and the stock market. The coin came down for the stock market because at that time Lord Thomson had just bought *The Times* and created *The Times Business News*, thus expanding the market for aspiring financial journalists.

JD *You were one of the original intake?*

JC Yes, I was one of the first to arrive. This was in 1967. They initially started with people transferring over from the *Sunday Times*. I did the column which they now call Tempus (a share comment column) and I also later had my own share tipping column. As a result I quickly discovered that I was just as good at the job as the people I was writing about. This is the point as a journalist that one ceases to wish to communicate. At the time I had forgotten my ambition to be out by the time I was 30, but it soon popped up again and I realised that managing money myself was the way out for me. At the same time, I was approached and reintroduced to somebody I'd been to school with, who wanted to set up this sort of business and offered to back me. I thought about it for six months and then said "yes".

JD *Who was that?*

JC A man called George Steer who had been at Kleinworts, but was now working for Bonas & Co, who are one of the world's largest syndicate diamond brokers. They wanted to diversify into new areas, including investment management, and that's how it happened. We were one of their early diversifications. While I was on *The Times*, as you can imagine, I had an open door to the chairman or managing director of every public company in the country. I also met all the main stockbrokers and merchant banks. The one thing I decided early on was that I wasn't working for any of that shower, which left only one thing, which was to be independent. And George kindly set me up. Well, I put in some money myself, which I had to borrow, as my finances then were not as they are now.

JD *There was no family background in the investment business?*

JC None at all, except that my grandmother had a portfolio with a stockbroker. She was unusual in that she made her own money. She was finance director and part owner of a private company in the 1920s, which for a woman was extremely rare. So there was a portfolio, which was partly passed on to my mother, which was where I'd begun to learn about it. I became fascinated in the markets from the age of 11.

JD *What fascinated you?*

JC I don't know. Do you remember how you became interested in things when you were at prep school? Just curiosity, I expect.

JD *What effect did Winchester have on these impulses?*

JC Well, it did not manage to drive my enthusiasm away. I spent my time trying to make a few extra pennies. For example, I managed to acquire the franchise to run the book on the scholarship election. I remember dealing in second-hand books, too. This was back in the late 1950s. Some innocent entrepreneurs in publishing started something called the National Book Sale, which was originally surplus stock to the trade. Wells [the school bookshop] used to get into this in a big way, and I discovered that it was possible to buy an armful of books at sale price and take them up to March Gilbert, a second-hand bookshop by the cathedral, and flog them for profit. So I suppose I had commercial incentive even then.

It fructified a lot more when I was in Turkey. From my predecessor I inherited a little sideline, changing money for British residents and visiting businessmen. I discovered something that 15 years of expensive education had not taught me, which was that there's a lot of money to be made if you can find buyers and sellers at a price that leaves room for entrepreneurs to make something in the middle. At the time, the Turks, in their great naiveté, were quoting an exchange rate of 25 to 37.5 for the pound. As you can imagine, that spread left something for everybody.

JD *What subjects did you read at university?*

JC English Part One and History Part Two, having read Classics at school. I got a scholarship to Cambridge. I wanted to do modern languages but nobody would let me at school because they said it was too easy. "Go away and teach yourself in your spare time!" At Cambridge they said: "Our courses are all rather medieval. You're a man of the present moment." They were both right.

JD *One of the interesting questions people want to know about successful investors is whether the feel for the business is something you are born with or acquire. Which was it in your case, do you think?*

JC I feel for it. Like backing horses, which I started very young, it is about judgement and the trade off between risk and reward. The two disciplines are parallel. It doesn't really matter what your background is. Of my directors, the one who has been here longest, George Luckraft, started with us as a student in vacations. He was still at Cambridge when he started and because he was working for us and found the City interesting, he switched to studying land economy, didn't do any work and got a third. Nigel Thomas went to London University and read economics. One of my most successful contemporaries at school was Anthony Milford, who spent all his time playing bridge and going racing.[2]

JD *When you set up the business, what were you hoping to do?*

JC Well, what we thought we were going to do was different from what we actually ended up dong. We thought that we would start with investment management, and that this would lead on to a Slater–Walker

---

[2] Milford was a fund manager with the Framlington group, where he ran a highly successful, but volatile, fund specialising in healthcare stocks. He regularly played bridge for England in the 1960s and early 1970s.

type operation, putting together deals. Don't forget this was the late 60s, and this kind of business was all the rage. Fortunately, I discovered early on that I was very good at investment management, and didn't have time for anything else. George Steer wanted to get involved in one or two deals, but it wasn't a great success. In fact, it became a waste of time and we stuck to our last, at which we were quite good.

JD *Where did you start?*

JC I was a hermit crab in the office that belonged to a small broking firm in New Broad Street. We used their office and used some of their services. When I say "we", it was actually just me, as the admin side was contracted out at that stage. I eventually graduated to a part-time secretary, and she sat there solemnly operating my typewriter, which had a peculiarity – I'd had the @ sign replaced by the Turkish 1. I've still got it, a curious feature.[3]

JD *Who was your first client? How did you get hold of them?*

JC I collected some from George Steer's group, Bonas. The top man there was called Benjamin Bonas, and he found one or two amongst their contacts, I found one or two amongst my contacts, and then we advertised – a very small advert in *The Times* – and I picked up one or two people who'd read my column and seemed to think I might know what I was doing.

JD *Did you set out thinking, "I'm a clever fellow and I can make more money than everyone else?" Or was there something more deepseated?*

JC I set out thinking that I was a better judge of shares and potential share prices than quite a lot of people doing the same job. I did not set out to make a lot of money. I set out feeling there was a very considerable hole in the market and that people who in those days had £20,000, which is now the equivalent of about £200,000, got pretty well looked after in every aspect of life except their share portfolios. I reckoned it should be possible to make a reasonable profit with that sort of money. These are people who would have had their money with brokers, or would just read the papers and do it themselves. That's what quite a lot of them did.

---

[3] Carrington says he speaks Turkish, Finnish (linguistically a close relation to Turkish) and a little Hungarian, a characteristically idiosyncratic choice.

JD *And from the beginning you were always equity focused?*

JC It's the way I was brought up by my grandmother. It was most odd when people started talking about gilts and things like that.

JD *This was the early 70s. How did you go about looking for shares in those days?*

JC I knew a lot of the companies already. I built up a network of brokers fairly easily. One of them was my grandmother's old broker. He's dead now, but when he retired he became a consultant for us, a man called John Allday. The man who introduced me to George Steer was also a broker. He actually became a shareholder in the company. And one or two people I picked up because I knew them from *The Times*, it's as simple as that. One picked me, David Hunter from Henry Cooke. David was a very good broker. He walked into the office one day. He said: "We've heard what you're up to, and we'd like to deal for you." We're still very good friends. Until it ceased to be equity-based, we ran their firm's pension fund and tend to do a lot of business with them. David's son Rupert has just come to work for us.

JD *What was the first thing you had to learn?*

JC I had to learn the business from scratch. Within six weeks I realised just how much I didn't know. Mostly the practicalities of the business, simple facts like the liquidity of the market. The fact that the brokers' circulars which we got at *The Times* had been leaked to clients six weeks earlier. The fact that the way to act upon a circular was to find out about it before it was sent to any other client. I had to learn all sorts of realistic things like that. It's all very well, you can say something in theory looks cheap, but if you can't actually buy the shares, it's no use at all.

JD *If you look at the portfolios you had then, would you recognise them?*

JC Yes. I did that about a year or two ago. *Plus ça change.* I've still got things that were around then. The philosophy hasn't changed.

JD *Did you have a theoretical framework for valuing shares in those days?*

JC In those days price-earnings ratios were the thing. Nobody was interested in yields, as they are now. I say now, but that might just be my age, because today the world is full of young fund managers, who may well be interested in something else now. But we were not interested in yields then. Remember that we were talking about the aftermath of the Labour government, and the only way you had to make a return was through capital gains, so you really did not worry about yields. Today with neutralised taxation, they are much more important.

JD *How did you cope with the fact that earnings figures are not necessarily very reliable?*

JC I was always looking for status change.[4] I still am. If you've read your *FT* today, you'll see a company called Bodycote [a metal technology company] on the front page of the companies section. That is a company which has just had a status change and which we own. What we saw there was a company which had changed and which I believed an awful lot of professional investors hadn't realised had changed. I also saw a wonderful high-quality earnings stream, coupled with a business which was extremely capital intensive.

JD *Is that good or bad? Some businesses just seem to consume capital* ad infinitum.

JC Well, if your costs are quantifiable and don't go on strike, and they can't just walk out of the door, I'm all for that. The great thing about capital is that if it is your main cost, there is none of the risk associated with labour, walkouts and what have you. Capital is more flexible, and your costs are more certain. In Bodycote's case, it means they only put in a plant if they know that the demand is already there.

---

[4] When shares are priced in a much higher (or lower) multiple of earnings than before, they are said to have experienced a status change.

JD *How long did it take you to develop a style of investing?*

JC Well, it probably was in the course of developing already. It's a difficult question to answer. It grew naturally. Remember that we had to live through the 73-74 bear market fairly early on. It turned out all right in the end. But it was tough. I'd started going liquid in September 1972. I started talking to fellow fund managers, and we all came to the conclusion that we couldn't find anything to buy, and if you can't find anything to buy it must be right to sell, so we started selling. I remember we went through the Three Day Week unloading shares. I stayed up all night working out what to sell. In 74 I started buying foreign stocks, which bolstered our performance quite a lot. Then in 75 we realised the market was turning, early, which was the right thing to do. We started looking for companies with cash.

JD *Any examples?*

JC I remember one called Benford Concrete. It was trading at 12 pence, but had 17 pence of net cash on the balance sheet at the time, together with a bunch of assets that were in for nothing. We ended up with a funny collection. The shares we bought didn't conform to our normal rules in any way. We coped and scrambled through somehow. But for the first seven years, we didn't make a profit on investment management. We had created a company with a bit of surplus cash in it, which we traded, and we lived off that. In late 74, we were bold and took for us a large underwriting position in an insurance company. I cannot remember which. We reckoned the market had gone low enough.

JD *You couldn't make much money. But you never lost faith?*

JC No. Stretched it from time to time.

JD *Your approach is to be equity-focused and you're looking for multiple changes. What else?*

JC Multiple changes are one of the things. If you want some more aspects of philosophy, we are not traders, we don't take short-term views, we don't buy something just because it is moving. What I always tried to do is introduce into private portfolios the kind of quality growth stocks institutions like, and put quality private investor stocks into institutional portfolios. We are also backers of management. Philip Darwin[5] always used to say that when you're buying a share, you're effectively lending money to the managing director, so if you don't trust him, don't buy the share. Management is the first thing I look at, and I work on the basis of extreme prejudice. That is one reason, incidentally, why we virtually never recruit anybody with experience from the City. I have enough prejudices of my own without importing another set.

The people I am prejudiced against are put on the banned list, also known as OMDB, for "over my dead body". The banned list has never let us down. It is a much shorter list than it used to be because I've been right. A lot of them have disappeared. The first thing I do when I have a new issue, if there's a name on the list in there, I won't touch it. Actually that was one of the good things about having a journalist's training, because by the nature of the job one had to involve oneself to some extent with bad companies. It was quite educational. The other thing which amazes me is how so many people in the City can be taken in. I think I can smell PR hype at a hundred paces, but there's still an awful lot of it about, especially in the Sunday press.

JD *What sort of companies would be on your blacklist?*

JC Well I remember the author Gerald McKnight, when we were both members of the Savile Club, was doing a book on the great money men of the day – Jim Slater, Pat Matthews, Oliver Jessel and others.[6] He asked my thoughts. This was about 1972. I said, "I'll tell you one thing. At least one, if not all of them, will precipitate the next bear market." He looked at me totally amazed. But he came back to me later and said: "Do you realise, I was shocked by what you said. These men were my idols and you said they've got feet of clay. Now I reckon that you're right." So I made it a rule never to touch anything Slater-Walker was involved with, knowingly anyway. Or Pat Matthews, do you remember that First National Finance Corporation? I tell you why. In that case it was a quite specific reason. I

---

[5] A former senior partner of the stockbroking firm, Laurence Prust.
[6] *The Fortune Sellers*, Michael Joseph, 1972.

only met him once. He was going on to me, giving me the razzmatazz about the company. He said, "We've got this property in the West Midlands". I said: "Where?" He said, "In the West Midlands". Again I said, 'Where?" So he rang up and asked: "About that property we've got. Where is it?" He'd never heard of Smethwick. A man who doesn't know the details of his business, forget him. So I avoided all those and kept out of quite a lot of trouble. I never bought a share in Ladbroke either.

JD *Why was that?*

JC Two reasons, really. One, I didn't like the style of the man who ran it. And two, because it was very much a creation of the broking community. It was very much a broker-created company. For a long time, for an entirely different reason, I would never buy BOC [the manufacturer of oxygen and other liquid gases] simply because I thought it was badly managed. There was no individual involved there. Mostly they were connected with people I didn't trust.

JD *This was based on meeting these people?*

JC Sometimes. Jim Slater I actually liked, but I didn't trust the people around him.

JD *What qualifies you to judge managers?*

JC I don't know. I've just found by experience that I'm a good judge of people. I don't know where it comes from. I know I've got it. I once gave my old friend George Blakey some good advice about a man he was preparing to do a deal with. I knew he was wrong even before I met him, because he was three-quarters of an hour late for lunch. I'm very old-fashioned. I can't trust a man like that.

JD *How does the economics of the business fit into your approach?*

JC We like growth situations. We like nice balance sheets. We love to find something we can buy and hold for years. This has been one of the main reasons for our success, I think. We're a complete contrast to stockbrokers and probably still are. I took on a client who had his money with a broker. The broker said: "I'll come up with the portfolio and go through it and tell you why I've bought the stocks." He did. It wasn't a bad list, but the reasoning for every share he had was that something was just about to happen. That's the broker's mentality, because they live on commission and turnover. They want to buy things where there's an out. I want to buy things where I can keep them forever.

JD *Do you have sectors you particularly favour?*

JC We are all of us much better on the whole with companies where the human added value is important, rather than, say, commodities. We've not traditionally had much in mining. We tend to be underweight in oil. We tend to be underweight in property. We've also all got our little peculiarities. We've traditionally been light in financials too, mainly because we've seen the City and realised how badly managed they are. We performed rather poorly in the first quarter of this year because the index was driven totally by the banks. We had been in banks. We weren't that foolish, but we got in so early. We thought they had risen far enough.

JD *Give me a couple of examples of things that worked and a couple of things that didn't work.*

JC Undoubtedly the greatest success has been in Williams Holdings. I bought in there for an equivalent of 3 pence or 7 pence or something, when Nigel Rudd took over the show. I owe this one to George Blakey, who's been very important in my life. He's a funny man, very strange, but a great lateral thinker. Anyway, he worked for a firm called Lyddon. W. Williams & Sons Holdings had been one of their corporate customers. Nigel Rudd and Brian McGowan were looking for a shell operation, and the rule was, and I think still is, that to take control of a shell company you have to make sure there is a certain minimum number of shareholders. They like to come to a company like us, with a lot of private clients, because they know that if they give us a large chunk, it can be spread over a large number of registrations. At one time, I think I had 18% of Williams. We made lots of money out of that one.

The other big success is probably Nokia. I have to put this one down to a broker. With Williams, we were shown the opportunity, but I had to do the work myself. Nokia came from, I think, the best stockbroker I've got. He's hardly ever wrong, a man called Harald Lundén in Stockholm, whom I've known for years. Harald rang me up one day and he said, "Look, I've been to see Nokia. They are flat on their back. But I can see the potential. You won't believe me, but I think you're going to make ten times your money." I said: "Harald, I trust you." I listened very readily, because I'm a great fan of Finland. I like that country because they get things right. Super country. Actually they made me 40 times the money, I think, over four years. I've still got some.

JD *That's two good ones. Any others spring to mind?*

JC I have been a great supporter of Importadora Y Exportadora Patagonia. That's a small chain of supermarkets in Patagonia which I found when they were absurdly cheap. One of my innumerable rules about investing is that I never invest in a country until I have been inside their supermarkets. They tell you a lot about the feel of a country.

JD *And what about things that haven't worked out?*

JC Well there are lots of them, but one tends to forget them. There was a dreadful thing called Bergen Brunswick, an American company. That was a complete disaster. What did they do? I cannot remember. Typically, of course, I've even forgotten why I bought it. Generally, one of the important things I tell both clients and my colleagues is that the hardest bit of this job is cutting losses. If you do that, it is relatively rare to lose a lot of money on an initial purchase.

The greatest disaster I've had was something different. That was Psion. I had it all the way up, the shares about quadrupled within the space of a few months, and I sold a few at the top, but basically I should have tried to sell all of them. It came all the way back down again. Much worse, I cut my losses and sold and it's now gone all the way back up again. That's one I got definitely wrong. There must have been some others. For a long time, we were able to boast that we have never had a stock go bust on us. But you write them out of your life. There have been plenty of quite nasty ones.

JD *You were into some of the emerging markets, especially Latin America, in a big way quite early on. How was that?*

JC Because I knew and liked the countries. I got interested in Chile initially, and Argentina back in the late 1970s, and I was in Chile again in the early 80s. Got the stock right, got the currency wrong. I also resumed going to Argentina in the 80s. One of the attractions for me is that South America is so underreported. And also so badly reported. The first time I went to South America was actually when I was on *The Times*. That was Columbia and Peru. The first time I went back again on business, I remember we had a meeting with a British ambassador and when the door was firmly shut, he said, "I must tell you, I'm not supposed to have political views, but it is our view that the *FT*'s correspondent here is basically a raving loony leftie." I found that people didn't understand how biased the reporting was. The first time I went to Chile I asked an ordinary man in the street what it was like under Pinochet. He said, "I'll tell you, this will now be the last country ever to go Marxist again." I said, "What was wrong?" He said he couldn't get any milk, he couldn't get any petrol, he couldn't get any sugar. It was basics, not ideology. Pinochet had a very simple policy. He wanted to make sure there was plenty of money in people's pockets and plenty of goods in the shops to spend it on. That isn't being a dictator in the sense that the BBC understands it. If you wanted a nasty country, it was Argentina under Galtieri, who really was a nasty thug.

JD *When did you start taking an interest in overseas markets?*

JC I was overseas focused from the very beginning. Far earlier than many much grander fund managers. In the 70s and 80s, institutions didn't like the dollar premium and tended to buy funds if they wanted overseas exposure. That didn't worry me. Another one of my successes was East Asiatic. It was a great Danish overseas trading company. It did very well in the 80s. I first came across it when I was in South America. A relation of a friend of mine, who'd been seconded to the World Development Fund from Schroders, told me about it, so I looked into it. In Denmark, up until the 80s, an apprenticeship in East Asiatic was regarded as equal to university qualifications. At that time the Danish market was closed. However, and this was a real coup, I found out that there was a theoretical listing in Paris. Nobody had traded it there for some years, but I wanted to buy, and we made a fortune because a year later the Danes opened their market. I wouldn't have found a company like that unless I had been a traveller.

JD *What about Japan?*

JC I've done quite well in Japan, but I wasn't as early into that. I was in by 1980, I suppose. I've had some good things. I've had one or two horrors in Japan. But the best decision we made was to get out a few years ago. I'm not bad at Japan. I can understand how the Japanese investor thinks, to some extent. I'm not so good at the United States. It's not a natural market for me. I have bad feelings towards it, and I don't like it very much. As a race, Americans are unbelievably thick, slow, stupid and sometimes corrupt. That's my personal view. It is not quite the worst investment of all. That is an Australian resource stock listed in Vancouver.

The other market I am hopeless at is Hong Kong, I just don't understand it. Everything one buys is some sort of property-related company, and as a matter of principle I don't really understand property. In the 70s I made a lot of money in the Hong Kong Shanghai Bank and in the 80s I made a lot of money in another bank which did extremely well. But they're the exceptions that prove the rule. In principle, I shy away from it.

JD *How do you and your colleagues split the management of your funds?*

JC The way we run the business now is that essentially the clients are divided up between us. Everybody makes a contribution. I'm winding down towards my retirement. The plan is that I shall cease investing in the UK and I shall hand over those portfolios. But I shall carry on with the global fund for a while. I've done enough, 26 years, 27 years. Long time now.

JD *What do you tell your clients when they come to you?*

JC I tell them: "My job is actually to lose you less money that you would do on your own." I am lucky because most of my clients come to me. I don't have to go out and find them. The longer they have been with me, the less I find I need to talk to them. You can't tell clients this, but the primary service you provide is your clients' education. The level of ignorance about investment in this country is a scandal of the education system. People simply are not taught. 95% of the population who leaves university still thinks that the best investment is the one with the highest yield! Unbelievable. It has been said by one or two of my staff that the seminal experience in their early days in the company was hearing me firing a client – for being ignorant and a pest!

JD *Do you believe in market timing?*

JC Yes, to a point. For most of my career, we have tracked the overbought/oversold index. It's a rough and ready guide. We don't try to trade without it, but all that happens is that when it is overbought, it gives us some price targets. On the other side of the coin, have you seen the chart of the market going back to 1970? Did you notice the crash in 1987? No. Market timing is not that important because we're not traders. One of my first clients, who was actually a very old friend, called Julian Board, and a pretty good investor himself, gave me a piece of good advice. He said: "You're a profit snatcher. Stop it." It is a very good piece of advice, something I have to tell the clients all the time. In the stock market a loss is a loss, a profit is a profit, whether it is realised or not. It's very hard to tell people. I once met a potential client who had one of those portfolios which you could see had been bought in the 1960s. He said: "What are you going to do with this?" I said: "Sell virtually everything." He said: "Sell?" I said: "They're showing losses." He said: "I've been in business 30 years and I've never sold anything at a loss in my life and I'm not going to start now." I said, "You've got losses, whether you like it or not. And whether you take them or not." But he wouldn't understand me. He didn't take me on.

JD *Do you believe in efficient markets?*

JC No, absolute nonsense. Most of these academic theories arise from the fact that the large institutions, particularly merchant banks, are trying to justify the fact that they haven't done as well as their publicity machine says they have. The words "merchant banker" are my language is roughly the equivalent of "*Guardian* reader". They're both extreme derogatories.

Anyway, those who can do, them who can't teach. That answers that one.

Actually, I'm being ever so slightly unfair on academics. You know we act for two Oxbridge colleges? One of them has an economics Fellow, who has actually made some very, very clever investments. He's wrongheaded in many ways but very shrewd. He's made quite a lot of money, and he gave me some assistance in creating a recovery fund which I would never have dared to do on my own.

JD *Do you do any technical analysis with charts?*

JC Yes I do. Not as a primary source, but I will nearly always look at a chart before I act. I would never buy a share in Japan, for example, without looking at a chart. You go to Tokyo, I mean, people don't believe this, but have you noticed? Here, outside a tube station you buy an *Evening Standard*. Tube stations in Japan, you buy a chart book. There are other things with Japanese stocks, but the chart's got to be right. The next thing I look at is my usual prejudices, such as who are sponsors, if there are one or two banks there that I won't touch. The third thing I look at is percentage of foreign ownership. The last thing I want is to buy the shares the Japanese don't want themselves. My other great disaster, incidentally, was that I found Nintendo. I went down to Kyoto to see the chief executive. He'd never seen a shareholder before, let alone a foreign shareholder. When I said I wanted to buy some shares, I was met with polite laughter. My colleagues said I must be mad, but I made four times the money in six months! I thought that was good, but if I had held on to them, it would have gone up 56 times. Oh, and I was offered the UK agency as well! So that was a disaster.

JD *What about the state of the economy? Do you spend time thinking about that?*

JC Some aspects I look at. I do keep note; I don't hang on every word, but it's always been one of my philosophies that rising growth and falling unemployment is bad for markets, as it squeezes margins and means, as is beginning to happen now, that money is being diverted from financial securities to real assets. Of course, the thing about the stock market most people don't understand is that it is a place of last resort, where you go when there is nowhere else to put your money. Even very intelligent people don't understand that the way the economic condition affects the stock market isn't as simple or precise as they think. "The country's in a terrible mess, so why is the stock market booming?" That sort of thing. I am scornful of people who base all their decisions on that kind of thinking.

JD *You don't spend your life worrying about what Alan Greenspan is going to do next?*

JC No, there's traders to do that. I find a lot of clients get very nervous about the volatility of the markets. I have to explain carefully that an awful lot of money in the stock market is geared or borrowed money which they don't understand. If it's your own money you have in shares, then you don't have to worry. The people who are worrying and dashing about are people who are 90% geared which means a fall of 10% will wipe them out. Most people, the sort of clients we have, don't understand what Greenspan and the traders are up to, but then they don't need to understand that. It shouldn't concern them.

Far more important than macroeconomics, particularly if you're looking at emerging markets, is to take note when there's been a fundamental legal change which in some way encourages buying of shares in a country. This gives you a wonderful opportunity because nothing happens for months, then it all happens in a rush. It happened in Finland. It happened in Sweden. If the government takes some action which long term increases or reduces the supply and demand for shares, that's very important.

JD *When did you first realise that this was happening in emerging markets?*

JC I know the moment I realised it which is when I started going round Polish companies, where I never believed this would happen. I did believe it would happen in Hungary. I was on record as saying in 1981, because I knew Hungary very well, that I believed that by 1990 it would be either not Communist any more or at least neutral. What I didn't see was that it would happen to all the others as well. I thought Hungary was a bit different.

Clients are very nervous about volatile markets like Poland. They don't ring up Warsaw to see if their shares have gone higher, so they worry. A very important thing about our business, which is quite different from people running unit trusts or corporate funds, our clients know what is in their portfolios, so you've got to err on the cautious side. I wouldn't buy in South America for a long time without getting the clients' permission first. Simply because I know it was a recipe for trouble. One notices that running unit trusts as well. It's easy to take a loss in a unit trust. It's harder with private clients. That's why I always warn clients: "Don't be surprised that the first sell note you get after putting your cash in, you'll almost certainly make a loss." This business is trial and error. I say: "We should get 60% right, we hope to get 70% right, 90% is spectacular; if it's 100%, we're cheating." It is important to condition them.

JD *Do you use derivatives?*

JC No. We have done them in the past. We did a bit of traded options in the early days, but I'm very unconvinced by it all. Before we sold the business, we had quite a lot of capital in the company. From time to time we would buy a Footsie to put on our own book if things looked nasty. Derivatives are an expensive broker's toy.

JD *You don't have much capacity to use gearing in your type of business?*

JC No, we don't. I was always habitually geared myself, personally. It's produced an enormous change in my attitude since I've sold out and had more money than I want. It does alter your attitude. For the better.

JD *Where do you get your ideas?*

JC I still read quite a lot, but I much prefer doing things face-to-face. We are apparently notorious in the City. We've been told that we get more ideas here on our own than other fund managers. Clients are important. An intelligent client in business will let us know about something that is happening in his area which often produces a sound investment. One of my clients put me into something which had been a great success in the States which I'd never heard of called Xilinx. It's a computer company. He did so simply on the grounds that one of his ex-students had gone to work for him and was telling him what a good company it was. The other great source is that we do a lot of company visits, learning a lot more about their customers, competitors and suppliers than they do about us. When you've been doing it for 30 years, as I have, you don't actually know where the ideas come from anymore. I get fewer of my ideas than the others from brokers. I do get some from brokers. Inevitably, you only get to know about new issues from brokers, for example. I'll tell you about my reading habits. I abandoned all Sunday newspapers three years ago. Partly because they are merely vehicles for public relations companies, partly because newspaper managements realised they were missing a trick on Saturdays and have made their Saturday sections much better. The only things I really want to read about, I read in the *Spectator*.

JD *What do you look to learn from company visits?*

JC Between the five of us, we probably see upwards of 20 companies a week one way or another. For example, when I was in Argentina and Brazil and although I was primarily there about my own business, apart from having a holiday I still managed to fit in several company visits. The one thing brokers are told is that I have nothing to do with finance directors. That's for analysts to talk to. I'm not interested in their numbers. The broker's analysts can tell me. What I want to know is what the guys are like and their strategic thinking. I like a nice pleasant chat. When I was in Argentina, one company chairman wrote to me and said what a refreshing surprise it had been. When young Americans come in all they want to do is their number crunching, but I came in and talked to them about the history of the company and his brother who won a Nobel Prize and things like that. I also like to go on my own. I loathe collective meetings with other investors asking dumb questions. So I don't go any more to brokers' lunches. I go occasionally to a presentation and I might go to a factory if there is something specific I wanted to see. But if you go with other people, other people get the same answers to your questions.

JD *Is investment an art or a science?*

JC I say, "No, it's trial and error." Where most people go wrong is their failure to cut losses. Not understanding the way share prices work. It's basically the failure to realise that a loss is a loss whether you crystallise it or not. It's also about people, judgement of people, which apparently I've got. You've got to be risk-prone. You've got to understand risk. You've got to be your own man, really.

JD *What do you do with your own money?*

JC Some of it is in equities. Some of it, as I'm getting older, is in bonds. A lot of it is in Hoare Govett's floating rate note, for capital gains tax reasons. Otherwise, I buy race horses and I travel.

JD *Are you in favour of the current cult of performance measurement?*

JC I'm all for it. The problem is that the All-Share Index is no longer a good measure because of its weighting. In an ordinary portfolio, you can't attempt to replicate it, so you're always out of line – sometimes you're out of line for the good, and sometimes for the bad. I have to tell clients it's only a rough guide. I say when we underperform it, we're not doing as badly as you think, and when we overperform we're not doing as well as you think, so it's very artificial. We need an unweighted index for private investors. As a matter of principle we have always measured against the All-Share Index and we are very proud of our outperformance for the vast majority of clients. In the early days, there were a lot of performance fees around, which I am against, because it produces a conflict of interest, particularly between clients. We take a straight percentage fee on the size of the fund. That's enough incentive.

JD *Is investment harder now or easier?*

JC I think it's probably easier. It is easier, I think, because the world has changed. You now have a whole world that is basically committed to market economics. It's taken some variables out. I mean, who's afraid of a Labour government now? It seems the market isn't. I am. I think they are a bunch of shits. I also don't want to see hereditary peers abolished. That's my number one reason. The other thing I hate to see is the prospective abolition of hunting. Not because I hunt myself. Indeed many who hunt I loathe. But simply because I am a countryman and I resent having the urban majority dictate to the rural minority.

JD *What about insider information?*

JC Don't think I've ever had any in my life. In any case it's not our style, we're not buying for short term. My idea is to find investments. Oh, inside information is around and always will be. I'm not quite sure of the ethics, particularly for broker analysts. Some analysts have problems deciding what is inside information and what is not.

JD *Tell me finally about horse racing and what you have learnt from it?*

JC I got interested about the same age as I went into the stock market, about 11. I didn't understand either at the time but became much better informed. I've been owning horses since 1969. For fun, of course. You don't own horses to make money. I've got shares in ten horses in training, and sort of one and a half brood mares. The majority are trained by Peter Makin. He's a very good, underestimated trainer. Betting is another thing. I think I'm good at that. The satisfaction is seeing through the hype and proving one's judgement. It's all risk and reward, really.

CONCLUSION

Carrington is one of the few originals left in the fund management business. Behind the banter and the splendidly, politically incorrect views lies a shrewd investment brain. Note in particular his observations about the right and wrong way to run an equity investment portfolio:

- Avoid fashionable or heavily promoted shares. Don't buy a share just because a broker says something is about to happen.

- Don't be surprised to make a loss when you start out. Even the best investors cannot pick winners 100% of the time.

- A loss is a loss, whether or not you realise it. Cut your losses.

- Don't snatch your profits. Let them run.

- People matter. Stick to backing managements you can trust.

- Be honest about your blind spots.

8. JIM SLATER:

To ground zero and back

To meet Jim Slater now, exuding as he does the easy charm and confidence of the seriously affluent, it is not difficult to imagine that he was once the most talked about stock market operator of his day. More difficult to recall is that the same man was also the most famous single casualty of the great stock market crash of the 1970s. It is now nearly 40 years since Slater left the City, a self-confessed 'minus millionaire', his financial empire Slater Walker close to collapse and his onetime reputation as a 'Midas of the financial world' sorely tarnished. His fall seemed to many to mark the end of a particularly flamboyant chapter in the history of the financial markets.

The months that followed were difficult ones for Slater personally. He had two court cases to face: one minor, one potentially very difficult[1]. The Department of Trade and Industry produced a report that criticised some of the company's activities. The press pored over his business dealings, looking in retrospect to puncture the reputation for financial wizardry that previously they had done so much to promote. For someone who had only months before been lionised in the newspapers and courted by some

---

[1] One, brought by the DTI, resulted in Slater being fined £15 for 15 technical breaches of the Companies Act. The court accepted that the offences were purely technical, there was honesty of purpose and there was no question of personal gain. The second and more serious case was brought by the Singapore government, which wanted to extradite Slater to face charges of fraud and conspiracy in connection with a share incentive scheme at an obscure Far Eastern company called Spydar. Magistrates in London dismissed the charges saying there was no case to answer.

of the country's most illustrious banks, the sudden reversal of fortune must have been a shattering experience.

Yet Slater, a man who could charm the birds off the trees, is nothing if not resilient. At the age of 82, he has more than restored his financial fortunes and has long moved back into the investment world, although in a very different capacity from before. The devil-may-care financier of the 1960s re-emerged in the 1990s as a champion of the country's private investors, writing a series of well-received popular books on investment and devising a pioneering new statistical publication on all the London market's listed stocks which won many converts in the fund management community. More recently, in the less favourable market conditions of the new century, while continuing to back a small number of listed stocks, he has carved out yet another career as an active entrepreneur, helping to create a number of new businesses and funds.

Slater's legendary charm and determination remain undiminished, as does his enthusiasm for the markets. For a while, after the collapse of Slater Walker, Slater kept his head down, writing a series of children's books, learning to play bridge and setting about restoring his finances through property deals. But, as anyone who knows him will testify, the stock market remains one of his great passions in life. The favourable conditions of the 1980s and 1990s – a long bull market, with falling inflation and low interest rates – inevitably set the sap of such an inveterate enthusiast rising. His personal investments during this period put him comfortably back in the millionaire class. His books, media articles and public appearances meanwhile earned him a new generation of followers, and to this day, he remains a popular source of inspiration and advice for many private investors.

You do not need a degree in human psychology to suspect that Slater's efforts to stamp his name on a new method of picking stock market winners, as he attempted to do in the 1990s, stemmed in part at least from a desire to rehabilitate the public reputation he once enjoyed as the country's most famous stock market guru. Because of the history of Slater Walker, and the methods it adopted, he remained for many years a controversial figure whose name continued to attract strong reactions – both positive and negative – from those in the professional investment business. Such controversy has slowly waned with the passage of time. In 2002 he once again became a director of a small public listed company, something which for many years many would have regarded as unthinkable.

Even during his darkest days nobody ever doubted that Slater understands the ways of the market inside out. Investing on his own account, and for a number of family and friends, he made back in the 1990s' bull market a good deal more than he lost in the 1974-75 market collapse, when he was primarily a corporate dealmaker, not a professional investor, as he is now. Having once calculated that he was worth £8m at the peak of his fortunes in the early 1970s, Slater won't quantify his wealth today but his days of being a minus millionaire are a distant memory. My guess is that he is now worth about £30m.

HOBBY TIME, WITH NOUGHTS ATTACHED

For someone who endured such harrowing times in the 1970s, Slater has aged well. He lives contentedly with his wife Helen in Surrey, writing the occasional magazine article, keeping an eye on his portfolio of direct investments, dealing in a small number of shares for his own account, and pursuing his other interests, of which bridge and salmon fishing are high on the list.[2] Two days a week he is in London for business meetings. He is a tall man, with a ready smile, and a reputation for being both loyal and generous to his friends. Apart from his impish sense of humour, Slater's great personal attribute is the ability to concentrate intensely on what he is doing. He was an exponent of focus long before it became a fashionable management concept in the 1980s.[3] In business meetings, from personal experience, I can attest that his attention to detail can sometimes come across to those who don't know him as needlessly abrupt. He is not the world's greatest listener, and woe betide anyone who clicks a biro, or indulges in some other form of distraction, during a meeting.

---

[2] Slater claims to have popularised the business of timesharing for salmon fishing enthusiasts. He still retreats regularly with his son Mark to Tayside and Speyside to indulge in his hobby.

[3] I am referring to his personal approach to business. Slater Walker was a monument to the difficulties that a company can get into by trying to be and do too many things at the same time.

Slater named his first book about investment, *The Zulu Principle*, to reflect an attitude to life that he says has guided him for many years. Essentially, the Zulu Principle asserts that everyone can become an expert on something, and turn it to their advantage, by the simple device of choosing a relatively obscure subject and finding out more about it than anyone else. "It is," says Slater in his autobiography, "the same principle as using a laser beam rather than a scatter gun, and is analogous to Montgomery's excellent strategy of concentrating an attack." Do a few things well, in other words, not a lot of things badly. With this in mind, when he was still running Slater Walker, he set up a foundation to help develop outstanding talent in two activities close to his heart: tennis and chess. Nigel Short and Tim Henman were both early beneficiaries of his initiatives, and although neither quite made it to the very top of their chosen sports, both exceeded anything that other English pretenders to world crowns had achieved in their chosen fields for at least a generation. The Slater Foundation continues to support talented youngsters and individuals who, for whatever reason, are facing exceptional suffering.

The paradox is that it was only at an age when most men have retired to tend their gardens that Slater himself found the time and financial freedom to devote himself full time to codifying his lifetime's experience of following the stock markets. A typical day for Slater now starts at 7.00 a.m., when the Australian markets, in which he owns some shares, open. Once the London markets opens at 8.00 a.m. he will put in a call to one of the two stockbrokers that he uses regularly. He works from home, in a book-lined study in his house in Cranleigh. After years of surviving without a computer, he now uses an online service, Digital Look, to stay in touch with the share prices of companies he owns. He mainly relies on his brokers to keep him informed about the things he needs to know. He prefers to deal with the smaller broking firms: "I find you get more attention being a big fish in a small pool." One of his brokers, Giles Hargreave, is a fellow member of his bridge club, the Portland in Mayfair.

His brokers know which companies he is interested in, and ring or fax him whenever there is any news to impart. (There is an unconfirmed rumour that, prompted by the success of his website, he may now even have an email account.) "I ring my broker in the morning to get the prices, and then I get them again from another broker maybe a quarter of an hour later. It's not that I distrust any of them, but they ring me, so I always check the prices again and they've usually moved a bit. Anything which happens during the day concerning any share I am interested in, I know I am going to get covered very strongly and very quickly." Overall, when he is at home, he reckons that he is on the phone to each of his brokers up to eight times a day. "Quite often when I am dealing in something, the calls may be all about one transaction, just to be updated on prices." When he is away fishing or abroad, he still rings up twice a day to stay in touch.

Each day, Slater also gets a daily summary and valuation of his various broker accounts. Once a week he sits down and does a detailed review of his investments, including his pension fund, which he has always managed himself. He says that he deals "nearly every day", but not in great quantities. There are also new issues to look at. For many years, he also ran, unpaid, portfolios for his family and his secretary, among others. He reads a number of newsletters, and devours most new books on investment that come out. Although he actively monitors his share holdings, he says that he is no longer involved in as many shares as he was. He currently follows fewer than 20 shares in any detail, and most of those will be companies that he knows intimately. Given the many headwinds that have prevailed in the stock market since the bursting of the Internet bubble in 2000, he trades much less actively than he did. Apart from a small handful of favourite UK stocks, in three of which his holdings are sufficiently large to require market disclosure, if he wants to invest in UK smaller company shares these days he is mostly happy to do so through the Slater Growth Fund, a unit trust run by his son Mark on principles his father helped to shape.

REALLY ESSENTIAL STUFF

In addition to his own dealing activity, Slater is particularly proud of having devised *REFS*, or Really Essential Financial Statistics, to give it its full name. This is a monthly statistical service which Slater created and originally developed in conjunction with Hemmington Scott, a firm of financial publishers. When it first appeared, *REFS* was an innovative and comprehensive addition to the ranks of information sources available to active investors. Nearly twenty years on from its first publication, and despite multiple new sources of competition from Bloomberg and others, *REFS* continues to provide Slater with a steady stream of royalty income, a testament to the quality of his original creation. Its aim is simple: to bring together on one page, for every company quoted on the London Stock Exchange, all the key numbers and ratios that a serious private or professional investor needs in order to form a judgement about the attractions of a share. In this respect, it is quite like Value Line, a well-established subscription service for investors in the United States, on which it is to some extent modelled.

In addition to providing core background information on companies, Hemmington Scott also analyses the *REFS* database to provide a monthly list of tables which rank all the UK quoted shares in a series of different valuation criteria. These include market capitalisation, relative strength, return on capital, dividend yield, earnings growth, price to book value ratios and gearing (the ratio of debt to a company's shareholders' funds). For each of the main market indices, the reader can quickly see for themselves which shares have done best for each of these various measures. In effect, what *REFS* does is provide a regular screening service of the kind that many professional fund managers carry out for themselves, and make it readily available to a wider audience. The service is too expensive to become a mass market product, but some private investors swear by it, and it can still be found in professional fund management houses, notwithstanding the ready availability of more formidable real time electronic information sources such as Bloomberg. Professional investors like the handy and accessible format in which the information in *REFS* is presented. These days there is an online service too, updated day by day.

Although Slater uses *REFS* to help provide the data for his own stockpicking methods, the service itself has a much wider application, as a single sourcebook in which an investor can find, in one place, so many relevant details such as brokers' earnings forecasts and details of company directors' dealings. Many other commercial services provide this kind of information, and *REFS* itself can be accessed via the Internet, but many subscribers still prefer to receive the latest information on a monthly basis in two chunky sets of covers.[4] Devising and refining the formulas to create a usable and commercial publication took many months of Slater's time, as well as a considerable investment by the publishers.[5] It remains an impressive publication.

Slater seems more than content with his life now. "My health is not bad for an old guy, and I still have plenty of energy. I love the market, just as I like playing bridge. The stock market is a big game, and fortunately I play it well, much better than I play bridge. There is always something going on. Last week for example," he told me in December 2011, "Spanish Mountain Gold, my largest personal holding, announced new and much larger resources and Agrifirma, the Brazilian farmland business I helped to found, recently announced a wonderful deal with a leading private equity group in Brazil. Shortly afterwards Jim Rogers, another smart investor I much admire, joined the board of Agrifirma's former parent company, Genagro."

"So my business life is ongoing. My business partner Ian Watson and I get on very well together. Our skills are complementary and it is very much a case of one and one making three. In both of our main businesses, Spanish Mountain Gold and Genagro, we have very happy teams who are both effective and fun to work with. Many of my friends have retired, and some only work one day a week. They think I am mad to go on as I do, and I think they are mad not to. I don't know who is happier. I guess we are who we are; I just love the day-to-day involvement."

"Now that I have reached my 80s, I plan on spending more of my time developing the Slater Foundation. Its aims are twofold: to alleviate suffering and to encourage excellence. We try to make very specific person to person donations. My daughter Clare and my daughter-in-law Diane are helping me to find the right candidates. I call them my angels. I hope that together we will be able to make some gifts that are really worthwhile."[6]

---

[4] A third, optional volume covers stocks listed on the AIM market in London.

[5] Slater says one of the main benefits of devising the data requirements was that he was forced to sit down and clarify some of the fuzzy areas in his thinking about investment, such as what is really meant by return on capital employed.

[6] More details can be found at **www.jimslater.org.uk**.

HOW IT ALL BEGAN

Slater first became seriously interested in the stock market when he was an executive at Leyland in the early 1960s. It was while there, he recounts in his memoirs, that he decided to try to apply the Zulu Principle to the business of share selection. While recovering from illness in Bournemouth, he bought back issues for two years of the *Stock Exchange Gazette* and the *Investors Chronicle*, and ploughed his way through them all, looking for the common threads that explained which shares had been most successful. He had already decided that small- to medium-sized companies with rising earnings were the place where he should look for an edge.

Within a relatively short period of time, he decided that he had a system which worked, at least when tested against historical experience. He persuaded his bank manager to lend him £8000 and invested it, along with £2000 of his savings, in the shares of a company, Bernard Wardle, which happened to supply parts to AEC, the Leyland subsidiary where he worked. Shortly afterwards, he formed an investment club for executives within Leyland, and later wrote to Nigel Lawson, then City editor of the *Sunday Telegraph*, proposing to write a monthly share-tipping column that expounded his new system of share selection. It was the profits he made from Wardle and other investments that eventually provided him with the capital to start Slater Walker.

In his first column, which went under the *nom de plume* of Capitalist, Slater set out his methods, which he said were based on looking for shares that combined an above-average earnings yield (what we would now call a low price/earnings ratio) with "above-average growth prospects". He set out what he then regarded as nine important investment criteria:

1. The dividend yield must be at least 4%.
2. Equity earnings must have increased in at least four out of the last five years.
3. Equity earnings must have at least doubled over the past four years.
4. The latest chairman's statement must be optimistic.
5. The company must be in a reasonable liquid position.
6. The company must not be vulnerable to exceptional factors.

7.   The shares must have a reasonable asset value.
8.   The company should not be family controlled.
9.   The shares should have votes.

With its list of rules, and the high degree of confidence with which they were pronounced, this was a typical Slater effort. In the two years that the column ran, the results were more than satisfactory: a return of 68.9%, Slater calculates, during a period when the market rose by just 3.6%. How far he actually followed these methods while he was writing the Capitalist column, and why they worked, is one of the things that the financial journalist Charles Raw set out to question in his highly critical account of the early years of Slater Walker.[7] One of Raw's allegations was that Slater used the publicity that his column afforded to support his own share dealing activities. There would have been nothing illegal about this, even if true, but it put, in Raw's view at least, a question mark over the real extent of Slater's investment expertise.

Slater has always denied the thrust of Raw's allegations, but in his autobiography conceded that in hindsight his position was open to abuse. 'The standards observed by people giving investment advice to others, and by journalists writing about shares, have changed in recent years,' he wrote. 'This is a necessary and highly desirable process. Looking back on it, it is obvious that there could be conflict of interest if anyone advises others on shares and buys some of them himself. Similarly it is clear that there could be a conflict of interest if someone buys shares and recommends them in a newspaper. But at that time Stock Exchange investment was relatively new to me, and I had evolved what I thought was a particularly attractive and unique system, which I intended to share with my friends and others who were interested. Looking at it with hindsight, and with consciousness of today's different standards, I can see how it could be open to a different interpretation.'

When Slater first fell from glory, there were many in the City who, from envy or conviction, were not inclined to give him the benefit of the doubt. Although what Slater the professional investor does now is very different from what Slater Walker the business was doing all those years ago, one thing

---

[7] *Slater Walker: An investigation of a financial phenomenon* (Andre Deutsch, 1977).

which has not changed is that he still loves to talk about the shares he has bought and sold. He knows the value of having his favourite shares talked about in the press and in the markets and is assiduous at protecting his public image. Because of the evident potential for conflicts of interest, however, in anything he writes for publication now he is careful to say openly when he owns the shares that he has tipped. He avoids dealing personally in the shares for a few days before and after the appearance of his articles.

THE SLATER WALKER STORY

It is with his investment philosophy now, as he has refined it over the past few years, that this chapter is mainly concerned. This is not the place for another history of Slater Walker, fascinating though that period was. But the outline of the story can be quickly told. Slater was an ambitious young accountant who by his late 20s had become a rising executive at AEC, the commercial vehicle subsidiary of Leyland; as an amateur investor he started writing a share-tipping column for the *Sunday Telegraph* under the pseudonym Capitalist; and finally the impatient entrepreneur threw in his job to start his own investment advisory business, which soon became the financial conglomerate Slater Walker. Although it started in a small way, Slater Walker rapidly became a financial and industrial holding company which, it seemed, was ready to try its hand at anything and everything.

In the space of just a few years, with the help of a rising share price and the support of an extraordinarily enthusiastic fan club in the financial press, it made a series of acquisitions, launched a number of new unit and investment trusts, obtained a banking licence and came close to pulling off three ambitious mergers – first with Pearsons, then with Warburgs and finally with Hill Samuel. It also moved into mining, finance and property. For a while it was deal-a-minute stuff. "There was no formula," Slater said later. "It was simply a question of keeping a completely open and receptive mind, and being alert to all possibilities."

In many ways, we can see now that Slater was merely doing in England what the great conglomerate kings of the day were doing in the United

States at the same time: exploiting febrile stock market conditions to build a multi-faceted corporate empire through a series of market-financed acquisitions. What is difficult to understand now, for anyone who did not live through the heady bull markets of 1968-72 and 1971-72, is the huge impact that the activities of Slater Walker had at the time on the City and the prevailing economic climate. Slater's impact was quite out of proportion to the size of his business. (Note the number of times that Slater's name was brought up voluntarily, in one context or another, by other subjects of this book!)

While the company presented itself as a sharp and predatory animal which had ambitions to shake up the management of some of Britain's sleepy large companies, and liked to cock a snook at the Establishment in the City, in reality Slater Walker was more of a vehicle for a group of clever and ambitious young financiers to engage in a decade of opportunistic deal-making.[8] This was an activity for which Slater, with his quick mind, his nose for figures and talent for self-promotion, turned out to be ideally qualified. For a while, he could do no wrong, becoming, even by his own account, a dangerous believer in his own publicity. The newspapers drowned him in adulation, lovingly recounting his every word on what was happening in the markets.

When, in January 1973, Sir Patrick Sergeant, the City Editor of the *Daily Mail*, a longstanding confidant, reported Slater's view that the market was set to fall by 10%, the news duly sent share prices tumbling. However, it was not long before Slater Walker started to overstretch itself financially. It also rapidly outgrew the ability of Slater and his associates to control it. In its hurry to make waves, it also happily took advantage of the rather relaxed laws which then governed City behaviour.[9] When Slater Walker

---

[8] Although some think it has pejorative overtones, the term 'wheeler dealing' does not seem inappropriate as a description of what Slater Walker was doing, conveying as it does an impression of constant activity.

[9] Slater's verdict: "Many of our ideas were highly innovative. In the takeover field we introduced a number of new techniques, which in some instances helped to shape the present Takeover Code. When we were on the other side, competitive merchant bankers knew that we were around. On the other hand, we tried to be rather too clever in some instances by adopting the minimum disclosure required by the law rather than a higher level to make the nature of our activities completely clear."

crashed, it crashed in style, providing moralists with plenty of ammunition to deplore the iniquities of the City.

Slater himself was wiped out, largely by virtue of the fact that he had borrowed heavily to buy agricultural land and paintings at the height of Slater Walker's success. In this, he was nothing if not consistent. Throughout his early career, he had financed most of his stock market investments with borrowed money, a course of action that testified to his capacity for taking risks and his huge faith in his own abilities. In 1972, he had decided that the stock market was heading for trouble and began to liquidate most of Slater Walker's holdings in favour of cash and property. Farmland was one favoured asset. Asked by an eager associate how much land he should be buying, Slater characteristically replied: "Don't stop till you reach the English Channel!"

In 1973, he started to liquidate his property holdings too, but in the fevered circumstances of the time found himself unable to get out in time to save his overgeared financial empire. In 1975, after a number of private discussions with the Bank of England, which was struggling at the time to contain the secondary banking crisis, he resigned from Slater Walker, announcing to the press that his liabilities exceeded his assets by £900,000 (the equivalent of nearly £4 million today). Slater Walker was soon broken up and its various component parts either dissolved or absorbed by other companies.[10]

Whether or not Slater Walker could have survived, had the 1974-75 stock market and property crashes been less savage in their intensity, is not easy to say. Slater's own conclusion, in his autobiography *Return To Go*, was that Slater Walker was very much a phenomenon of its time. It rose to giddy heights on the back of the 1968 and 1972 bull markets only to be levelled to the ground by the property and stock market crashes of the mid-1970s. He concedes that the company lost "its social justification" when it started having to liquidate its investments to survive. He also failed to recruit enough good managers "of the right moral fibre and ability" to run the business. It is hard to disagree with anything in his verdict. If Slater

---

[10] With the consent of the Bank of England, management control of Slater Walker was handed over from Jim Slater to his friend Jimmy Goldsmith. The most durable side of the business has proven to be the unit trust business, which lives on today under new ownership as Britannia Investment Management.

had stuck to his last, which was backing his judgements about the markets, picked some better associates and set his corporate sights rather lower, the story might well have had a different ending.[11]

The one thing that Slater has never lost is a reputation for being an acute reader of trends in the financial markets. The *Investors Chronicle* once observed that 'for ten years he was the shrewdest judge of financial markets in the Square Mile'. His own conclusion was that although he was "too inclined to take a short-term view of everything" at that stage, he did have "hair-trigger reactions in market terms and tended to act almost instantly". The great irony of Slater's ten-year City career is that he was one of the first to foresee the coming stock market crash, but proved unable to escape from its effects, having fatally overgeared both the company and his own financial affairs. When the crunch came, and liquidity dried up, he was unable to realise value for his assets. As can be imagined, the experience has coloured his subsequent approach to investing in the stock market.

HUNTING FOR CHEAP GROWTH STOCKS

There is still a broad similarity between the basic stock selection method that Slater proposed in his early columns as Capitalist and the much more sophisticated methodology that he had developed subsequently. This methodology is built around what he now calls "the PEG factor". This is the ratio between the expected growth rate of a share and its price/earnings ratio, a ratio which many investors have looked at over the years, but which Slater has adopted and developed in his own distinctive way. The easiest way to illustrate this is with a simple example. If a company has earnings that are expected to grow at 15% this year, and its shares are selling at 15 times its expected earnings, then it has a PEG factor of 1.0 (15 divided by 15 is one). If the same company was selling at 10 times its earnings, its PEG factor would be 0.67 (10 divided by 15); and if selling at 20 times its earnings, it would be 1.33 (20 divided by 15).

---

[11] Slater came close on two occasions on pulling off a merger between his business and much larger companies, including Hill Samuel. Had they succeeded, his subsequent career would have been very different.

What Slater is looking for are companies with low PEG factors – the lower the PEG, the better. What constitutes an attractive figure depends on the market environment, and in particular on the prevailing level of interest rates. In 1998, when this book first appeared, his basic rule was not to buy a share with a PEG above 0.75; ideally, he said he preferred it to be below 0.66. In 2011, with interest rates having fallen to historically low levels, his view now is that a PEG of 1.0 would be acceptable for the right company. Even so, with so many headwinds facing the equity market, he has still not been finding much in recent years that is "glaringly attractive" in the quoted company universe. The essence of his approach, however, remains unchanged: to look for companies which are growing fast, but whose growth potential is not yet valued fully by the market. A different way of expressing this is to say that he is looking for cheap growth shares, ones with earnings that are growing faster than their price/earnings ratios.

It is still at heart the same approach – "above-average growth" and "above average earnings yields" – that he developed in the early 1960s. "To me," says Slater, "a low p/e ratio and a high growth rate has always been the right combination, no doubt about it. That, of course, is what a low PEG is." Note that he does not say, like conventional value investors, that a low p/e ratio is in itself an attractive quality for a share. Nor does he say that growth shares per se are attractive. Such shares may or may not be bargains. The distinctive feature of his method is that what matters most about a share is the relationship between the p/e ratio and the future growth rate of the company.

As he has developed the ideas for his books and other publications in recent years, Slater has refined his stockpicking system further. In his first book about investment, *The Zulu Principle*, first published in 1992, he again came up with a list of features, this time 11 in number, which he urged investors to look for in a share. These he said reflected the 27 years' experience of investing he had accumulated since setting out his first list. They remain the core elements of his investment approach – a considered verdict, if you like, to contrast with the untried hypothesis he was essentially working with in his Capitalist days.

The key elements in the list, of which he declared the first four to be "by far the most important", are:

STEADY GROWTH IN EARNINGS PER SHARE OVER AT LEAST FOUR OF THE PAST FIVE YEARS

Slater mentions 15% as the minimum growth rate needed. A shorter record can be acceptable in exceptional circumstances: for example, where there has been a sharp acceleration in earnings growth due to some new factor.

A MODEST P/E RATIO IN RELATION TO THE EARNINGS GROWTH

This is where the PEG factor comes in: the lower, the better. Slater adds the further suggestion that the p/e ratio should stack up favourably against the average p/e for the market and the company's industry. Note that he does not use historic p/e ratios, based on reported earnings, but prefers the prospective figure, based on brokers' estimates of what a company's earnings per share are likely to be (for the 12 months ahead).

A POSITIVE CHAIRMAN'S STATEMENT

If the chairman is pessimistic, Slater points out, then the obvious implication is that the "earnings growth could be at an end".

STRONG LIQUIDITY, LOW BORROWINGS AND HIGH CASH FLOW

Investors should look for self-financing companies that generate cash, and avoid highly capital-intensive businesses which "simply eat cash while others spit it out". Slater suggests that borrowings should not exceed 50% of net assets.

A BUSINESS WHICH HAS CLEARLY DISCERNIBLE COMPETITIVE ADVANTAGE, SUCH AS STRONG BRAND NAMES OR DOMINANCE IN A PARTICULAR MARKET

The point about such companies, says Slater, is that they are far more likely to be able to sustain their record of earnings increases into the future. The capacity to employ capital at a high rate of return – which he defines as over 20% – is "one of the surest marks of a true growth stock".

SOMETHING NEW, TO GIVE YOUR SHARES 'A STORY'

This may be a new factor affecting a particular industry, a new product or simply the arrival of a new chief executive with a good track record. But something, observes Slater, has to "form the basis of the story upon which the shares will be bought". Of the various options, new management is the best because the effects can be "so far-reaching and are ongoing".

A SMALL MARKET CAPITALISATION

As "elephants don't gallop", says Slater, investors looking for growth shares should aim for companies outside the main market indices. At the time, he recommended an upper limit of £100 million.

HIGH RELATIVE STRENGTH

This means shares which have recently performed well relative to the stock market as a whole. If the shares are not keeping pace with the market, you should be "on red alert", says Slater. As a rule of thumb, rule out companies whose shares are trading more than 15% below their maximum prices in the past two years.

A SIGNIFICANT MANAGEMENT SHAREHOLDING

Look for companies, says Slater, in which the management has a significant holding of shares "relative to their personal finances". The ideal is a holding of around 20%, large enough to make the managers highly motivated, but not so high as to enable them to block a bid.

Out of his original list of rules, Slater has since deleted any reference to specific dividend yields. He has also relaxed the £100 million threshold for market capitalisation. All that matters for his methods, he says now, is that the dividend is growing broadly in line with a company's earnings. He downplays published asset values and the traditional value investor's criteria, such as price to book values. 'Although you should welcome the comfort of a strong asset position,' he says in *The Zulu Principle*, 'remember that book values are often unreliable. A property value could easily be overstated, whereas an excellent brand name may be in the books for next to nothing.'

BEYOND THE ZULU PRINCIPLE

In a later book, *Beyond the Zulu Principle*, Slater added yet more refinements to his stock-picking model. Most of the book is devoted to explaining how investors can relate his ideas to the information that they can find in *REFS*, his monthly statistical publication. But he also adds some extra rules and observations based on his experience in actually trying to apply his share selection criteria in a systematic way to his own investments. This has led him to modify some of his earlier comments.

Among the more interesting of his observations are these:

- Most of the growth companies which meet his criteria are to be found in just a few sectors, of which services, drugs and healthcare, media, electronic and electrical equipment, pubs and restaurants, and retailers are the main ones.

- Almost all companies, he says, are "cyclical to some extent", but "companies in highly cyclical industries rarely become great growth stocks". This is another way of saying that he sees little value in steel, chemicals and other companies of that sort.

- Companies which have the ability to "clone" an activity such as a shop, restaurant or indoor tennis facility and open more of them across the country can produce "exceptional" earnings per share growth. In other words, a successful formula that can be repeated without much additional effort is a fairly reliable path to rapid share price appreciation.

- Stocks that meet the basic Slater criteria for a growth stock are in a minority. In early 1996, for example, only 50 of the top 100 shares, 90 of the next 250 largest companies, and 160 of the 377 remaining smaller companies in the FT All-Share Index qualified as growth stocks according to his methods. Among the minnows outside the FT All-Share Index, only 60 out of 700 companies made the grade.

- Applying the PEG criterion in a rigorous fashion further reduces the number of qualifying stocks. In early 1996, the average PEG in the UK market was about 1.5. Slater says that low PEGs work best where p/e factors are in the range of 12 to 20 and earnings per share are growing from 15 to 30% a year. He says investors should steer clear of companies whose prospective p/e ratios are above 20. The reason is that growth rates above 30% are unsustainable and p/e ratios of more than 20 are too demanding.

- Return on capital and profit margins are key characteristics of the "great growth stocks". Very low margins add to the risk of an investment, while very high ones attract competition. The trend of a company's margins is crucial, since falling margins can be "the first and only warning signal that a company is losing its competitive advantage".

The biggest change in *Beyond the Zulu Principle*, and one which he expanded on in an article in *Professional Investor* magazine, is the much increased emphasis on a share's relative strength. In his first book, Slater says that "poor relative strength" should not put an investor off. Yet now he says that positive relative strength over both the previous three- and twelve-month periods has become one of his "mandatory requirements" for picking a share.

In coming to this conclusion, Slater has been influenced not just by his experiments with the *REFS* database, but also by the findings of Jim O'Shaughnessy, a successful American investor who has conducted some exhaustive research into what have been the most successful share selection criteria in the US market over the past 40 years. His research, published as a book, showed conclusively that positive relative strength was a feature of nearly all the most successful investment strategies which O'Shaughnessy tested.[12] This has confirmed Slater's view that, in a bull market at least, investors cannot afford to ignore it. More recently he has been impressed by the findings of another American researcher, Richard Tortoriello, an analyst at Standard & Poor's, who also found that relative strength over shorter periods was an important predictor of future returns.[13]

---

[12] The findings are summarised in O'Shaughnessy's book, *What Works on Wall Street* (McGraw-Hill, 1966). This contains page after page of detailed numerical analysis of the effects that applying different investor criteria, such as high and low p/e ratios, would have had on a portfolio of US shares. The research is based on the computerised database of historical share prices kept by Standard & Poor's over a 43 year period.

[13] The details are in his book *Quant Strategies for Achieving Alpha* (McGraw-Hill, 2008).

Apart from relative strength, the other requirements on which Slater says he now insists are:

- a low PEG factor
- no selling of shares by directors
- cash flow greater than earnings
- an identifiable competitive advantage
- gearing of under 75% (unless cash flow is particularly strong).

Other factors which are desirable but not mandatory are:

- an accelerating trend in earnings per share
- a cluster of directors buying their company's shares
- dividend payments
- a low price to sales ratio is a good "value filter"
- a new story.

WHY IT WORKS

What is the rationale for PEG factors – and why should they work? The answer lies in one of the oldest and best known tenets of investment. The way you make money from growth stocks is by buying them when they still have several years of growth ahead of them – but before the market has fully appreciated the sustainability of that growth potential. What investors are looking for is the "double whammy" effect which comes from (1) the market recognising that a company is set for a period of future growth in earnings; and (2) the market also deciding to acknowledge the value of that growth in the way the shares are valued.

In Slater's words: "There are only two basic reasons for a growth share appreciating in price. The first is earnings growth and the second is the increase in multiple that the stock market awards to the company." Of these, it is the "status change" in the multiple – the moment when a share ceases to be priced at, say, 15 times earnings and moves to 25 times earnings – that often accounts for the greater part of the investor's return.

The PEG factor is at bottom a statistical device for trying to identify the conditions in which a re-rating of this sort is likely to happen. In Slater's words, it identifies shares which are "pregnant with possibility".

What distinguishes Slater's approach from others who look at earnings forecasts and multiples in a less methodical way is that at any moment he can compare the latest consensus earnings forecasts across the entire universe of stocks. By looking at rolling 12-month forecasts each month, he is effectively comparing "chalk and chalk, not chalk and cheese". What he means is that, since companies report their results at different times of the year, those who rely on historic p/e ratios are often looking at data which is some months out of date. Those who look at prospective p/e ratios are similarly looking at a forecast which may cover anything from one to 12 months ahead.

There are two technical drawbacks which make PEG ratios not so simple to calculate. One is that they are based on forecast earnings per share; that means to use a PEG ratio you have first to obtain brokers' estimates of forecast earnings which is not always easy (unless you are a subscriber to a service such as *REFS* or *The Estimate Directory*). Second, there is the risk of error. Not only are earnings, as Slater himself admits, relatively easy to manipulate if companies want to disguise their performance, but the estimates are only as good as the brokers are able to make them. A number of recent studies have highlighted how unreliable and inaccurate broker estimates of future earnings can be.

By concentrating on consensus forecasts, and looking at rolling 12-month forecasts rather than simply calendar year forecasts, Slater aims to eliminate some of the risk of mis-forecasting but he does not deny that the risk remains. One way he seeks to reduce it in his own investing is to add some subjective weighting of his own to the question of which brokers are more likely to be well informed about a company's prospects. That is something which can only come from experience.

REALITY TEST

As with all investment methods, the only sure way of testing them is to try them out in the real world. Slater can point to sound evidence that his PEG methodology is capable of producing good results. Analysis carried out by Hemmington Scott on its *REFS* database showed that stocks selected by applying a series of filters derived from Slater's methods have subsequently performed consistently better than the market as a whole. *Tiptracker*, an independent (but now defunct) publication which monitored the performances of all the UK's leading share tipsters at the time, arrived at the same conclusion. If someone had selected a portfolio based on a purely mechanical application of the main Slater criteria at the start of January 1996, it would have produced an overall gain 15 months later of 25%, with three gains of 100% plus (British Borneo Petroleum, Parity and Blacks Leisure), although there were also 11 shares that recorded a loss if sold on a similarly mechanistic basis. No other tipster, the newsletter concluded, had achieved such a good record over the same period.

Slater has published three selections of share tips in his books and newspaper columns. One, which he featured in his book *Beyond the Zulu Principle* in November 1995, consisted of four companies: Parity, British Borneo, Business Post and Rutland Trust. By June 1997, the four shares had risen by an average of 180%. The second, a New Year's list in the *Financial Mail on Sunday* featured eight companies. By June 1997, the six remaining shares (one was taken over and one was later recommended as a sell) had risen by an average of over 100%. In January 1997, he repeated the exercise, picking six shares in all, including two of the shares he had selected the previous year. Six months later, the shares had risen in value by 14%.

Finally, there is the experience of his son, Mark, who runs the Slater Growth fund, in which stocks are primarily selected on Slater's "growth with value filters" formula. The fund had an excellent start. A return of 60% in its first year was certainly eye-catching, making it the best performing equity fund in its first 12 months. Results since then have been more mixed. Having tracked the market for a number of years, its performance picked up dramatically in the autumn of 2009, when Mark Slater refined his methodology once again, to incorporate a stricter stock selection discipline, more closely attuned to his father's stockpicking criteria. He also took on board some of the findings of Richard Tortoriello in the book on quant strategies mentioned earlier. As of 15 November 2011 the fund was ranked 1st out of 277 UK equity funds for its performance over three years, according to the fund analysts at Trustnet. Detailed analysis by the multi-manager team at Hargreaves Lansdown confirmed that the fund's recent record reflects genuine stockpicking ability rather than simply style effects (meaning the happy accident of a fund being in the right sectors at the right time).

There is no doubt however that the Slater method, for all his concern with margins of safety, involves a degree of risk, as conventionally measured, which is higher than many investors may want to tolerate. The kind of companies that the PEG method throws up tend to be small, fast-growing companies, which are precisely the kind of share which is likely to be adversely affected by a deep recession or market setback. Their share prices often have large spreads and poor liquidity which means that if they started to fall, they can fall faster than the market and prove difficult to sell. Experience has shown that the method works better at some times than others. For most of 1996, for example, Slater's filtering system struggled to come up with many qualifying companies from the main FTSE 100 index. He has had the same experience in 2011. Some of the biggest winners Slater has had have been "concept" stocks, such as themed sportswear shops and restaurants, which can fall out of favour with the fickle consumer public just as quickly as they have caught on. They can be vulnerable to an inverse "double whammy" effect if trouble hits, with falling earnings coupled with a status change in reverse.

As with any investment, however, it is easy to become transfixed by the risks. There is nothing wrong with taking above-average risk if you know what you are doing and you anticipate an above-average reward. The point here is that Slater has never pretended to be interested in finding shares for long-term investors. His interest is in finding shares that are going to move sharply in the short to medium term. He is after rapid capital growth, on the basis that you only need a few really big gains to compensate for indifferent performance elsewhere. If the risks are high, so are the potential rewards. Provided you follow the discipline of cutting your losses and running your profits on the big winners, as the most successful card players and punters do, you can expect to come out as a substantial winner overall.[14] This is a point that is much easier to explain to those who have experience of playing cards or betting seriously in any form, but which tends to pass by those who have not.

What his filtering methods aim to do is weed out many of the bogus stocks whose growth turns out to be based on creative accounting rather than substantive business growth. There is less evidence to conclude how good it is at identifying when to sell shares. The early successes were publicly tested in a particularly buoyant stock market. There have also been the inevitable duds, such as Grosvenor Inns (he cut the loss at only 4%). What Slater can claim to have demonstrated successfully is that the method does identify correctly some of the best performing shares in the market while they are still in the process of being re-rated, which is exactly what the method sets out to do.

FINDING A DISCIPLINE THAT SUITS

It is perhaps worth making the point that Slater has never said that his methods are the only way to make money from the stock market. On the contrary, he explicitly concedes that there are several ways of trying to make money from stocks and shares, and indeed attempts to give some general advice on each of them.[15] He distinguishes several approaches: picking dynamic growth shares, investing in cyclical shares, looking for asset situations and following charts (also known as technical analysis). He himself has experimented with lots of different approaches in his time, and allows himself more latitude in choosing shares than he advises

---

[14] Slater refers to S.J. Simon's classic book, *Why You Lose At Bridge*, in which Simon advises players who want to make money at rubber bridge to walk away when they are having a bad run at cards, but stay late when they are on a hot streak. This is despite the knowledge that in theory the cards have no memory.

[15] Nor does he confine himself to the stock market. *Investment Made Easy*, another of his books, is a wonderfully clear introduction to such things as life insurance, pensions and unit trusts.

readers of his books. For a while, he was very interested in high yielding shares and the simple, but far from infallible, system developed by Michael O'Higgins in the United States for exploiting their apparent underpricing.[16] More recently he has set out detailed criteria he looks for when identifying value stocks and gold shares, in which he has become a significant investor in recent years. These lists all start with a number of clear statistical filters.

The important thing, he emphasises, is "to find a discipline that suits you and stick to it. Modify, temper and refine it as you learn by experience, but you must have a method." His own preference has always been for growth stocks. It is the discipline that best suits his optimistic temperament and is also the approach where he believes his screening methods give him an advantage over the rest of the market. The trouble with investing in cyclical shares, he says, is that you have to get your timing exactly right to be able to make a lot of money consistently. If you are looking for asset situations, on the other hand, the problem can be that you have to wait an awfully long time before the value is recognised in the share price. With growth shares, the payoffs can come much more quickly, especially if you can catch the status change.

As should be clear by now, Slater is someone who places huge store on analysis and logic. Intuitively, he wants to believe that there are discoverable rules which hold the key to successful investment performance. His is fundamentally the attitude of the successful backgammon or bridge player: whoever can calculate the odds better must come out on top. When he was a boy, Slater wanted nothing more than to become a professional chess player. He is also the man who, when challenged to play Monopoly for a publicity stunt, sat down to work out exactly how to play the game, based on a detailed analysis of which

---

[16] O'Higgins produced impressive historical evidence to show that anyone who systematically picked the six highest yielding shares in the Dow Jones Index at the start of each year could expect to outperform the market in the succeeding 12 months. Like most rule-based systems of this kind, no sooner had the apparent anomaly been discovered than it ceased to work reliably. In the UK, the highest yielding shares in the Footsie index underperformed for two years in a row, thanks largely to the disappointing performance of two specific stocks, Hanson Trust and British Gas.

properties on the Monopoly board offered the highest potential returns on investment.[17] Anyone who follows his methods must be prepared to do a lot of homework and be comfortable with figures.

A second point Slater says he is personally adamant about now is building in "a margin of safety" in his investment strategy, just as Ben Graham, the father of modern security analysis, insisted any intelligent investor should do. It was precisely his indifference to the downside risks of market speculation that proved so costly to Slater in his early career, so this newfound emphasis on risk aversion is hardly a surprise. Growth stocks are inherently risky, and the important thing for an unseasoned investor is to add some protection against picking the wrong ones.

The safety net in his methods comes principally from four sources:

1. His insistence on companies having a consistent record of growth, not just one or two years of exceptional growth. This tends to eliminate the "shooting stars" – companies that roar ahead for a brief while, only to disappear almost as quickly as they appeared on the scene.

2. The requirement that growth stocks should not be priced too highly by the market (the low PEG factor).

3. The emphasis on a record of strong cash flow. "What all the good growth companies tend to have as a common feature," says Slater, "is very strong cash balances. Cash flow is what they are all about."

4. Good relative strength. Of all Slater's criteria, this is one that many investors find the hardest to grasp, since it is to some extent counter-intuitive. How can a share which has performed well relative to the market in the past still be a better bet than one which has done less well? Yet in a bull market, at least, says Slater, relative strength is one

---

[17] The calculations are described briefly in *The Zulu Principle* and at greater length in *Return To Go*, which is itself of course a reference to the Monopoly board. The conclusion is that the properties on light blue sites (e.g. The Angel, Islington; Euston Road; and Pentonville Road) offer the best potential returns, followed closely by the orange sites. However, the orange sites are the best buy overall because there is a greater chance of landing on them.

of the most powerful screening factors there is – so much so that while he may relax some of his other criteria in exceptional circumstances, he now says he never relaxes his rule that shares must have outperformed the market over the previous year (and preferably over the previous three months as well).

"You don't want to be buying a share, especially a growth share, unless it is moving up," that is the kernel of his advice. In his view, it is powerful supporting evidence that a status change may be about to happen. Unlike the out and out contrarian instincts of other investors, he believes that there can also be safety in numbers, or the company you keep as an investor. Contrary thinking only works, he said once, when the timing is absolutely right: you have to be prepared for a long wait. With its emphasis on relative strength, his style of momentum investing has turned out to be supported by a fair deal of empirical evidence. Analysis of historical trends in market ratings suggests that, while you want to avoid excessively popular shares (i.e. those with very high p/es or very low dividend yields), there are also clear benefits to be had from being in shares that are already starting to move. This ties in with the fact that Slater has never really been a long-term investor: his average holding period is rarely more than two to four years. Mostly, he says, he wants to see results on a one- to two-year horizon.

Slater says he sees his investment approach now as a two-track one. The function of the PEG factors is to find the shares that have the kind of undervalued growth potential that he is looking for. The other tests that he applies are then designed to guard against the risk that the potential is simply too good to be true. In some ways, it is like making a series of bets. The more tests that a share passes, the more risk that the investor has laid off. A good bridge player, Slater observes, uses the information from the bidding and each trick that is played as clues about the location of the key cards. In investment, too, once you have your basic idea, you are still in the hunt for further clues. The financial statistics provide most of the answers, but it doesn't stop there. You have to keep on top of the news flow and try to ferret out as much information as you can. Slater has the clout to be able to ring up many of the companies he follows and ask to lunch with the chairman if something untoward has happened. This is not an option that is open to many of the ordinary investors who now follow his methods, but suggests there is much that even ordinary investors, with a bit of effort, can do to help themselves.

PLAYING THEMES

In practice, how does Slater pick his own shares? The monthly screenings in *REFS*, he told me, are one of his regular sources of ideas, but by no means the only thing that triggers his interest in a company. What he looks out for in particular are: (1) dealings by directors; (2) significant changes in brokers' forecasts of future earnings; (3) results that are out of line with the anticipated results at a company; and (4) good relative strength. It was the buying of shares by directors that originally alerted him to one of his biggest successes in the 1990s, a company called Blacks Leisure, which he first started buying at around 70 pence (on its way to over £5).

The company displayed all the necessary elements for success using his methods. "In January and February 1996, five directors bought shares at an average of 67 pence. The relative strength of the shares improved and a few months later, when the shares were about 130 pence, the company announced that earnings per share (EPS) were up by over 400%. Brokers' estimates for the following year were then revised upwards again, and a year later EPS increased by a further 175%. A wonderful example of keeping an eye on directors' dealings." Even after dropping back to 450 pence, the shares were still up by around 500% in the space of only 18 months.

This was a classic example of the virtuous circle which investors hope to benefit from by buying a small company as it enters a period of rapid growth. In many cases, says Slater, several factors move together in a natural progression: the directors buy, the relative strength improves, better results are announced and future forecasts are revised upwards. What you need in order to pick up early on a big move of this kind is the signal that something is about to happen. You still have to do your homework, but the important thing, says Slater, given how many companies there are quoted on the London Stock Exchange, is to have an early warning system in place. Then you know where to focus your attention.

Slater also likes to pick out and play one or two general themes in the market. One such theme in the mid-1990s was the rapid growth in High Street and out-of-town sports retailing from which both Blacks Leisure and another Slater favourite at the time, JJB Sports, benefited.[18] The key moment was the Football League's decision to give BSkyB the television rights for top division football in England. It made certain, says Slater, that the sport would in future be run and marketed in a far more aggressive way. The drive to improve the merchandising of sports equipment was one of the biggest and most obvious secondary effects. The sudden surge in value of quoted football club shares was another aspect of the same phenomenon. To pick up on these emerging trends early enough to profit, you have to be alert to what is going on.

A second theme that Slater was early to appreciate was the problem that computer users face with the so-called 'Millennium bug'. He cannot remember where he first heard about the huge cost that users faced to reprogram their computers to cope with years that begin with a 20 rather than a 19, but he quickly discovered that the problem was on a much larger scale than anyone had acknowledged in public. This reinforced his interest in computer support companies such as Parity and DCS, which both scored well on the PEG test when Slater first looked at them. They would be, he thought, among the most important beneficiaries of the mad scramble by industry to get their computers sorted out in time for the new century.[19]

A third theme that was "beginning to brew" in Slater's mind when I spoke to him for the original edition of this book was that of education under the newly elected Labour government. He expected the government to be more radical in trying to reform the educational system than most people expected, and began to look at one or two relatively small companies which provide educational materials and training, and which could be expected to benefit from the policy changes. This led him later to acquire a sizeable stake in a company called Education Development, Once he has identified general themes of this sort, his technique is to keep tabs on the companies

---

[18] Appendix 6 describes how Slater used the data in REFS to help him find JJB Sports.

[19] In practice fears that the Millennium bug would cause widespread havoc turned out to be a non-event, but not before industry had spent many millions of pounds on trying to anticipate the problem, to the benefit of the companies Slater had invested in.

which stand to gain and monitor their valuations closely, so as not to miss any opportunity to buy if and when they pass the PEG and his other tests.

Inevitably over the years, as market conditions have changed, different themes have come to shape his portfolio. Slater and his son Mark made a lot of money during the Internet bubble by creating a fund to invest in small startup companies and selling it on while Internet mania was at its height. But he was also quick to see that once the bubble burst in 2000, the nature of the investment game was bound to change. For the last decade, he has gradually shifted the emphasis of his investment activities away from individual shares towards larger, direct investments which seek to capture broad sectoral themes, of which the so-called 'supercycle' in commodities has been the most conspicuous. An investment in a biotech venture had limited success, but a mining venture called Galahad Gold, which he and his business partner Ian Watson founded in 2003 and later listed on the AIM market in London, was markedly more successful. When the company liquidated five years later, the investments were sold for an average of four times their original cost, generating tenfold (and in some cases much higher) gains for the original shareholders. Soon afterwards the two men founded a farmland investment company, Agrifirma Brazil, which is transforming thousands of hectares of scrubland in Brazil into productive farmland. (In 2011, following an $80 million investment by a large Brazilian private equity fund in its transformational land subsidiary, the company was renamed Genagro Ltd.) Slater has also helped to set up two thematic unit trusts, Junior Oil and Junior Gold, both managed by his son-in-law Angelos Damaskos. The first invests in small oil exploration stocks, the second in gold mining companies that Slater expects to profit from the rising price of gold.

OTHER ASPECTS OF INVESTING

Like Colin McLean, Slater is much less keen on meeting management than he once was. He reckons that it is too easy to be impressed by a charismatic company executive (such as he himself once was!). His own investment appraisal is 80% based on financial analysis and 20% on his perception of management. His reasoning is that "my perception of the figures is infinitely less likely to be wrong than my perception of the management. My wife tells me I am not very good at judging people. I will meet management as part of getting involved. It also helps me to get good feedback on a company's competitors. Of course, you can meet an exceptional executive, but the danger is that if they are charismatic and good, they can persuade you to forget your own judgement and the figures. The other point is that the playing field is not always level. They are seeing you on their own ground, and it is not too difficult to impress somebody in those circumstances." Slater says that little things about a company – how the receptionist answers the phone, what its literature looks like – can often give you a better idea of how efficient the company is. "If I found people were sloppy, that would put me off."

He also has some advice about the ideal size of a portfolio. He says it is all very well for "investors of the calibre of Keynes and Buffett to advise concentrating on just a few stocks", but most investors naturally have rather less confidence in their ability. Slater advises anyone with a portfolio up to £50,000 to invest in ten to 12 shares; with £500,000, he reckons 15 shares is more appropriate; and for anyone with £1 million, 20 or more may be best. Of course, this is based on cost, not market value. The whole point of investing is to find some really big winners and run the profits. In this way, the chances are that a successful share may soon account for 20 to 25% of the value of a portfolio.

When it comes to selling shares, Slater reiterates his longstanding advice to "run profits and cut losses", but says the main reason to sell is if the story which persuaded you to buy the share in the first place has changed. If a company's profits start to falter, a major new competitor enters its business or the company loses a major source of business, it may make sense to sell the shares. In any event, investors should keep an eye on what is happening to the PEG factor. "A PEG of 1.2 is as high as I would personally allow," he says. The market average PEG has been around 1.5 recently, and he believes investors should sell if their shares cross that threshold. However a deterioration in the relative strength of a share is not necessarily a cause for concern but may become so if it persists for long.

CONCLUSION

Jim Slater is a fascinating phenomenon, both as a man and as a public figure. Nobody has ever doubted that Slater is clever. His command of the technicalities of investment analysis is formidable. Nobody who reads his books, or looks at the detail which has gone into the production of *REFS*, can fail to be impressed by the clarity of thought and expression that they display. A common view, from which I suspect Slater himself does not dissent, is that in his early days he was often too clever for his own good and his judgements were not always sound. It is no surprise that the old City, with its cosy monopolies and leisurely ways, found his impatience and early success painful, partly because it showed up their own limitations.

As Establishments always do, having failed to embrace him in his heyday, they turned on him when adversity struck. If he is now enjoying his successful public rehabilitation, and the money his stock market expertise has brought him, he has, I think, ample reason to be satisfied. Those who, on the strength of the distant past, are still inclined to write him off as "just a promoter of shares", rather than a serious investor, seem to be making the classic investor's mistake of letting past prejudices cloud the current reality. The ability to build momentum around a company he has started or owns has always been part of his methods. Whereas forty years ago that may have been considered ungentlemanly behaviour by stalwarts of the old City of London, it is today a recognised and routine part of the marketing strategy of any self-respecting investment bank or brokerage. Disclosure of his personal holdings has taken the force out of past criticisms of his regular media articles about his favourite shares, and his views certainly remain much in demand.

What remains striking is how many professional investors admit to having been affected by the Slater phenomenon in their formative years as investors. In his Slater Walker days, he set a tone for the way that the markets were then thought to operate which, whether they liked it or not, others could not afford to ignore. There is piquancy in the fact that today his ideas are again permeating the City. In recent years his passionate crusade against the excesses of the European Union has found much greater support than when he first started to broach the subject in the

1990s. So strongly did he feel about the threat that the European Union posed to Britain's interests that in 2000 he published at his own expense 500,000 copies of a tract entitled EU Cannot Be Serious: The Truth About Europe, in which he inveighed against the continued encroachment of EU regulations on Britain's independence and warned – prophetically –against the risks posed by the proposed adoption of the euro as a single currency for Europe. Answering his own question about whether monetary union could be justified, he replied; "There would be some savings on business transaction costs. It would be easier to compare European prices with our own. We would not need to incur the cost of changing pounds into other Eurozone currencies. However when put on the scales against being forced to accept the wrong interest rate for the UK, the loss of exchange rate flexibility, higher taxes, higher unemployment costs and massively increased regulation and bureaucracy, there is an overwhelming case against joining." Subsequent events have amply vindicated this stance.

As for his stockpicking methods, Slater has always had a rare talent for promotion which he continues to use to good effect. But there is no question that his methods have a sound empirical foundation. It is no accident that the largest investment banks all now produce the kind of quantitative analysis which was still seen as pioneering when he first unveiled it in *REFS* and his books. Whether it is possible for others to apply the Slater methods profitably year in, year out is by its nature harder to test. The success of his son Mark's fund, and that of the gold and oil funds run by his son-in-law, does suggest that Slater methods are capable of being transferred across the generations. Of his stock market selections, such evidence as there is points to the successes more than compensating for the inevitable occasional picks that didn't work out. Nobody who backed him on Blacks Leisure, on JJB Sports or on Parity, to take some early examples, or followed him more recently into Andor Technology and Domino's Pizza at an early stage of their stock market runs, is likely to want to complain. General stock market conditions, having been so buoyant in the 1990s, have been less favourable in the last few years to stockpickers. Jim Slater has always been the first to say that you have to tailor your investment strategy to prevailing market conditions. On this count, as on others, he speaks from a deep well of experience that money alone can never buy.

9. MARK MOBIUS:

Global stock seeker

Whoever it was who first dubbed Mark Mobius "the Indiana Jones of the investment world" undoubtedly deserves some sort of brilliancy prize. The image of a rugged guy with a stack of academic qualifications fighting his way through a trail of war and mayhem in the remoter parts of the world looking for investment bargains is an inspired metaphor for what Mobius, the world's number one authority on emerging market investment, does with his time. There is certainly an element of hyperbole about it, but it is not as outlandish a metaphor as you might think.

Mobius has done more than anyone in the last twenty-five years to popularise a new way of investing. If the fashion for emerging markets amounts to a permanent revolution in the Western world's savings habits, as it certainly does, then Mobius can justly claim to have been well in the vanguard of change. This is a man who, as his promotional literature reminds us, spends 80% of the year in transit from one country to another, clocking up thousands of miles a year in his private jet as he spins around the globe, checking up on the far-flung investment funds he manages. His portfolios span all five continents and look very different to the global equity portfolios traditionally owned by investors.

Nor is the kind of speech that Mobius makes to his investors much like the conventional sales pitch you will hear from a fund manager seeking your money. Instead, he says things like: "The places I like to be are the places where nobody else wants to be. And I want to be there when there is blood on the streets. I'm happy when things are bad. It is a strange business. Problems, crashes, people jumping out of the windows. That's my kind of place. One guy in Thailand in the stock exchange put a gun to his head and said, 'Make the market go up, or I'll shoot myself.' Fantastic. That's the kind of market I want to be in."

There is, as those who are familiar with modern investment theory will know, method behind this apparent passion for danger. Mobius is no charlatan – anything but. His work rate and commitment to the job are unrelenting. What he is engaged in doing has the full support of both academic theorists and one of the few undoubted investment geniuses of the 20th century. Sir John Templeton, who first persuaded Mobius to take on the challenge of creating a new global emerging market fund business in the 1980s, stands alongside Warren Buffett and George Soros as one of the true great investors of the modern era. What Mobius is doing today, in extending the horizons of the mutual fund investor to new countries, is very similar in many ways to the pioneering efforts that Templeton himself made in the 1950s, when he launched one of the world's very first global equity funds[1].

It is Templeton's tried and tested contrarian principles of investment which also lie behind the seemingly unconventional approach that Mobius brings to his work as an emerging market investor. Templeton was a committed value investor, always looking for the cheap or bargain stock, regardless of where it could be found, and regardless of what fashionable opinion thought of it at the time. He was buying Japanese companies back in the 1970s, for example, when Japan was still known mainly for "its cheap and shoddy exports" and companies such as Toyota, now the world's leading car manufacturer, could be bought for just four or five times earnings. Thirty years on, Mobius is doing the same thing, but with the big difference that he has far more markets to look at and more money to invest. He is painting the same strokes as Sir John Templeton, but on a broader canvas.

---

[1] I am talking about the modern era. In the late nineteenth century, investment trusts like Foreign & Colonial were doing exactly what Mobius is doing now, pioneering investment in the emerging markets of the day, such as the United States.

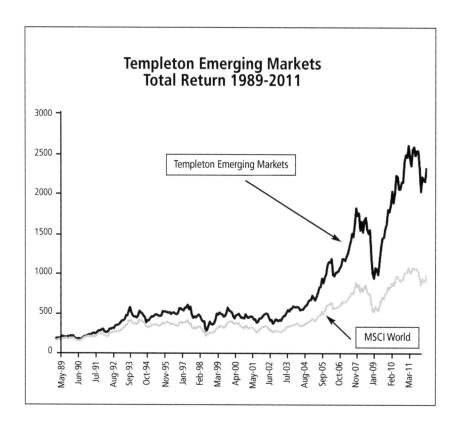

Emerging markets are volatile by nature, which is why the record of Templeton Emerging Markets Investment Trust has been up and down since its launch. What marks out all the funds managed by Mark Mobius, however, is that they combine above-average performance with below-average volatility.

What Mobius has done for the investment business in the last twenty-five years is two things. One is to demonstrate that it is possible to apply conventional investment principles to countries where until quite recently only the very brave would have dreamed of looking to invest. And the second is to convince a wide swathe of sensible people, from thrifty middle-class investors to worthy professionals such as actuaries and pension fund trustees, that it is rational to put their money into such unlikely havens. If Warren Buffett is right to say, as I noted in the introduction, that investment management is 75% marketing, and only 25% performance, then Mobius has undoubtedly earned his place in the rankings of the world's top investors on that score alone.

Although there were many sceptics in the early years of the emerging markets phenomenon, the record now brooks little argument. Mobius and the other pioneers of emerging investment markets have done a remarkable job in transforming investors' attitudes about what is, and what is not, an acceptable place to invest your money. In 1986 barely $5 billion was invested in emerging market funds. Ten years later, the figure had risen to more than $100 billion. Today the comparable figure is more like $500 billion. What we have seen in the last quarter of a century, in other words, is a quite profound change in the pattern of global equity investment, and with it a rewriting of the rules about what risk and reward for equity investors mean.

The Franklin Templeton group remains one of the leaders in the field. In 1998, when the first edition of this book came out, the emerging markets division which Mobius runs had $14 billion of funds under management, spread across 35 funds. In 2011 that figure had nearly trebled, to $40 billion, and the number of funds to 60. The performance of his funds in the early years was often extraordinary. In its first ten years the return on Templeton's main US emerging markets fund was 647%. At the end of 2011 the total return achieved by the Templeton Emerging Markets since its launch in 1989 was a fraction under 2000%, a twentyfold increase over 24 years, equivalent to a compound rate of return of approximately 13% per annum.

It is true that the returns have been far from consistent. Emerging markets are more volatile by nature, and have experienced several phases of poor performance. Between 1994 and 1998, for example, several markets fell by more than 50% in a year, a real rollercoaster ride. During the two big bear markets of the early twentieth century (2000-03 and 2007-09), emerging markets fell further and faster than the US and UK stock markets. The aggregate returns since the stock market peak of 2000 however remain substantially better than from mainstream equities. When the sector hurts, Templeton funds suffer along with the rest. But any investor who joined the bandwagon of the last two decades has still enjoyed one of the greatest investment rides over that period, and those who have travelled with Mobius have done so with less turbulence than many of his rivals.

Yet when Mobius was asked by Sir John Templeton to start an emerging markets fund in 1987, hardly anyone in the investment business had heard of him. In fact, only a handful of people could justly claim to know what was meant by 'emerging markets'. The phrase had only been coined the year before, as a euphemism to disguise the fact that most of the countries in question were regarded at the time as some of the worst credit risks around. The Third World was how most people described countries such as Brazil, Indonesia and India, and the idea that such places, whichever euphemisms you might choose to describe them, were a safe and acceptable place to invest your pension fund would have been – and indeed was – initially greeted with incredulity.

If the concept itself was hard enough to sell, barely eight months after Mobius accepted his new assignment, the world stock markets promptly had their single worst day in history. The October 1987 crash on Wall Street sent the Dow Jones Index tumbling by more than 20% in a single day, dragging nearly all other world stock markets down with it. The ensuing crisis of nerves threatened to strangle the new fund at birth. "If even Wall Street is that unstable," investors could reasonably ask, "what on earth am I doing giving someone money to invest in the Bangkok or New Delhi stock market?" The first emerging markets fund which Mobius set up for Templeton consequently had what he admits was "a disastrous start". Despite being oversubscribed at launch, it was down 20% at the end of its first year.

Yet, miraculously, the new fund not only survived its baptism of fire, but has gone on to become the cornerstone of an operation which now spans more than 40 countries. In his first year, Mobius could find only six countries that met his specifications of being both an emerging market and a place with the necessary legal framework to make it a safe place for investors to commit their capital. Since then, as more and more countries have decided to welcome foreign portfolio investment, the list of qualifying countries has expanded steadily. They include not just what one might call the 'First Division' of emerging markets, places such as Brazil, Taiwan and the Philippines, where capitalist ways are relatively well rooted and understood, but more exotic locations such as Botswana, Colombia and Sri Lanka, where the political climate was traditionally seen as highly hostile to outside investment. The collapse of the Berlin Wall in 1989 added a further raft of former Communist countries, such as Poland and the Czech Republic, to the list of those which are now in the market for equity capital from overseas investors. In 2011 Mobius is spearheading the launch of a new fund that will take his investment teams into a range of new "frontier markets", countries such as Nigeria, Kazakhstan and Egypt, which did not even qualify as emerging markets when he started out.

Global fund flows have played a significant part in the economic development of emerging market countries. In real terms much more capital has flowed out of the United States and Europe into the emerging markets in the last twenty five years than the entire amount of money which Europe received from the United States under the post-war Marshall Plan. Although the annual rate of new net investment in emerging markets slowed from its peak in the early 1990s, the total invested continues to grow by billions of dollars a year. Evidence of the change in sentiment which Mobius and others have wrought is how many fund management companies now routinely offer emerging markets funds to their investors. Some specialise in single countries; others, including Templeton, prefer to offer mainly general diversified funds, covering a number of different countries or regions. Many fund managers also run funds which specialise in buying the debt issued by developing countries. Pension funds and other institutional investors have accepted emerging markets as a legitimate investment class. Emerging markets investment, in short, has become big business.

Just as every new sport needs its superstars, so this new branch of investment management has also created its own need for heroes. With his distinctive shaved head, a wardrobe full of Thai suits and a private jet to whisk him round the globe, Mobius from the outset has been a talisman for a new breed of professional investor, one who lives on a plane and spends his days meeting companies and quite literally shuffling funds around the globe — from Jakarta to Santiago, from Moscow to Mexico City. Indiana Jones really is not a bad metaphor for it all, even if the reality of his life is inevitably a good deal more mundane than the glamorous picture that the image evokes.

CRAZY BUSINESS, CLUED-UP GUY

It does not take long to realise that Mobius operates in a different world to that inhabited by most of the other investors in this book. His book of press cuttings, which his secretary in Singapore kindly sent me one day, tells its own story. Most professional fund managers are lucky to rate the occasional mention in this or that specialist investment magazine; not Mobius. Here we have pieces in such diverse publications as the *Wall Street Journal*, the *Jerusalem Post* and *GQ* magazine. One piece has Mobius and his distinctive shining pate starting out from the cover of a man's magazine called *Adonis*. Being the world's best known emerging markets authority requires a high profile and attracts a lot of media attention.

"Lives there an investor who wouldn't envy Mark Mobius his job?" asked one of many gushing magazine profiles quoted on the blurb of his book about emerging market investments. "There he is, touring a rubber plantation or a bicycle factory in China, motoring through Turkey... talking to a businessmen in India... inspecting a factory in Brazil... or taking a breather in London." The picture of a man passing his working hours on some kind of permanent Baedeker tour, bestowing the gifts of capitalism on the poor and needy, is not quite how Mobius himself sees it. The reality is that a lot of his time is spent worrying about how to deal with the latest example of incompetence, corruption and/or fraud in the countries where his investors have their money. Push behind the carefully constructed marketing profile, and what emerges is a much more interesting and multi-dimensional picture of what being an investment icon actually involves.

One thing about Mobius which is not exaggerated by the press cuttings is his extraordinary peripatetic lifestyle. Not for him the luxury of spending a whole day, as Ian Rushbrook was wont to do, sitting in his office and doing nothing but think. At the age of 75, Mobius keeps up a daunting travel schedule which would test someone half his age. He has property in Hong Kong and Singapore, but most of his time is spent either on the road, or in the air, visiting companies, talking to clients and spreading the gospel of emerging markets investment to anyone who cares to listen. He is unmarried and brave enough to venture the opinion that families get in the way of work.

I can vouch for the fact that he is permanently on the move. When I met him in London for the first time, I told him I wanted to send him some written questions about his investment methods. He asked me to fax them to his Singapore office which I did a few days later. From there, his secretary passed them on to him in Moscow, where he was paying a fleeting visit. He typed out his answers on his personal computer during his plane journey across Siberia the next day, and faxed them back to me from Tokyo, which was his next stop. He has a policy of trying to answer every message that is sent to him within 24 hours.

The next time I caught up with him, it was in London, where he had come to speak to some of his institutional clients. I asked him then what his schedule was. "Last week," he replied, "I was in Hong Kong, making a few company visits. Then I left for Tokyo. We have a new office there and I had to talk to them about selling emerging markets funds. Then I headed for Antwerp to meet with one of our joint venture partners in a tea plantation project in Vietnam. Then I headed to Paris for a half-day talk with two of our clients, and then here to London to talk to clients. Tomorrow, I head off to Turkey to talk at a conference and also to do a few company visits. Then I will go to Germany to visit some relatives for the weekend. Then I will be back here [London] for a board meeting of our funds; then to Egypt – more company visits – and Jordan, Lebanon for the same purpose; then Ivory Coast to look at that market and also to talk at a conference; then back to Singapore."

How, you might ask, can anyone organise a coherent working life in this kind of working environment? The answer, obviously, is "not easily". It depends, says Mobius, on three things: personal discipline, good organisational support and the power of modern communications. Mobius's schedule is planned up to four or five months in advance. He says he tries to organise his trips so that he does not spend "too much time crossing time zones". He tries to time things so that he will be in South America in winter and the Northern Hemisphere in the summer, as he does not enjoy "extreme cold", but says that "it is not always easy". Much of his travelling is done in one of the company's two private jets, although for longer journeys he prefers to fly on commercial flights, to avoid the hassle of having to organise refuelling, pilot rotas and so on. "It's not all luxury flying on a private jet," he reminds me. "I have to make my own soup and do my own cooking." The great advantage of the private plane is that he can get from point A to point B at his own convenience and bypass the chaotic transport systems of many of the countries he is forced to visit. In countries such as Russia, he adds, it is also safer to have your getaway plane ready. Wherever he goes, however, he says he insists on finding time to work out in a gym for at least an hour every day.

As well as the secretaries in his seventeen offices dotted round the globe, Mobius relies on modern telecommunications equipment to make his life work. Wherever he goes on his travels, he is pursued by a steady stream of messages from the network of offices in the Franklin Templeton group. Reassuringly, it turns out that even this hugely disciplined modern globetrotter, in the days before email and instant internet access, used to have the same trouble as the rest of us in getting things to work. "What should happen is that I plug into my hotel PC through AT&T and then get on the Internet," he told me, as we sat down for our second meeting in his London hotel in 1997. "Unfortunately, it doesn't always happen that way. So then I have to get on the phone to Hong Kong and find out what the problem is, what modem should I be using, what speed, and so on. When I finally get in, I have a whole stack of faxes from my analysts, so I will speak to them, dictate over the phone, send courier packages, do whatever has to be done. It doesn't all work smoothly." Today, these early troubles with technology may be a distant memory, but they have been replaced as headaches by "information overload", the curse of the modern era of instant communications. "Now, it's email, iPad, cellphones, everything. There's been a crazy revolution in communications", Mobius observes. "Today I'm dealing with two or three hundred emails every day."

With a portfolio that spans so many countries, Mobius cannot possibly hope to keep on top of all that is happening in every country where he has funds invested. In addition to his regular company visits, he relies heavily on the team of local analysts that he has built up in all of the bigger countries where he invests. Although the emerging markets funds are run as an independent operation, they rely heavily on the infrastructure and support of the Franklin Templeton organisation. Whereas it is just about possible for one person with a bare minimum of research and administrative support to run a specialist UK equity fund, that is not an option for someone trying to invest all round the world, as Mobius does.

"The way it works is this," he told me in 2011. "Of course, there's no way that I could manage the 60-odd funds that we have under management myself. What we do is we have a pretty disciplined process, where we have a system of analysing companies, which is documented in a very well worked out, standardised documentation format, that's used all around the world. That goes through a process of criticism, and analysis, by a team of people. Then it gets added to an action list, which is used for filling our portfolios. Then both analysts and portfolio managers select from that action list. No one can buy a stock unless it is part of the action list,"

"Then of course we have price limits set for each stock, and so right round the world, 24 hours a day, somebody is selecting a stock from that action list, which has been of course approved by me and my senior colleagues. It all goes through the Hong Kong office, where they have a 24 hour order system, and farmed out to each of the offices around the world that deals with trading. So, if it's in Asia, it goes to Hong Kong, or if it's Latin America, it goes to Miami or Fort Lauderdale, and if it's in Europe, then it goes to Edinburgh, Scotland. That's the way we manage the whole process. My role is more to make sure that we're sticking to the discipline, to make sure we're getting good value, and then also draw out the creativity and the abilities of all these people that we have. We have a terrific team of people, who are very well-educated and highly professional. It's really grown into something much, much bigger than we ever imagined."

This is obviously not the kind of investment process that a private investor can hope to replicate. Given that the only practical way for most people to invest in emerging markets is through a fund managed by an investment management firm, it pays to pick one with the right amount of resources and a clear and consistent investment discipline. The way that Mobius has gone about it is to build a network of analysts and support staff in all the main regions that he follows. In the Templeton system, the analysts are the ones who mostly come up with the stock selections in the countries on their watch. His job is to manage the team, lay down the investment discipline they have to follow and give them general pointers of where to focus their attention. He now has 48 analysts dotted around the world in Hong Kong, Singapore, Vietnam, India, Dubai, South Africa, Argentina, Brazil, Poland, Russia, Korea, Turkey, Romania and Austria.

With the exception of Russia, each analyst is responsible for between two and five countries. Their job is to find shares that look cheap when measured against the established criteria which every fund in the Templeton organisation is required to pursue. As a matter of policy, Mobius insists that each office should have at least one local person who knows the language and business conventions of the countries or the region they are in. The Templeton policy is to visit every company in which they have made an investment at least once a year. Mobius makes as many of these trips himself as possible, usually accompanied by his local country analyst.

The analysts work on a bonus system which is based on how much money the stocks in the portfolios they run have made in absolute terms. Mobius does not think much of the modern craze for measuring everything against benchmarks — a problem which is compounded in the case of emerging markets by the fact that there are a number of rival indices, each giving a slightly different perspective on how well the emerging markets have performed. His point is that what should matter to investors is how much money they make in absolute terms, and the risks involved, not how their managers have performed against everyone else. In a business where short-term performance measures are increasingly widely used, Templeton has a long-term perspective to investment, and measures results over five-year periods.

The analysts have to make their share recommendations in a standardised format, and with a standard amount of supporting documentation. "The decisions are really made by the analyst. If his documentation is good and the recommendation is reasonable, then it is very difficult for me to say no," says Mobius. "If I suspect the numbers aren't right, or it is incomplete, then we can reject it. But if it is well documented and makes sense, and it looks like a bargain, then we will buy it." Mobius will quiz his analysts about their thinking, and offer general thematic advice. "Thailand's come down by 30%, don't you think you ought to fly over there and see what's cooking, that sort of thing." Turnover is relatively low. "We only get rid of people if they are lazy, and they're not willing to work. That's the only reason. Not because of their performance or anything like that, because we know that if somebody works hard, tries hard and is motivated, he will be successful. It doesn't require a genius to be a fund manager. It just requires hard work, diligence and willingness to get out and learn and keep an open mind. Open-mindedness is very important."

The rest of Mobius's time is spent on the road, visiting companies in countries where he has invested, talking to clients and banging the drum for emerging markets investment. He says his aim is to stay out of the office as much as possible, partly in order to escape the minutiae of day-to-day administration. The priority "is to stay focused on the important things, which is finding the stocks that are cheap", and to make sure that his investors understand what is happening to their money. Emerging markets are inevitably more volatile than mainstream stock markets, and there is a big education job to be done in making sure that those whose money is at risk don't panic unduly when the inevitable crashes in particular markets occur. Because the Templeton approach is based on contrarian principles, buying at times of maximum pessimism and selling at times of maximum optimism, there is always plenty of explaining to be done.

That is no doubt one reason why marketing plays such a big part in Mobius's life. It seems a moot point whether fame found this outward-looking personality, or if it was the other way round. Anyone who agrees to have an entire advertising campaign built around the image of his bald pate – not a feature that most men want to advertise – is clearly not averse to personal publicity. There are times when the public persona which he adopts to promote the business seems to have taken on a life of its own. For example, when I mentioned to him that in the cuttings there seemed to be several different versions of what he studied when he was a graduate student at the Massachusetts Institute of Technology, he replied without a hint of embarrassment: "Oh, I tell a different story every time. At the moment I tell people that MIT was Made In Taiwan." This is a reference to the fact that Mobius spent several years working in Taiwan, first for a British stockbroking firm, Vickers da Costa, and then running a fund management company, before he joined the Templeton group. In fact, he studied development economics and physical sciences at MIT. Mobius has spent most of his working career in the Far East. It was while running his own consulting firm that he was asked by a Chinese client to look into the prospects for stock market investment in the region.

One legacy of so many years spent pitching the case for emerging markets to sceptical audiences is that Mobius has acquired a list of snappy one-liners he likes to bring out to illustrate his arguments. For example, he often describes the ideal investor in emerging markets as "young babies aged three months old; they can't redeem shares and they think long term". On another occasion, he quotes with approval a line he attributes to Marlene Dietrich: "It is amazing what you can achieve with discipline and the right packaging." This is a line that might make a good motto for the whole Templeton story in emerging markets. Mobius is such a disciplined individual that some might call him a control freak. He has a nice sense of humour, but in conversation gives away few clues about his personality.

RISK AND REWARD

The paradox is that Mobius spends much of his time trying to tell investors of all the risks that are involved in investing in emerging markets; yet the worse he paints the picture, the more his investors seem to love it. The first few years of the emerging markets craze were so spectacularly successful, with several markets regularly doubling or more each year, that much of his time was spent trying to lower expectations to more realistic levels. In one seven year period early on in the fund's life, the Turkish stock market rose more than 3000%, Chile by over 2800% and Mexico by nearly 2000%. As markets never run in straight lines, a sell-off was inevitable. It eventually took place in 1994, prompted by the unexpected devaluation of the Mexican peso – which reawakened all the nagging doubts investors had about the stability of the countries they were investing in – and the unrelated but equally unexpected decision by Alan Greenspan to raise American interest rates. Although investors became more wary of what was still a new investing fad, not everyone stopped thinking that emerging markets were a modern Klondike. Mobius himself said of the time: "The honeymoon period – when things were going up 200%, 300% a year and everyone was saying 'let's have a party' – is over. Now we have to deal with reality."

Fifteen years on, emerging markets have continued to mature. While individual country markets are still capable of making spectacular gains in a year – in 1996, for example, both the Russian and the Venezuelan markets achieved this feat – the days when the diversified funds can hope to achieve such gains are a thing of the past. But those who understand the dynamics of emerging markets, he argues, can still hope to do very well out of investing there, if they know what they are doing and have the patience to wait for results. An average compound return of 20 to 25%, which is roughly double the average return achieved by stock markets in America and Europe, was the kind of target he had in mind in the 1990s. Today, in a world of much lower interest rates, where mainstream equity markets have struggled to deliver positive returns at all, that might be more like 10 to 15% per annum.

Emerging markets will always be a bumpy ride, and you do need patience and strong nerves to ride out the volatility. In 1997 Mobius told me he expected there to be another crash in emerging markets at some stage which will "discourage everybody" and make it a great time to start buying all the cheap companies all over again. That crash duly materialised less than a year later, creating what Mobius conceded was a "crisis of confidence amongst many investors". The Asian crisis of 1998 was a painful episode for the region, and caused big losses for investors who were caught by surprise by the ferocity of the downturn in countries such as Thailand and Korea. Many Asian countries, excited by the success of their export-led economies, had expanded too fast and become dangerously reliant on cheap credit. The bubble duly burst – a forerunner in some ways of the much greater debt crisis which was to engulf many developed countries in 2008.

The philosophy that Mobius shares with his mentor Sir John Templeton is that you have to be an optimist at heart to be an investor. "The fact remains that there are always problems, but we are entering an era which is perhaps unparalleled in the history of mankind. With better communications, improved travel, more international commerce and generally better relations between nations, the opportunities for mankind and for emerging market investors are better than they have ever been before." And there is always the consolation – another central tenet of the Templeton philosophy – that markets go up more often than they go down. "The odds are in our favour, as long as we use common sense and are selective in what we do."

THE CASE FOR EMERGING MARKETS

Although in market terms the early years exhibited signs of being a craze, the increase in emerging markets investment is not an accident. There are sound economic reasons behind it. A number of different things have contributed to its sudden growth in popularity over the last ten years.

Mobius himself lists the main ones in his books, together with a huge amount of supporting statistics. The growth factors include:

- Faster economic growth. Emerging markets have been growing at twice the rate of the developed economies. The underlying reasons include: growing populations, the spread of cheap telecommunications, increased trade and pro-Capitalist government policies. All these factors hold out the promise of rapid growth in company earnings.

- An increasing number of countries have realised the importance of having stock markets to raise finance to support the growth of their economies. They are opening their markets to foreign investors and slowly putting in place the legal and regulatory systems to support them. The number of quoted companies in these countries continues to grow every year.

- In terms of investment maturity, these countries still have a long way to go. In the average emerging market, the value of all the shares on their stock market is still only a fraction of the country's Gross National Product. In the big three markets (the USA, London and Tokyo) the ratio is nearer 90%. Over time, the two ratios can be expected to converge, implying better returns for investors in the smaller countries.

- Another contributory factor has been the quiet but important revolution in the theory and practice of investment management in the West, which has encouraged scores of previously parochial investment institutions such as pension funds to risk committing funds overseas, often for the first time. The ending of exchange controls in the UK in 1979 was one of the key milestones in the development of a new climate of opinion which has created what amounts to a new industry of international cross-border equity investment.

Financial academics have done their bit for the cause by demonstrating that there are substantial diversification benefits to be had from investing overseas in markets which are not well correlated with those of the investor's home country. Historically, the evidence suggests that while the UK market closely follows what happens in New York, for example, there is less of a correlation with what happens in emerging markets. The divergence in performance used to be marked, but has become much less so as financial markets and capital flows have become more globalised. When Mobius started out, in any given year emerging markets were more likely to move in an opposite direction to Wall Street and London than they were to move in the same direction. The Indian stock market and Wall Street, for example, were negatively correlated for some years: one went up when the other went down. A pension fund in, say, the UK could reduce the risk in its portfolios simply by adding some emerging market exposure. Although emerging markets typically now move in the same direction as the bigger markets, though not to the same degree, this is no longer such a compelling argument.

At bottom, the case for emerging markets can be summarised very simply. Higher economic growth and more trade promise higher investment returns than you can get in the main stock markets, while diversification can reduce the apparent risks of investing in even the most improbable countries to an acceptable level. This is pretty much what the experience of the past twenty five years has turned out to be. In addition, Mobius points out, valuation ratios in emerging markets are often lower than in the developed markets such as London and Wall Street. As the markets become better known, then investors can reasonably look forward to p/e ratios rising and dividend yields declining – the kind of status change which so excites Jim Slater when he finds it in a company. What Mobius and his fellow investors in emerging markets are looking for is a status change in whole countries.

Table 9.1 shows Mobius's calculations of how some of the various emerging markets compared in valuation terms at the end of 1995. What is striking is not just the disparity between ratings in the emerging markets and their larger brethren, but the huge diversity in ratings between different emerging markets at any one time. There are always going to be markets which are cheap and those which are going to be expensive. Given the volatility of these markets, there is therefore a strong case for spreading your risk across a diversified fund rather than trying to cherry pick the best ones and running into trouble. The flip side of the spectacular gains which have been achieved in some emerging markets in the last few years is that when they crash, they tend to crash in a big way.

Table 9.1 Emerging market valuations as at 29 December 1995

Country	Price/ earnings	Country	Price/ book	Country	Dividend yield
Emerging markets					
Argentina	15.0	Argentina	1.4	Argentina	3.5
Brazil	36.3	Brazil	0.5	Brazil	3.4
Chile	17.2	Chile	2.1	Chile	3.5
China (Shanghai)	10.4	China (Shanghai)	1.3	China (Shanghai)	4.6
China (Shenzhen)	6.6	China (Shenzhen)	1.4	China (Shenzhen)	5.0
Colombia	11.3	Colombia	1.0	Colombia	2.6
Greece	10.5	Greece	7.8	Greece	4.5
Hong Kong	14.3	Hong Kong	1.8	Hong Kong	3.4
India	14.2	India	2.3	India	1.8
Indonesia	19.8	Indonesia	2.3	Indonesia	1.9
Jordan	18.2	Jordan	1.9	Jordan	1.9
Korea	19.8	Korea	1.3	Korea	1.4
Malaysia	25.1	Malaysia	3.3	Malaysia	1.7
Mexico	28.4	Mexico	1.7	Mexico	1.1
Pakistan	25.1	Pakistan	2.2	Pakistan	2.4
Peru	14.5	Peru	2.8	Peru	1.3
Philippines	19.0	Philippines	3.2	Philippines	0.6
Portugal	14.8	Portugal	1.5	Portugal	3.3
Singapore	17.8	Singapore	1.7	Singapore	1.3
Sri Lanka	8.1	Sri Lanka	1.2	Sri Lanka	3.0
Taiwan, China	21.4	Taiwan, China	2.7	Taiwan, China	1.2
Thailand	21.7	Thailand	3.3	Thailand	2.2
Turkey	8.5	Turkey	2.7	Turkey	4.4
Venezuela	12.0	Venezuela	1.6	Venezuela	2.6
Average	**17.1**	**Average**	**2.1**	**Average**	**2.6**

Source: Adapted from *Mobius on Emerging Markets* (FT Pitman Books, 1996)

Table 9.2 shows six examples of the year-by-year returns from a number of the smaller emerging markets, with the comparable figures for the Tokyo, London and New York markets.

Table 9.2 Market returns by country (% return: main markets)

Year	1991	1992	1993	1994	1995
Brazil	173	3	99	69	-20
Greece	-19	-27	22	2	10
Turkey	-27	-45	254	-40	-11
Singapore	25	6	68	7	7
Taiwan	-1	-27	89	22	-31
Venezuela	48	-42	-7	-26	-29
Wall Street	31	7	10	2	38
Tokyo	9	-21	26	22	1
London	16	-4	24	-2	21

Not much pattern or uniformity of performance there!

While it is broadly true that markets in the same regions tend to move more closely together, it is by no means an iron rule. For example, in 1995 and 1996 Hong Kong performed strongly, while Japan languished and the Thai market fell by 60% in a matter of months.

It is impossible to distinguish the rise of the emerging markets as an investment class from the ideological changes which have swept away so many previously invincible-looking political regimes in the last 15 years, including those behind the Iron Curtain. The irony is that many of the worst regimes in Africa and elsewhere were supported by well-meaning but misdirected aid from the developed countries. Having studied development economics at MIT at a time when it was still a growth subject, Mobius says he knows better than most what a blind alley the aid programmes and the theories of investment-led acceleration into growth that were fashionable at the time have proved to be.

His conclusion now is uncompromising: "People realise that Socialism and Communism has been a bitter, expensive failure. All of the forces that supported a Socialist kind of thinking – government aid, taxation of the rich, takeover and nationalisation of enterprises – all these policies have been disastrous and a lot of money has been thrown that way for no good reason. And now people are waking up to the fact that it is people which create development. It is not aid programmes. It is not steel plants. They were focusing on the wrong thing. What they are doing now is focusing on markets, which are created by people – unless you have that, you don't have anything."

The power of modern communications has been a powerful force in spreading change through many former Communist countries, and its effects do not stop there. Governments in emerging markets are paying more attention to the need to respect the law, and to behave in an honest way. "The fact that a government is corrupt to the core is now in the news," says Mobius. "People know about it. That is really healthy." The appearance of newspapers which are genuinely independent of the state is also good news: "Crooks can run, but they cannot hide any more." In the first edition of the book he added this prediction: "China will be the next regime to go. The press are like flies, mosquitoes biting in every direction. China is trying to get them off, but it can't." That prediction has only partly been supported by recent events.

Emerging markets are more risky than they appear if you confine yourself to looking only at the volatility of the performance statistics. Although they have superior long-term growth prospects, historical research shows that there is no automatic correlation between economic growth and investment returns. The economic crisis that rippled out from Thailand to infect Korea, Indonesia and other Asian countries in 1997-98 demonstrated convincingly that growth can never be taken for granted. You also have to consider a host of other factors which raise question marks about the real risk of investing in places where in many cases even such basic assumptions about the way we run our business affairs as property rights and contract law have yet to be fully adopted. Corruption, fraud and incompetence, although reducing, are still very much the order of the day in many countries. And as a lot of governments have embraced capitalism out of expediency as much as from conviction, the idea that all of them are heading down an irreversible road towards fully blown capitalist ways is an illusion.

Mobius does not downplay the importance of the risks. One reason why he insists on spending so much time visiting companies in person is that there is no other way to find out what is really happening to the companies he has his money with. In many emerging market countries, there is little or no financial press. Accounting standards are still either rudimentary or, where they do exist, the way they are applied is far from uniform. In China, reports Mobius, most accounts are still drawn up by hand. And there are inconsistencies all over the place. In 1995, for example, Argentina banned inflation accounting just as Venezuela announced that it was making it compulsory. Rules governing the release of financial information are also haphazard or non-existent, so insider dealing is a frequent problem.

In many places, says Mobius, it is still difficult to get accurate share price quotations. Published economic statistics are also frequently virtually useless. Quite often, as happened in Hungary a few years ago, different government agencies can give totally divergent accounts of the state of the economy. And then there is the ever present danger of fraud. "Emerging markets are not the only place where one can be defrauded," Mobius writes in his book, "but given their relative newness and fluid regulatory structure, it pays to be on the lookout." While most host governments have realised the value of treating outside investors "fairly and honourably", the exceptions can, he says, be "egregious" (for which read "appalling").

TAILOR-MADE RESEARCH

Overall, Mobius makes the point that many of the normal rules of investment do not apply to emerging market investment: you really need a new mindset before you start. The major risks are systemic ones, and the list is "long and daunting". Thorough research is still the key to finding the best bargains, but it has to be research with a difference. The Templeton philosophy is based on long-term, "bottom-up" stock selection, using traditional value criteria and a willingness to invest at times of "maximum pessimism". The team of analysts Mobius has uses a "country scan" to screen all the listed companies in a market and also compare valuations between similar stocks in different countries. From these lists, they then pick the ones that look the most undervalued, for which they prepare ten years of financial information – ideally, five years of historic figures and five years of prospective earnings projections. Shares must meet at least two of these three basic requirements:

- They must be cheap relative to their price history, the p/e history or to other comparable stocks.

- They must have good growth prospects, with at least 20% per annum average growth expected over the next five years.

- They must be cheap in relation to the company's net tangible assets.

Mobius summarises his approach like this: "Whenever you can buy a large amount of future earnings power for a low price, you have made a good investment." The emerging markets are one of the few places, it turns out, where it is still possible – assuming you believe the figures – to find shares that meet the strict basic value criteria laid down by Ben Graham all those years ago. But even this does not mean it is always possible to find enough good stocks to fill a portfolio. Although Mobius aims to keep his funds fully invested, for long periods he has kept quite a high proportion of the funds (up to 40% at one point) in cash, simply for lack of opportunities.

The routine of regular company visits is designed to ensure that Mobius and his analysts can see for themselves what companies are doing. As the published figures are often so unreliable, this is in part simply a precaution against deception. But Mobius also likes to see how the managers behave in person, and looks for small telltale signs of trouble. Quite often, he says, he finds himself as investor playing the role of morale-booster: "The times when we have made the biggest successes have been times when things were really down and even the managers of these companies were not confident. When there is a big loss of confidence, and problems abound, these are the times when we usually are happiest investing." The emphasis on company visits is, says Mobius, the most distinctive feature that he has added to the Templeton philosophy of investment. In 90% of cases, he will not buy a share until he has visited the company. He regularly visits over 300 companies a year. "When we visit companies we like to thrash out some hard facts as well as getting a feel of how the company is run. This may include querying some information included in the annual report or asking the management to elaborate on future plans. We also like to gauge how competitive a company is with other similar companies in other countries. We like managers that seem to have facts at their fingertips and seem enthusiastic about having foreign funds investing in their companies."

In addition to the visits and the financial analysis his analysts carry out, Mobius relies on a network of local informants for insights into the dynamics of business in any area he is visiting – who knows whom, who pulls the strings in the government, that sort of thing. His team also use technical charts to study historical price movements and "for insights on when to buy a share that we have isolated as being a bargain". Nevertheless, despite all this homework, Mobius calculates that at least 20% of the stocks he buys will turn out to be mistakes, "often because of poor corporate performance and companies' lack of regard for minority shareholder rights".

Implicit in the Templeton method is a refusal to lay down strict asset allocation rules – say, 40% to the Far East, 30% to Latin America and 30% to the rest of the world – and then go out to look for bargain shares in those markets. Its predominantly 'bottom-up' style means its allocation of funds is driven by where it happens to find stocks that are cheap. A glance through the way its portfolio has changed over the years shows that this discipline is taken seriously. By value, to take just one example, the Emerging Markets Investment Trust had 17% of its funds in Turkey in its second year, 1990, but only 5% in 1994. Even today, when the fund is much bigger, Mobius and his team are still making big geographic bets. In 2011, for example, more than 20% of the fund's assets were in China and Hong Kong.

Looking through the lists of companies that Templeton owned in the 1990s (see Appendix 7), the inherent caution of Mobius's approach was evident[2]. Apart from the significant holdings of cash, the biggest holdings were in local telecommunications companies, which can be expected to grow strongly on the back of economic growth, almost regardless of their efficiency. There were also big holdings of banks, whose success is also tied to economic growth and, in the Far East, significant shareholdings in some of the better-known property and trading companies, such as Cheung Kong Holdings and Hang Lung Development. The relatively large holdings in Hong Kong are explained by the fact that, after the market crashed in 1993, well-established companies were trading at prices which were artificially depressed by anxieties leading up to the formal return of the territory to the Chinese in July 1997. As the handover approached, and the market rose sharply, Mobius started to sell his Hong Kong holdings and look for better bargains elsewhere, including Mexico, Thailand and Colombia.

However, what is also evident from the funds' holdings is that the bottom-up method which Mobius adopts can produce some big bets on individual countries as valuations change. If you analyse how the holdings of the Templeton Emerging Markets Investment Trust were concentrated geographically alter its launch in 1989, it shows that the balance of his holdings moved decisively towards Argentina (briefly) in 1993, Hong Kong in 1994 and Turkey in 1995. Just as striking is the number of new countries that have been added – Chile and Hungary in 1991; Indonesia, Korea and Pakistan the following year; Venezuela, Poland and Sri Lanka

---

[2] The latest weightings are widely available from the websites of research portals such as Morningstar, Digital Look and Trustnet.

the year after. Brazil, Hong Kong and Turkey are among the countries which he has held and added to most consistently in the first ten years.

The changes in the portfolio illustrate how the contrarian philosophy laid down by Sir John Templeton – "buy at times of maximum pessimism" – can indeed produce spectacular results at times. For example, Mobius made a big investment in Argentina just before the tub-thumping Peronist Carlos Menem took power, at a time when inflation was at 2000%, and most smart money was fleeing the country, fearing that Menem would stick to his word and in Mobius's words, "dig a grave of state ownership for the Argentine people". In fact, as we now know, Menem did a complete U-turn once he was in office, sending the stock market up by 500% in three years. Mobius made a similar bet in Manila when he bought a big chunk of the Philippines telephone company while a political coup was in progress. The stock's rating soon jumped from six times earnings to eighteen times earnings as the political uncertainty disappeared.

After the big initial welcome that outside portfolio investors such as Templeton received in many of the emerging markets, Mobius says he detects the beginning of a change in attitude in some countries, especially former Communist ones. He describes how one of his analysts walked into the office of the manager of one of the big Russian steel companies. Before he could open his mouth, the manager said: "I want to ask you a question. I want to know, is the destruction of the Russian economy by you capitalists on schedule?" To which his colleague, being "a wiseacre", says Mobius, replied: "No, it's not on schedule. It is ahead of schedule." The dangers of hostility are always present, and always liable to spill over into unhelpful acts.

Hostility does not matter in itself as much as the consequences. "I think the honeymoon period [in emerging markets] is beginning to come to an end because now that we have more money and more markets, we have become targets," says Mobius. "People are beginning to think they can steal and cheat and lie. When people used to ask me what to do about that, my flip answer used to be: 'I lie, steal and cheat right back at them.' But that of course isn't really the answer. The answer is you have got to start holding them to fire and say, 'We represent money of innocent investors who assume that they will be treated fairly. If you do something to try and steal our assets, we are going to try and do something about that.' We have become much more activist in this area since we started. We have quite a few cases pending against companies asking them to make good money because of their back door dealings."

Half a chapter in one of his books is devoted to a detailed account of Templeton's long and drawn out attempts to win legal redress from a Turkish utility company, Cukurova Elektrik, in which Templeton bought a minority shareholding. Trouble started when the Turkish government decided to privatise the company and a Turkish private company, run by the Uzan family, took control of the business. Within months, the company was in trouble. Allegations of malpractice started to fly thick and fast, with some accusing the family of using World Bank loans to speculate on the foreign-exchange markets, and similar abuses. Templeton's initial attempts to register its shares in order to attend and vote at the company's shareholders' meetings were blocked, effectively disenfranchising them. Although the government threatened to take away the company's licence, it proved unwilling or unable to move decisively against the family. The case rumbled on unsatisfactorily for years, and Mobius was eventually forced to abandon it and take a serious loss.

His way of dealing with this kind of problem now is to try to insist on certain preconditions before he will invest. The first and most important is that his custodian bank must be able to operate freely in the country – which is why his emerging markets fund has never invested in Nigeria, for example. "No reason why not one day. Iran and Iraq, too."* Without tangible proof of ownership, and some form of legal entitlement, shares can simply prove to be worthless. The second leg of his strategy is to press persistently for the development of a proper market infrastructure and a legal framework to match. He sees liquidity – the ability of an investor to buy or sell shares at will – as the best form of protection the emerging market investor can have. He rarely misses an opportunity to lecture governments on the need to establish a credible legal and market framework if they want to retain long-term equity funding.

The one constant in Mobius's approach is that he makes no attempt to hoodwink his investors about the risks they are taking on in investing in some of these exotic locations. His argument is that investors must adopt a genuine long-term approach, which includes accepting that they may not be able to get out quickly from markets which deteriorate suddenly. He told *Barron's*, the US stock market weekly, that all prospectuses should tell potential investors: "Don't expect to get out during a downswing. Don't take money out of a fund when markets are going down. If you want some cash, take it when the markets are good. Think like we think. Give us money when markets are bad. Don't trade these funds. Invest with a five-year time horizon." Finding the right kind of investor, in other words, is just as hard as finding the right places to put their money. Emerging markets investment is full of such paradoxes.

UPDATE (2012)

As noted earlier, the frontier markets funds Mobius now runs do invest in Nigeria.

10. CONCLUSIONS:

How you can profit

What conclusions can one draw from the experiences of the successful professional investors profiled in this book? What does it take to achieve exceptional success on the stock market? And what lessons can ordinary private investors learn from those who have achieved it? These are the questions that I attempt to address in this final chapter. At the end of the chapter, I also provide a summary of some of the more important pieces of advice that the experts have gleaned from their many years of experience.

BEWARE THE HOLY GRAIL

The first lesson, which may disappoint some, is that there is no single blueprint for success in stock market investment. The personalities and investment styles of those who have mastered the art of picking stock market winners are as different as they are alike. Some, such as Ian Rushbrook and Jim Slater, are essentially loners. Others, including Mark Mobius, Anthony Bolton and Michael Hart, have shown that it is possible to produce excellent results by applying individual judgement to the work of large, disciplined research teams. Specialist investors, such as Colin McLean and Nils Taube, who work in small collegiate groups, bouncing ideas off a few close colleagues, fall somewhere in between.

Some of these exceptional professionals have made money for their funds by buying small companies; others have done it mostly through the purchase of blue chip shares. Michael Hart has had success in gearing up his investment trust to take bets on currencies and the overall direction of the market. A stockpicker such as Anthony Bolton or Colin McLean would not dream of trying that approach. Meanwhile Mark Mobius is taking bets on companies in faraway places which most of the others would never think of owning. While Anthony Bolton spends most of his working day talking to companies, it was rare for Ian Rushbrook to meet one from one week to the next.

At one level, the diversity of these practices merely emphasises that the great attraction of the stock market is that there is more than one path to success. Investing in shares is a classless activity in the sense that the rewards are open to all. There is nobody who cannot, in principle, profit from the market. There is no law that prohibits you from buying a single share, or from buying a thousand, if you can afford it. Nor can anybody say with absolute conviction: "This is the only way to do it." (If anyone does say that to you, then the only sensible response is to make your excuses as politely as possible and pass by on the other side.)

But this multiplicity also reinforces the important point that nearly all successful professional investors develop a characteristic style and approach to the markets which is very much their own. Once they have found a method with which they are comfortable, they tend to stick with it. Not that the best investors don't change the kind of shares they invest in in response to changing market conditions. That is the essence of the game. But they all have a chosen method which they apply in a thorough and disciplined manner. The ones who are most successful, I have noticed, are frequently those whose organisations allow them to invest in a way which avoids the conflicts of interest that bedevil the rest of the professional fund management business.

Most of the most successful investors are completely absorbed by what they do: even those like Ian Rushbrook, who have made millions from their expertise, still find the lure of the markets compelling enough to drive them to their desks each day. (He had been known, I am told, to visit his office on Christmas Day.) At an age when most people have retired, Mark Mobius is still careering round the world on a crazy travel schedule. The flip side of the extreme pressure is the intense satisfaction that comes from knowing that they are doing a difficult job well.

THE NATURE OF THE GAME

As this is a book about exceptional investors, it is inevitably about the ways in which they differ from their many less successful counterparts. But it is worth emphasising again that most professional fund managers do not invest in the stock market in the same way that private individuals do. The livelihood of an average professional fund manager does not depend primarily on how much money they make for their clients in absolute terms. What matters most is how well they have performed in relative terms: is it better than the market averages? Is it better than the majority of the other professionals in the game?

Once you set your sights on doing better than the average, which is what many private investors also seek to do, it very much changes the nature of the game. It is open to question whether seeking to outperform the average in the equity markets is actually a sensible objective for many investors. Not for nothing is some 30% of all pension fund money in the UK now invested in index-tracking funds, which seek to emulate the performance of the equity markets but not to outdo them. An increasing amount of private investor money is also starting to flow into index-tracking unit trusts and exchange traded funds.

The argument for such funds, in essence, is that the risks and costs of chasing higher performance are so often not worth the effort. There is a remarkable consistency about the findings of research into mutual fund and unit trust performance in the United States and the United Kingdom. After you have taken into account management fees and transaction costs, at least three-quarters of all such funds fail to provide a better return over time than the main market indices.

Similar results have been found in research into the performance of professionally managed pension funds.

However, that such evidence is so overwhelming is not an argument against an active investment strategy. Far from it. Just because something is difficult does not make it impossible or irresponsible. What it does help to explain is why there are so few consistently exceptional track records in the professional fund management business. Those who produce such results are rare beasts. They themselves are the first to admit that the game they are playing – trying to do better than their competitors, year in year out – is not an easy one. Michael Hart speaks for many professional investors when he says the single most important lesson he has taken from his career is "how difficult it all is".

THE FALLACY OF EFFICIENT MARKETS

But don't be tempted into thinking that it cannot be done. If there is one thing which unites all the investors in this book, it is their disdain for the academic theory of 'efficient markets'. This is the notion that the stock market is a highly competitive place where all available information is rapidly and efficiently absorbed by thousands of expert investors. The practical consequence is that most shares will be fairly priced at any point in time, and it is therefore difficult, if not impossible, to secure an edge in performance without some obvious cause (such as trading on inside information, or assuming an above-average degree of risk).[1]

In fact, most expert investors these days start from the assumption that markets are broadly efficient, in the sense, as Ian Rushbrook said, that investors collectively do not leave a lot of "free lunches" lying on the table. Where they part company from the theory is in their belief that such opportunities do still regularly arise; and that it is possible to exploit them

---

[1] This is inevitably something of a simplification. In fact, it is conventional to distinguish between three kinds of market efficiency – strong, semi-strong and weak.

for profit. Anyone who has worked in the City for more than a short period knows that the stock market is not and never will be wholly efficient in the sense that the academics mean.

Colin McLean, probably the closest to a theorist of investment of all the investors I have profiled, put it well when he said: "We do not need long-term studies to tell us what is plainly obvious from examination of any day's trading – much of what happens to the stock market does not make a lot of sense." (This is rather akin to Dr Johnson's effective demolition of nominalism, the fashionable 18th-century philosophical argument that objects only exist in the perception of others. He kicked a stone and said: "I refute it thus.")

There is plenty of evidence to support Ian Rushbrook's considered view that share prices are more volatile than they should be if the markets were really efficient. In particular, it is clear that that market's response to events is often exaggerated: investors become over-gloomy about bad news and over-confident about good news. There is a herd instinct at work whose practical effect is to accentuate the cycles of the stock market and to create buying opportunities for those who can distinguish underlying value from current market sentiment.

The important thing for investors is to know how to spot and profit from these opportunities. As Anthony Bolton was quick to realise when he set out on his career, if outperformance is your objective, the key to success is, by definition, to do something which is different from what the vast majority is doing. All the investors in this book have in their differing ways taken this philosophy to heart, and it remains the key to extracting the maximum value from stock market investment.

DEFINING CHARACTERISTICS

Here are some of the ways in which I believe the investors in this book have succeeded in differentiating themselves from the pack:

ANTHONY BOLTON Makes a virtue out of looking for undervalued or neglected shares, using intensive research and industry knowledge to distinguish shares whose unpopularity is the result of sentiment from those which are shunned for sound reasons. The underlying rationale is the simple, demonstrable truth that in the short term stock markets tend to react to news in an exaggerated way.

COLIN McLEAN Differs from the average fund manager both in the depth and sophistication of his research and in making larger than average bets on a relatively small number of companies. Concentrates on a few companies and sectors where he believes he enjoys an appreciable advantage over other analysts.

MICHAEL HART Foreign & Colonial has many of the characteristics of an index-tracking fund, with a widely diversified portfolio across many international markets. Yet it has been able to deliver additional returns through its ability to use gearing of various sorts to make bets on currencies and by going against the herd to buy shares when markets are falling.

IAN RUSHBROOK In his early years, did well by taking relatively high-risk bets on small companies. Now enjoys an advantage over his competitors by virtue of his sophisticated modelling techniques and a willingness (impossible for most professionals) to make only a handful of decisions each year. Also marked by an unusual identity of interest between his own and his investors' preferences.

NILS TAUBE Distinguished from most of his competitors by the quality of his contacts, his unparalleled experience and the ability to see and exploit underlying trends and anomalies across national borders. Essentially an ideas-driven investor who, like Rushbrook, enjoys an unusually free hand in deciding where and when to invest.

JOHN CARRINGTON Differs from many professional fund managers in the way that he has placed quality of service for his clients above expansion of his fund management group. An expert in smaller companies and obscure overseas markets, he makes a point of avoiding fashionable and heavily promoted shares.

JIM SLATER Scores an edge by investing in a limited number of shares, with no agency conflicts and a screening system which, having developed himself, he understands better than anyone else and can access before anybody else. Also has exceptional analytical skills.

MARK MOBIUS Benefits from a unique and well-founded contrarian investment philosophy and an organisation which is structured so as to enable him to extract the maximum value from it. A defining characteristic of the Templeton approach is a recognition that the best time to invest is when others are at their most pessimistic, a philosophy which sounds simple but in fact requires rigorous self-discipline to put into practice.

WHAT IT TAKES

The success of the Templeton philosophy raises an important point about temperament. It is natural to think that successful stock market investment is primarily a matter of technique, of reading balance sheets, of understanding economic trends, and so on. There is no doubt that these skills are necessary and becoming increasingly important. All the best investors are comfortable with numbers, can analyse balance sheets and are familiar with the language of business and economics.

But it would be a mistake to think that these skills alone hold the key to success as an investor. Colin McLean has a highly sophisticated system for analysing company figures, but concedes its main use is to spot shares which are worth avoiding, not to find those which are worth buying. Ian Rushbrook is an expert manipulator of statistics and economic data, but it is his experience and intuitive feel for value which was ultimately more important in determining his investment choices. The same goes for Nils Taube, with his deep personal memory bank of companies and their trading history.

What all the great investors share is an acute appreciation of what risk and reward in the stock market really means. Technical skills play a part in this: not for nothing did Ian Rushbrook say that he learnt most of what he knows about risk management from playing poker. But temperament is equally as important. The one quality all the investors in this book seem to agree on is that the ability to act in an unemotive and dispassionate way is critical. It is all too easy to become emotionally involved in the shares you have bought, and to be swayed by what you read in the newspaper or by what other investors are thought to be doing. But until you have developed the ability to stand out against conventional opinion, and come to terms with your own fallibility, then the one certainty is that you are going to find it difficult to achieve consistent above-average results from the stock market.

WHERE PRIVATE INVESTORS CAN PROFIT

At first sight, that may sound discouraging for private investors. There is no reason, however, why individual investors need to worry over-much about how seemingly complex the business of professional investment has become. As Jim Slater argues, the reality is that ordinary investors have huge advantages over professional fund managers, if only they are willing to make the most of them. The greatest advantage is simply that the ordinary investor has no need to abide by the rules of the professional game.

As the sole arbiter of your investment performance yourself, you are potentially in a position to do all the things that the professionals cannot in practice do, even if they tried. For a start, no private investor has to try to outperform the market: your livelihood does not depend on relative success. Your main concern is the absolute level of return you make on your money, and the risk you have to take to achieve it. That is why it is a perfectly rational decision to put all your money into an index-tracking fund, and just take the returns that the market as a whole offers. Even Buffett, the greatest active investor of them all, now says that this is the sensible way for many investors to proceed.

Second, private investors are one of the few classes of investor who can often afford to take a genuinely long-term view of their investments. While many professional investors say publicly that they adopt a long perspective, in practice most are still bound by the tyranny of shorter-term performance measurement. They cannot afford to let their short-term performance drop below the market averages for long, as it is more or less bound to do if they are genuinely investing for the longer term. Yet a policy of buying good companies and holding them for the longer term is still a sound and proven way of achieving a good performance.

Third, private investors are not burdened with the sheer size of portfolios with which most professionals have to grapple. The bigger the fund, the harder it becomes to sustain an edge in performance. The only choice then lies between taking bigger bets on individual shares and making more bets on a greater number of shares. The latter route inevitably increases the risk of underperformance. It is rare for a private investor to want, or need, more than say 20 companies in their portfolio. If they are sensible, they will try to make this advantage count. As Ian Rushbrook's success with Personal Assets demonstrated, you don't need to be buying and selling shares every day in order to capture the benefits of being in the equity market: the savings in transaction costs alone can add up to 1 or 2% a year to your returns.

THE NATURE OF THE GAME

The good news, as Ian Rushbrook also observed, is that the stock market is essentially a "nice casino" where, on average, anyone who plays can expect to make money over the medium to longer term. His argument that the greatest risk a stock market investor faces most of the time is not being invested in equities at all is demonstrably true. The market is cyclical, and always will be, but a crash like the one which wiped out Jim Slater in 1974-75, as the one which followed the collapse of Lehman Brothers in 2008, are thankfully once-in-a-generation experiences.

More often than not, the market moves in cyclical patterns around an underlying growth trend. These patterns can be quite sharp: movements of 20-30% up or down are quite common. But the important point is that the underlying trend is upward. Over the long term, equities have produced an annual real return of around 7 or 8% per anum. In the bull markets of the 1980s and early 1990s, with interest rates and inflation falling, the rate of return has been 50% higher again: 12% per annum. When markets are rising at the pace they have been since 1982, the most important thing has been to be fully invested.

It will have made a difference whether or not your money was primarily invested in small companies rather than in large ones, or in America rather than the UK. It will certainly have made a difference depending on who you invested your money with. The Church Commissioners, for example, were poorly advised in the late 1980s and made an awful mess of their investment strategy, taking large amounts of money out of the stock market to invest disastrously in property. They were not alone. But, unless you were particularly unlucky in your choice of adviser or fund manager, how much money you made in these markets will essentially have been a difference of degree, not of direction.

That is why one of the oldest pieces of advice to anyone starting to think about the stock market is simply: "Don't confuse a bull market with evidence of investment expertise." Those who put their money with the best professionals, such as those featured in this book, have been doubly blessed. They have enjoyed the benefits of being invested in the equity markets during one of their strongest and most sustained periods of growth this century; and they also have had the benefit of exceptional managers adding to those already significant returns. (Since then of course, the stock maket's returns have been much poorer, as invariably happens following periods of exceptionally strong returns. The result is that many lauded professionals have been exposed as human after all.)

As will be evident from their comments, most of the investors featured here were becoming concerned by the current levels of the main equity markets at the time I first spoke to them. As professional investors, they knew that the recent rate of returns available from equities could not be sustained indefinitely. At some point, the rate of return from the stock market must revert to a level that is consistent with the long-run historical average. But none of them were foolish enough in 1997-98 to say categorically when the necessary correction would come: they know that bull markets, like individual share prices, tend to run longer than anyone at the time imagines is possible.

Even Nils Taube, who correctly foresaw the 1987 crash, and says there are only a handful of exceptional years when the overall level of the market is important, was not yet convinced in mid-1997 that we had reached a point where the markets were so overpriced that you could bet with confidence on their imminent fall (although he had taken out a small put option which would payout if the US market were to fall). Even when the markets do fall sharply in the short term, the long-term case for investing in equities remains powerful, but it is important, as John Carrington observes, to adjust one's expectations about the scale of what might be achievable, and the length of time it might take to materialise.

AVOIDING MISTAKES

If there is no surefire way to succeed in the stock market, there are still scores of surefire ways to fail, even in a bull market. If the majority of professional investors fail to do better than the market averages, as they consistently do, then the potential pitfalls for the unwary are even greater. The challenge for any investor today is not only to decide how attractive shares are as a class, but how they can avoid making the kinds of mistakes that are likely to cost them dear. For all but the very best professionals, investment is still very much what Charles Ellis, the consultant cited by Ian Rushbrook, calls "a Loser's Game".

What are the most common mistakes that investors make? In no particular order, here are the ones most commonly mentioned by the eight experts I have profiled: selling too early; following the herd; failing to cut losses; overtrading; falling for a persuasive management. The point that they all make, however, is that mistakes are inevitable. Investing is not a business in which perfection can ever be achieved. A strike rate of 50% is good, and 65% is exceptional. The important thing is to learn from the mistakes and not to be discouraged by the occasional failure. It is uncanny how often the success of an expert investor, when you come to analyse it, comes down to the success of a relatively small number of individual shares. Uncanny but not altogether surprising. As Peter Lynch, one of Anthony Bolton's guiding lights at Fidelity, explains in his book *Beating The Street*, this is at bottom simply a question of mathematics.

Suppose you invest £1000 in each of ten shares and hold them for three years. At the end of the period you find that nine of the ten have gone nowhere – they are still the same price that you paid for them – but the tenth share has risen tenfold. How well have you done? Do the sums, and you will find that you have made a gain of 90% over three years, equivalent to a compound annual rate of return of 23%! Not bad. Even if three of your ten original picks go bust and you lose all your money on them, the compound rate of return is still 17% per year, excluding any dividend income. Of course shares that rise tenfold – what Lynch calls "tenbaggers" – are not all that common. But nor are they as rare as you would think. For example, take a look at the list of biggest gainers in Michael Hart's portfolio at Foreign & Colonial, or at some of Nils Taube's great winners. The moral is clear: It pays to look for shares that have the potential for step changes in capital value.

This does not mean throwing caution to the winds. Diversification is an essential requirement for controlling risk in any investor's portfolio. But the logic of Anthony Bolton is inescapable on this point. Exceptionally good ideas are hard to come by, so when you think you have found one, it makes sense to make a significant investment in it. The stronger your convictions, the more money you should be prepared to put behind your judgement. This does not guarantee success, but it does ensure that if your judgement is good, you will reap an appropriate reward. A few big winners will go a long way towards paying for indifferent performance elsewhere, especially if you are rigorous about cutting your losses on those that fail to work out. The fact that specialist fund managers such as Colin McLean and Nils Taube often have lopsided-looking portfolios is no accident. It is the logical consequence of making selective bets on a few sectors where they believe they have a real understanding of how the hidden value in the shares they like is going to be released. It also protects them from the risk of investing blind in things they do not understand.

One reason why consistent outperformance is difficult is that good ideas tend not to last forever. Investment styles come and go. A particular investment approach works well for a while. As a result more and more investors adopt it. The prices of the shares which this method favours rise and before too long it naturally ceases to work as well as before. Something like this happened to the traditional value investing methods pioneered by Ben Graham in the United States. Similarly, growth shares had an exceptional run for a time. Then they faltered. Now they are back in favour again while value investors have had a tough couple of years.

One of the key messages from the experience of the investors in this book, however, is that relying on valuation indicators alone to guide the choice of shares is usually a mistake. While financial ratios are critical in determining whether or not a share is worth buying at any given moment, more important for longer-term success are the underlying economic characteristics of the business. That is why, for example, many expert investors now routinely give more credence to cash flow than they do to reported profits. Good businesses, especially those with strong franchises or powerful brand names, will tend to generate surplus cash flow over time.

BACKING YOUR OWN EXPERTISE

What private investors clearly lack are the information resources available to the professional fund management organisations. Only a seasoned traveller with substantial means is likely to be able to make sensible choices about what to buy if they are investing in emerging markets, for example. And the same is true, to a varying extent, if you are investing in companies in your own home market. A subscription to Jim Slater's *REFS* will help in the UK, but even *REFS* still only represents a fraction of the information which is potentially available to the professional investment management firm.

It then becomes a matter of choice how far you are prepared to go in picking companies about which your knowledge is not as full as it might be. The ideal, as Anthony Bolton says, is to confine your investment only to those companies where you do have specific and detailed knowledge. The industry in which you yourself work is the obvious starting place. There will be many occasions where someone who understands the dynamics of a particular business will find himself well placed to judge if another company in the business is undervalued or not.

Shoppers are in principle just as well placed as stockbroking analysts to judge the calibre and success of retailers whose shops they visit. Nils Taube, with his international perspective, was one of the first to make money out of buying supermarket shares, but anyone who visited Sainsbury's or Tesco in the 1970s could have made a lot of money by predicting that their particular kind of retailing was going to prosper in the medium to longer term.

The drawback of backing your own knowledge is that there will often be times when the sectors you know about are not throwing up any bargains at all. In that case, the choice lies between investing elsewhere – where by definition you have no edge – or sitting on your hands and doing nothing at all. Doing little or nothing is not such a bad policy, as Ian Rushbrook has demonstrated. But if you are going to invest elsewhere, it pays to put your money with a professional whose own investment edge you can readily discern for yourself. There are not that many around to make this as difficult as it might appear.

THE FINAL LESSONS

Here, by way of summary, are what I take to be 12 of the more important pieces of investment advice culled from the professionals in this book:

- Unless you have particular expertise in currencies or macro-economics, don't waste much time in worrying about the state of the economy as a whole.

- Trying to 'time the market', in the sense of deciding when it is going to rise or fall, is a largely futile endeavour. If the professionals cannot do it, the chances are you will fail too.

- Cut your losses and run your profits. Every successful investor attempts to do this, but be aware that it is not as easy as it sounds.

- In the long term, good companies with strong economics will do better than those with strong managements but poor economics.

- Trust your own knowledge of business and industry more than information from second-hand sources.

- Remember that stockbrokers make their money from commission. They have a vested interest in seeing you buy and sell shares.

- Don't take more risks than you are comfortable with. As J.P. Morgan famously advised, "Sell down to your sleeping level."

- Take reverses in your stride, if you can. Don't become emotionally attached to particular shares.

- Don't get too busy in managing your share portfolio. It is more profitable to make a few good decisions than a lot of second-rate ones.

- Beware of fashionable shares, and those which you are urged to buy because something is 'about to happen'.

- Investment styles come and go. Valuations change. There will be occasions when markets become over-excited, and others when they become absurdly pessimistic.

- When market valuations are high by historical standards, that in itself is no reason not to invest in equities, but it does argue for realism in projecting the scale of future returns.

These extracts are unchanged from those used in the first edition of Money Makers. *They still illustrate the essence of the professionals' approach, albeit that some of the examples may appear rather dated.*

APPENDIX 1:

Anthony Bolton

All fund management firms have to produce regular reports on their investment funds: for unitholders in the case of unit trusts, and for shareholders in the case of investment trusts. The following extract from the 1996 annual report of Fidelity's Special Values investment trust gives a flavour of Anthony Bolton's style, as well as details of his holdings at the year end date (31 August 1996). As the size of the fund has grown, so too has the number of shares it owns. Note too the absence of any of the 'blue chip' stocks which dominate the UK stock market (no Shell, no Glaxo, no BT). This underlines the fact that Bolton's method relies heavily on finding value amongst small- and medium-sized companies. The portfolio analysis also illustrates how far his holdings differ from the market as a whole – note the heavy weighting in service companies (43.9% against 25.0% for the All-Share Index) and the underweighting in consumer goods at that time (5.2% against 16.5%).

INVESTMENT MANAGER'S REPORT

Performance Review As shown in the Summary of Results on page 3, both the net asset value total return (+ 22.1%) and share price total return (+ 25.5%) of your Company have continued to outperform their benchmark index, the FTSE Actuaries All-Share Index (+ 15.8%). The strong performance of the portfolio can be attributed primarily to two factors. First, the generally positive economic and stockmarket background.

The environment has been one in which economic growth has gathered momentum, inflation has fallen and interests rates have been cut. The demand for shares has been helped by takeovers, companies announcing that they would be buying back their own shares, such as Barclays and Reuters, large inflows of cash into institutions and unit trusts and foreign investors increasing their exposure to the UK market.

The second factor which has contributed to performance has been the composition of the portfolio itself. The bias within the portfolio continues to be towards medium-sized and smaller companies and this has been a positive factor for performance over the last 12 months. In addition, a number of large holdings in the portfolio performed well during the year. These included **Misys**, a computer software company where good growth in profits was reflected in the performance of the share price. Prospects for **Mirror Group Newspapers** improved during the year as the newspaper price was subsided and the share price rose. Three other large

holdings, having performed well, were sold as we considered future prospects were by then reflected in the share price; **Burton Group**, the clothing retailer benefited from the recovery in high street sales, while **BET**, an industrial services company, and **Unitech**, a manufacturer of power supplies, were both the subjects of takeover bids which caused their share prices to rise.

While most of the holdings in the portfolio have performed relatively well, there have been some disappointments. The share price of **Wickes**, the D-I-Y retailer, fell sharply and was then suspended after it was announced that its accounts had failed to give a true picture and its profits had been overstated. The shares are valued at a price which your Board believes to be fair. **Amstrad's** move into mobile phones proved more difficult than expected and the share price fell back. Some companies announced disappointing profit results such as **Iceland**, the frozen foods retailer and **Body Shop International** and their share prices fell. These latter two holdings have now been sold.

With the portfolio outperforming the Index by a considerable margin, the Loan Stock gearing has achieved its objective of enhancing returns to shareholders. If the Loan Stock had not been issued, the increase in the net asset value would have been 20.1% instead of 22.1%.

Portfolio Review The structure of the portfolio has not changed greatly during the year. There are 149 holdings within the portfolio and the largest accounts for only 3.6% of your Company's assets. Portfolio turnover for the year was 55%. Stock selection remained primarily focused on small- and medium-sized companies with a market capitalisation from £50m to £500m. In seeking out 'special situations' we believe this area of the market offers a fertile ground for investment opportunities. This is partly a result of the tendency for other institutional investors to concentrate on larger or more familiar companies and thus place less research effort on smaller companies.

On the whole, those sectors which featured prominently in the portfolio a year ago continue to do so although individual holdings may differ. The complete sectoral breakdown is on page 11. The sectors emphasised in the portfolio include retail, media, computer software and oil exploration. Holdings in these sectors are a result of stock selection rather than to maintain certain sector weightings. Individual holdings within a specific sector can be held for entirely different reasons – they may, for example, be companies whose share prices are at a discount to their asset value, recovery or turnaround situations, unrecognised growth situations, companies where we believe there is corporate potential or unfashionable companies.

The one area where our exposure has increased is the insurance sector where we now hold a number of Lloyd's investment trusts. Following the difficulties in the Lloyd's insurance market in recent years, investment trusts were set up to invest in Lloyd's insurance syndicates. However, investors have been uncertain about the outcome of the rescue plan for Lloyd's. This resulted in many of the investment trusts selling at what we believed to be significant discounts to their true value. Subsequent to our purchase of such shares, confidence began to grow that the rescue plan would succeed. These holdings have on the whole performed strongly during the year.

London Insurance Market Investment Trust is now the largest holding in the portfolio and I am pleased to report that its share price rose 41% during the year.

A new holding in the portfolio is **British Gas**, which is now one of the top ten holdings. This is the only stock held in the portfolio which is in the FTSE 100 Index. During the year British Gas's share price significantly underperformed the general market. This was a result of an uncertain regulatory environment. However, we believe the share price has fallen to a level where investors have become too pessimistic about the company's prospects. We believe the potential rewards now outweigh the risks of owning shares in the company.

Oriflame International is now the third largest holding in the portfolio and is an example of an 'unrecognised growth' company. Using direct marketing techniques the company sells cosmetics in

Europe and is expanding in the emerging markets. Sales and profits have been growing strongly but the company is still relatively unknown in the marketplace and not widely followed by the stockbroking community. Consequently its growth has to some degree gone unrecognised, although this is beginning to change with the share price rising during the year by 68%.

Media holdings continue to form a significant part of the portfolio as in our view there are a number of good growth companies in the sector. These are attractive as they are experiencing strong growth in profits, and are generating cash which can be reinvested in their business, thereby limiting the need to borrow.

Some of the holdings in the sector which have performed well over the year include **Capital Radio** (share price up 45%), **WPP** advertising agency (up 41%), **Yorkshire Tyne Tees TV** (up 112%) and **Scottish Television** (up 43%). There has been some consolidation in the TV industry, with the regional ITV companies being taken over by competitors or by companies wishing to enter the industry.

Two of the holdings in the portfolio have benefited from corporate restructuring. **News International Special Dividend** is a special class of share issued by its Australian parent company News Corporation, the publisher of *The Times* and *The Sun*. These shares were trading at a significant discount to the price of News Corporation's shares despite the special class of share having similar dividend and asset entitlements. We believed that over

time this discount would narrow. During the year the parent company announced a reorganisation of its share structure which resulted in the company offering to exchange the shares we had at a significant premium. A similar situation arose with our holding in **Securicor** participating preferred shares. Here again the company sought to simplify its share structure and merge two companies, Securicor and Security Services. This resulted in the share price performing well.

One area where we look for value is among 'unfashionable' or 'controversial' companies. **T&N**, the second largest holding in the portfolio, fits into this category. It is now primarily an engineering company but used to be involved in asbestos, for which it faces liability claims. This has severely depressed the share price. The company has, however, developed an engineering business which has strong positions in certain sectors of the automotive industry. We believe the shares represent an 'undervalued' situation.

Another holding which falls into the unfashionable category is **London Clubs International** whose business is gaming. This has caused some investors to avoid the stock and not to appreciate the changes which were taking place in gaming laws as well as the growth prospects of the company. As a result we believed its shares were particularly undervalued at the time of purchase.

The portfolio has 8.2% of its holdings outside the UK. However, many of the holdings have businesses or some connection with the UK. **Tullow Oil** is an Irish oil exploration company with interests in Pakistan. The company is quoted on the UK stock market. **Energy Africa** is another oil company which, as well as having interests in Africa, has interests in the North Sea. **TNT** is an Australian company which has an involvement in logistics, such as parcel delivery, amongst other interests. The majority of profits are made in Europe. At the beginning of October, the company received a takeover approach.

Outlook The Manager will continue to seek out those investment opportunities which fit the description of a special situation. A bias towards small- and medium-sized companies is likely to continue although investment opportunities may also arise among larger stocks. In the past this style of investing has performed well in periods when the economy has been accelerating (and when investors look outside the market leaders). We believe that the portfolio is well placed to benefit from the promising economic outlook for the next year.

Fidelity Special Values plc
Portfolio Listing
as at 31 August 1996

Holdings by value	1%

London Insurance Market Investment Trust
Largest investment trust investing in Lloyds insurance syndicates — 3.6

T&N
Engineering firm with strong position in automotive components — 2.6

Oriflame International
Direct selling of healthcare and household products — 2.6

Securicor
Security services and 40% owner of Cellnet, a mobile phone operator — 2.1

Misys
Computer software, specialising in accountancy packages — 2.1

British Gas
Exploration, production and sale of gas mainly in the UK — 2.1

London Clubs International
One of the few UK quoted operators of casinos — 1.9

Berisford CV 5% ULS 2015
Owns Magnet, kitchens/doors, and Welbilt, cooking equipment — 1.9

News International Special Dividend Shares
Media company involved in printing, publishing and television — 1.8

Cairn Energy
Oil exploration and production with interests in Bangladesh — 1.8

TOP 10 HOLDINGS	22.5

Wembley
Leisure and property company, owner of Wembley stadium — 1.7

WPP
International advertising agency — 1.6

Nurdin & Peacock
Operates low cost cash and carry warehouses — 1.6

Shanks & McEwan
Waste management company — 1.5

ED & F Man
Commodities distributor and fund manager — 1.3

Aegis
Provides media planning and buying services — 1.3

Psion
Manufacturer of hand-held computers — 1.2

Tullow Oil
Irish oil exploration and production firm with oil fields in Pakistan — 1.2

APV
Designs and manufactures specialised process plant and equipment — 1.2

Norcros
Supplier of building materials. particularly for the interior of houses — 1.1

TOP 20 HOLDINGS	36.2

Yorkshire Tyne-Tees Television
TV broadcaster and producer of
programmes 1.1

International Business Communications
Provides information to business
through publications and seminars 1.1

Aurora Gold
Australian gold mining and
production company 1.1

Ashanti Gotdfields 'CDS'
Ghanaian gold mining and
production company 1.1

Huntingdon International
Provides biological safety
evaluation research services 1.1

Scottish Television
Regional *ITV* contractor 1.1

Chloride
Uninterruptible power supplies,
emergency lighting, alarms, batteries 1.0

Regal Hotel
Owns and operates hotels 1.0

Jarvls Hotels
Owns and operates hotels 1.0

Dorling Kindersley
Creates and publishes illustrated
books, CD Roms and videos 1.0

TOP 30 HOLDINGS	46.8

Chesterton International
Estate and consultancy services
and facility management 1.0

McDonnell Information Systems
Develops computer software and
installs hardware and related services 1.0

Hogg Robinson
Business services to travel,
transport and financial sectors 1.0

Cox Insurance
Insurance underwriter 1.0

Wickes
Operates chain of DIY stores 1.0

National Home Loans
Provides residential mortgages 0.9

Capital Radio
London-based radio station and
TV studio operator 0.9

London & Overseas Freighters
Owns oil tankers which are then
chartered 0.9

Betterware
Direct seller by catalogue of
housewares and consumer products 0.9

McCarthy & Stone
Designs, constructs and sells
retirement flats 0.9

TOP 40 HOLDINGS   56.3

Leigh Interests
Environmental services and extraction
and processing of coal   0.9

London American Growth Fund
Investment in US venture capital
situations   0.9

Willis Corroon
International insurance and
reinsurance brokers   0.9

Micro Focus
Produces compilers and
programmers productivity tools   0.8

Mirror Group Newspapers
Newspaper publishing and cable
television   0.8

Energy Africa
Exploration and productions of
oil and gas   0.8

Stagecoach
Provider of 'public' transport services   0.8

Development Securities
Property investment, development
and trading   0.8

Cadiz Land
Manages agriculture and owns
water rights in California   0.7

Electronic Retailing Systems (UK)
Produces electrical equipment for
retailers   0.7

Bulmer (H.P.)
Producer and distributor of cider
and premium branded drinks   0.7

Abacan Resource
Oil and gas exploration company   0.7

Hambro Insurance Services
Specialist insurance services   0.6

Electronics Boutique
Retails computers, software
and video games   0.6

British Biotech
Pharmaceutical research and
development   0.6

Kewill Systems
Provision of computer software
and hardware   0.6

Mowlem (John) & Co
Contracting, housing, scaffolding,
aviation, property and utility projects   0.6

New London Capital
Provision of capital to support
Lloyds underwriting   0.6

TNT
Australian company with interests in
logistics, including parcel delivery   0.6

Cape Industries
Manufacture of fire protection,
insulation and building products   0.6

Shandwick International
Public Relations consultancy   0.6

BCE Holdings
Developer of computer games   0.6

CLM Insurance Fund
Investment company mainly involved
in financing Lloyds underwriting   0.5

Graseby
Precision instruments/medical product
monitoring/environmental/defence
products 0.5

Kunick
Leisure services including
amusement machines 0.5

Kenwood Appliances
Manufacture and distribution of
domestic appliances 0.5

**Mercury European Privatisation
Investment Trust**
Invests in both UK and continental
European privatisations 0.5

Angerstein Underwriting Trust
Investment company participating
in Lloyds underwriting syndicates 0.5

Senior Engineering
Engineering products 0.5

CLS
Commercial property investors 0.5

Saltire
Distribution of electronic components 0.5

Tie Rack
Retailing of ties, scarves and
accessories 0.5

Unichem
Retailer and distributor of
Pharmaceuticals 0.5

Takare
Operation of nursing homes for
the elderly 0.5

Racal Electronics
Voice/data communications,
defence electronics 0.5

Canal Plus
French commercial pay-TV company 0.5

Heath (C E)
International insurance and
reinsurance broking 0.5

Tabacalera CIA 'Registered'
Spanish tobacco manufacture 0.5

Greycoat
Property investment and development 0.5

Caradon
Building and home
improvement products 0.5

Energy Research Group of Australia
Electrical equipment and
ticketing systems 0.5

Southend Property
Property investment, development
and dealing 0.5

WEW
Operating discount department stores 0.5

Lloyd Thompson
Wholesale insurance and reinsurance
broking 0.5

**Finsbury Underwriting Investment
Trust**
Investment company participating
in Lloyds underwriting syndicates 0.5

**National Parking Corporation
(unlisted)**
Car parking and breakdown services 0.4

Calm Energy Fully paid 1179/96
Exploration and production
of oil and gas   0.4

Life Sciences International
Scientific equipment and scientific
consumables   0.4

Masthead Insurance Underwriting
Investment company participating in
Lloyd's underwriting syndicates   0.4

Videologic
Multimedia technology for PCs   0.4

Liberty International
Holding company with interests in
shopping centres, property, financial
services   0.4

Ascot
Industrial holding company   0.4

Simon Engineering
Industrial services and
process engineering   0.4

Pet City
Retailer of pet foods, medicines
and accessories   0.4

JKX
Oil and gas exploration, production
and processing   0.4

Filtronic Comtek
Electronic components for cellular
telecommunications   0.4

Hazlewood Foods
Food manufacturer   0.4

Park Food
Supplier of hampers and other food and
non-food products   0.3

Quality Software
Specialist application software,
consultancy, training and maintenance 0.3

Cook (D C)
Motor distributor   0.3

TOP 100 HOLDINGS	89.0
OTHER HOLDINGS (49)	11.0
TOTAL PORTFOLIO	100.0

FIDELITY SPECIAL VALUES plc
Distribution of the portfolio
as at 31 August

	1996				1995
	UK %	Non-UK %	Total %	All-Share Index %	%
EQUITIES (including convertibles)					
Services					
Media	12.1	0.5	12.6	6.4	15.1
Support services	9.3	-	9.3	1.9	7.3
Leisure & hotels	8.0	-	8.0	2.1	7.3
Retailers – general	6.9	-	6.9	5.9	5.0
Transport	2.3	0.6	2.9	2.6	1.2
Retailers – food	2.0	-	2.0	2.6	4.2
Distributors	1.9	-	1.9	1.0	0.9
Other services & business	-	0.3	0.3	2.5	4.1
Total services	**42.5**	**1.4**	**43.9**	**25.0**	**45.1**
General industries					
Electronic & electrical equipment	4.8	1.2	6.0	2.2	12.0
Engineering vehicles	2.7	-	2.7	1.0	0.4
Engineering	2.4	-	2.4	4.2	1.6
Diversified industries	2.3	-	2.3	3.4	0.5
Building & construction	1.8	-	1.8	0.8	1.6
Building materials & merchants	1.8	-	1.8	2.4	4.7
Textiles & apparel	0.2	-	0.2	0.4	0.5
Chemicals	-	-	-	2.1	1.5
Other	-	-	-	1.2	-
Total general industries	**16.0**	**1.2**	**17.2**	**17.7**	**22.8**
Financials					
Insurance	9.3	-	9.3	2.1	2.1
Property	3.6	0.8	4.4	1.8	4.1
Other financial	2.7	-	2.7	1.0	2.0
Other	-	-	-	12.6	-
Total financials	**15.6**	**0.8**	**16.4**	**17.5**	**8.2**

	1996				1995
	UK %	Non-UK %	Total %	All-Share Index %	%
Mineral extraction					
Oil Exploration & production	3.0	1.2	4.2	0.8	3.7
Extractive industries	1.1	3.1	4.2	1.3	2.8
Other	-	-	-	7.5	-
Total mineral extraction	**4.1**	**4.3**	**8.4**	**9.6**	**6.5**
Consumer goods					
Healthcare	1.9	-	1 .9	0.7	2.3
Pharmaceuticals	1.7	-	1.7	7.9	0.8
Alcoholic beverages	0.7	0.5	1.2	2.8	0.7
Food producers	0.4	-	0.4	3.2	0.7
Household goods	-	-	-	0.5	1.9
Other	-	-	-	1.4	-
Total consumer goods	**4.7**	**0.5**	**5.2**	**16.5**	**6.4**
Utilities					
Telecommunications	2.2	-	2.2	5.2	6.1
Gas distribution	2.1	-	2.1	1.0	-
Other	-	-	-	3.9	-
Total utilities	**4.3**	**-**	**4.3**	**10.1**	**6.1**
Non-financials	-	-	-	-	2.2
Investment trusts	**2.7**	**-**	**2.7**	**3.6**	**1.0**
TOTAL EQUITIES	**89.9**	**8.2**	**98.1**	**100.0**	**98.3**
FIXED INTEREST (including convertibles)	**1.9**	**-**	**1.9**	**-**	**1.7**
Total portfolio 1996	**91.8**	**8.2**	**100.0**	**100.0**	
Total portfolio 1995	**89.6**	**10.4**	**100.0**		**100.0**

APPENDIX 2:

Ian Rushbrook

An extract from the 1998 Annual Report of Personal Assets, which illustrates three things: (1) Ian Rushbrook's highly individual approach to his job; (2) his low turnover of shares: and (3) the way that he uses his modelling techniques to support his investment strategy. The graphics showing the performance of his model are reproduced on page 68. I have also included the section which outlines the investment philosophy of Personal Assets, which is a rare model of clarity and consistency.

INVESTMENT REPORT

Life is full of minor miracles and I must begin by reporting one. Despite liquidity from 25% to 35% of total assets, Personal Assets had a good year in a bull market. The net asset value per share outperformed our benchmark by 3.1% increasing by 34.6% compared to the FTSE All-Share's 30.6%. Over the three years to 30 April 1998 (our preferred time-span for measuring performance) Personal Assets' net asset value per share grew by 96.8% compared to our benchmark's 76.7%, an outperformance of nearly 3,7% per annum compound.

Last year I lamented that my bearishness during the preceding twelve months had been a mistake. But I stayed bearish and increased our liquidity further. Again, it was a mistake. Over the last two years the UK market has risen by an astonishing 46%, and even Personal Assets' 57% rise in net asset value per share over the same period still leaves room for regret. Robin charitably comments that I have not been wrong – merely right much too early. If so, why have equities kept on performing so well?

The performance of Western stockmarkets has been driven by that of the US, which raced up by just under 40% in Dollar terms during the year. Continental Europe produced similar gains. However, this was in stark contrast to the Far East. In Dollar terms Japan fell by around 20%, Hong Kong by 30% and Malaysia by over 60%. It was like the movement of the tide, except that here the tide was one of money.

Japan's economy, the world's second largest, is in deep trouble. Far from growing, it may shrink this year. Overnight deposits earn 0.40%. Ten-year government bonds yield 1.57%. So Japanese banks and other investors have over the last few years discovered an opportunity too good to miss – US Treasuries, yielding over 6% in a strong currency and offering capital gains as well. The sums involved are huge. While Japan's GDP is around half that of the UK, the Japanese savings ratio is 14% of GDP compared to the US's 3.8%. Japan, therefore, saves twice as much actual cash as does the US. So is the remarkable performance of US financial markets due not to a 'new paradigm' but to something much simpler – a massive injection of additional liquidity?

There is no denying the US's economic health. Although in its eighth year of expansion, the US economy continues to grow without any obvious signs of increasing inflation. In the first quarter of 1998 GDP surged at a seasonally adjusted annual rate of 4.2%, up from 3.8% in the previous year. Unemployment stood at a 28-year low of 4.3% while inflation was running at only 1.4%. But can even this account for the strength of US equities? On the one previous occasion, 1961-64, when the US economy had this sort of growth while inflation stayed below 1.5%, the average price-to-earnings ratio was 19x and the average yield was 3.0%. Currently the S&P 500 Composite Index yields 1.4% and has a price-to-earnings ratio of 30X, having doubled in the last four years.

Something curious is happening and it is examined further in the accompanying Quarterly, 'New Paradigm – Or Old Bubble?'

Nearer home, the ratification of the Euro in May this year will be of great importance. Its launch on 1 January 1999 will create a single-currency zone comprising 11 countries. Euroland's $6000bn of GDP and 300m consumers will make it the world's second largest economy, just behind the US's $8000bn of GDP and 275m consumers. A lack of confidence in the proposed Euro seems to have been the main cause of Sterling's appreciation of 3% against the Dollar and 7% against the Deutsche Mark last year. This, coupled to UK base rates (at 7.25%, the highest in the developed world), attracted investors into gilts and other Sterling-denominated assets. In the future, however, we are likely to see increasing demand for the Euro and a relative depreciation of Sterling.

Compared to that of the US, UK economic performance has been positively anaemic. After six years of economic expansion UK growth this year should be around 2%, although any continued strength of an overvalued Pound could just tip the UK into recession. Headline inflation, at 4.0%, now stands at more than twice US and European rates.

This year saw a much higher turnover than usual in Personal Assets' portfolio. Last May we invested over 10% of our assets in adding to our bank holdings following the government's transfer of control of interest rates to a Monetary Committee of the Bank of England. This proved timely. Our purchases produced gains of 75% from Bank of Scotland, 47% from National Westminster, 44% from Royal Bank of Scotland and 37% from Barclays.

Towards the end of the year we increased our holding in British Petroleum and took a holding in Shell to give us a full weighting in the oil sector. We also added to our stake in British Telecom. During the year we switched our holding of 3i Smaller Quoted Companies into Advance UK Trust and acquired a 10% interest in Broadgate Investment Trust. Broadgate has a wind-up date in July 2002 and we bought it at a 16% discount to net asset value. Our long-standing commitment to investment management companies was reduced to a single holding in M&G following the acquisition of Mercury Asset Management by Merrill Lynch (which produced a gain of £1.2m, or 370% over cost) and Henderson Administration by AMP (a gain of £0.4m, or 140% over cost). We sold our Investors Capital Warrants at almost double what we paid for them, realising a profit of over £1.0m.

Of particular note is the appearance in the portfolio of 4 million Zero Dividend Preference shares (ZDPs) of Scottish National Trust, representing just under 26% of our total assets. Scottish National is a £600m investment trust that liquidates on 30 September 1998. On that date the ZDPs will be repaid at a fixed amount per share of 325.00p. They were acquired at a cost of 310.75p per share, giving us a gross redemption yield of over 7.25%. A holding of ZDPs is a particularly attractive way for Personal Assets to invest its liquidity, as the uplift to redemption will be received as a tax-free capital gain rather than as taxable income from deposits.

The last two Annual Reports showed our model valuations for UK equities, fixed-interest gilts and index-linked gilts for a three-year period. The models, however, proved quite useless this year in calling any downturn in the market. They simply showed equities as being even more expensive than previously.

There seems very little similarity between 1987 and now. In 1987, before the Crash, equities were 40% overvalued against long gilts. Equities then yielded 3.0% and long gilts just over 10% compared to 4.5% inflation. Today equities yield 2.8% gross (now worth only 2.3% to pension funds) and long gilts 5.8%, while inflation is 4.0%. Judged on their fundamentals, equities are even more expensive today than in 1987. Long gilts, however, are equally highly valued and it could even be argued that equities are slightly cheap by comparison.

Therein lies the conundrum. If long-term fixed interest rates are reasonable, then so are equities and we probably should not be 35% liquid. However, the world has enjoyed significant economic growth for more than half a decade. If inflation pressures emerge, central bankers will try to pre-empt them by raising interest rates. Inflation today is constrained by a strong Dollar, very weak commodity prices (in particular oil) and depressed Asian demand. But falling unemployment rates must eventually cause wage price inflation if growth continues at anywhere near current rates.

Equity market valuations tend to be high when economic conditions are good and low when they are bad. So an investor should, in general, gear up when economic circumstances are dreadful and go liquid when they are excellent. I cannot see how things can get better from here. So I intend to maintain liquidity at a high level. This means that we will underperform our benchmark next year if equity markets continue to do better than I expect. Protection of capital, however, I believe to be more important than short-term relative performance.

Ian Rushbrook
Investment Director

THE BOARD'S POLICIES FOR PERSONAL ASSETS

The Management Of Personal Assets Personal Assets is run by its Board. The day-to-day management of the portfolio is the responsibility of Ian Rushbrook, the Investment Director, and Robin Angus is a consultant to the Company and works alongside Ian on a part-time basis. The full Board meets monthly, the Edinburgh-based directors meet informally at least once a week, and we take all major decisions collectively. We are long-term investors and we measure our net asset value performance over rolling three-year periods against that of the FTSE All-Share Index.

The Board's investment philosophy

Our objective is to protect and to increase the value of our shareholders' funds over the long term and to achieve as high a total return as possible given our dislike of a level of risk significantly greater than that of investing in the FTSE All-Share Index. We distrust investment theories and 'investment styles' and in trying to achieve our objective we seek to be prudent and flexible and to use our common sense.

Guidelines for decision-making

There are, however, some guidelines which the Board follows in making investment decisions:

• *Meeting our shareholders' needs.* Personal Assets is managed as a flexible investment trust specifically for individual investors who may wish to invest a significant proportion of their capital in the Company as an alternative to holding a diversified equity portfolio. All our decisions are therefore taken with the needs of such shareholders in mind as regards both reward and risk.

• *Stable, long-term investing.* We dislike high turnover because it costs us money.

It also wastes opportunity, since good investments often take time to achieve their potential. It goes without saying that one needs good reasons to buy shares in a company. But it is not so often stated that one needs even better reasons to sell shares in a company one already holds.

- *Making worthwhile investment decisions.* It is difficult to make good decisions. Because of this, we work hard at the decisions we do make. We therefore want our decisions to have an appreciable effect on our net asset value per share, and it would be unusual for us to decide to buy or sell a quantity of shares which was worth less than, say, 2% of our shareholders' funds.

- *International diversification.* Most of our shareholders are UK residents or expatriates whose personal liabilities are denominated mainly in Sterling. We also assume that they may have invested a significant proportion of their net worth in the Company. The need for such shareholders to match their long-term liabilities with their assets therefore suggests that it is prudent for our portfolio to have a high Sterling content. Sometimes a degree of international diversification will be desirable in order to reduce risk. A suitable overseas (or non-Sterling) risk exposure for Personal Assets might accordingly be as high as 40% of total assets. But it might also be nil, because international diversification, like all investment strategies, is a means to an end and not an end in itself.

- *Recognising our own limitations.* We cannot hope to satisfy all our shareholders' needs. Personal Assets will never be able to offer one-stop investment shopping for global investors, although we do intend it to be able to supply most of the basic necessities of life for Sterling-based equity investors. We stick to what we know about and investors who want a stake in specialised investment areas should look for it elsewhere, over and above their shareholdings in Personal Assets.

- *Equity exposure, gearing, liquidity and derivatives.* Personal Assets is an equity investor. We therefore accept the basic risks of equity investment by maintaining, in normal circumstances, a fully invested portfolio. From time to time, however, markets may look particularly attractive and we may wish to increase our market exposure to more than 100% of shareholders' funds. This we will do through using either borrowed funds or derivatives (*futures, options, warrants and the like*). Alternatively, there may be times when the Board believes markets to be considerably overvalued. At such times we will either hold part of our resources in cash or use derivatives to lock in gains.

- *Bonds and currencies.* Owing to recent tax changes it is not tax-efficient for Personal Assets to hold fixed-interest gilts for capital gain and we will not do so. As regards currencies, if a foreign currency through the medium of which we held portfolio investments (at present this is only the US Dollar) looked unsustainably overvalued we would sell forward (if we thought it right to do so) all of our exposure to that currency, in order to lock in the gains we had made and to protect the underlying Sterling value of our foreign investments.

• *Unlisted investments.* The Board believes that for a trust like Personal Assets, investing in unlisteds absorbs more time and energy than it is worth. We shall therefore make no new unlisted investments and shall continue to value those we still possess on a very conservative basis until they can be sold.

• *Use of other investment trusts.* If we felt confident about the attractions of an area we had not invested in before, but lacked expertise in the area or could not commit to it sufficient money to achieve the degree of diversification of risk within it that we require, we would buy other investment trusts which provide the services we need.

Dividend policy

Our dividend policy is to pay as high a dividend as is compatible with our twin aims of ensuring that future dividend payments are as secure as they reasonably can be, and preserving a high degree of flexibility as regards investment strategy. We intend the present dividend of £2.30 per share to grow at least in line with inflation. It is also our policy never to cut the dividend rate. Shareholders can therefore be confident that each half-yearly payment will at least equal the previous one.

Personal Assets has a considerable advantage over most other investment trusts in that it has a much larger than average Revenue Reserve. Our Group Revenue Reserve now stands at £5.41 per share, well over double the current rate of dividend payment. In other words, we could pay dividends at the current rate for the next two years even if we had no earnings at all. This gives us the ability to maintain or increase the dividend even at times when we think it right to hold a portfolio with a much lower average yield than we do at present.

INVESTMENT TRUSTS FOR INDIVIDUAL INVESTORS

For whom do we run Personal Assets? Personal Assets is run for people who either possess a substantial amount of capital or hope to build it out of income. We want Personal Assets to provide for them an alternative to managing at least a substantial proportion of their own equity investments, whether directly or through professional advisers. In running Personal Assets we assume that our typical shareholder will pay Income Tax at 40% and will be exposed to Capital Gains Tax at the same rate.

This definition has bearing on our corporate actions where our shareholders' tax positions might be relevant. For example, such a shareholder would, we assume, be interested in having a PEP invested in an investment trust. Personal Assets therefore offers a simple, zero cost PEP, for which the unusually high minimum subscription level ensures that the Company can absorb without too much strain all the administration costs which would otherwise fall directly on the PEP investor.

Furthermore, it drives our attitude towards investment. Since the Directors and their families together own 29% of the Company, the investment policy we have adopted is the same as that which we would like to see followed on our own behalf.

Advantages of investing through investment trusts

For people with high incomes or substantial capital, the advantages of investing through investment trusts as opposed to managing their own portfolios directly or through a financial adviser are considerable.

• Such people often do not have the time or the specialist expertise to devote their full attention to their investment portfolios. Investment trusts offer them the benefit of full-time, professional portfolio management, while the direct relationship between the shareholders and the Board of Directors whom they elect (and who are responsible for performance) ensures accountability for investment decisions.

• Investors who manage their portfolios directly or through an adviser cannot offset the investment management and administration costs they incur against their taxable income. Nor can they offset the interest paid on borrowings for equity investment purposes. Investment trusts, however, can offset all such costs against their pre-tax income.

• People with high incomes are taxed at their top rate of Income Tax (currently 40%) on all realised capital gains in excess of £6,500 per annum. They therefore often find themselves faced with the unwelcome choice of either incurring unwanted tax bills or making 'tax-driven' investment decisions which in the end may cost them dear. Investment trusts, however, are wholly free of Capital Gains Tax on gains realised within their portfolios. They can therefore buy and sell investments as required *on investment grounds alone.*

Personal Assets for year to 30 April 1998

Company	30 April 1998 £'000	Purchase/ (Sales) £'000	30 April 1997 £'000
British Petroleum	2,362	589	1,239
British Telecommunications	2,273	553	1,131
Kwik Fit Holdings	2,094		958
Airtours	1,890		1,099
National Westminster Bank	1,797	407	730
Barclays	1,728	1,259	Nil
Rentokill Initial	1,704		890
Shell Transport & Trading	1,337	1,304	Nil
Scottish & Newcastle	1,316	19	951
Glaxo Wellcome	1,185		849
M&G Group	1,102		780
Broadgate Investment Trust	942	962	Nil
Royal Bank of Scotland	931	647	Nil
Bank of Scotland	921	525	Nil
Bass	738	(39)	558
General Electric Company	738		550
Tate & Lyle	585		551
Scottish Media	503	15	467
Ivory & Sime ISIS	464		365
Advance UK Trust	318	250	Nil
SEEL	168		168
Second London American	145	(55)	173
Investors Capital- Warrants	Nil	(2,273)	1,625
Mercury Asset Management	Nil	(1,530)	1,203
Henderson Group	Nil	(720)	581
Red land	Nil	(345)	350
3i Smaller Quoted Companies	Nil	(213)	226
Others	304	(48)	186
UK EQUITIES	**25,545**	**1,307**	**15,630**

Applied Power	1,610		940
Dover Corp	1,181		817
Bristol-Myers Squibb	1,013	12	638
Philip Morris	888		971
CalEnergy	781		964
Alltel Corp	767		582
Tyco International	Nil	(689)	489
USA EQUITIES	**6,240**	**677**	**5,401**
Scottish National ZDP	12,550	12,430	Nil
US Treas. Strip 0% 15/05/98	3,134	3,023	Nil
Net current assets	1,233	(5,601)	6,834
LIQUIDITY TOTAL	**16,917**	**9,852**	**6,834**
SHAREHOLDERS' FUNDS	**48,702**	**20.837**	**27,865**

Comparative values	30 April 1998	% Change over y ear	30 April 1997
SHARE PRICE	199.50	41.2%	141.25
NET ASSET VALUE/SHARE	180.21	34.6%	133.89
FTSE ALL-SHARE INDEX	2788.99	30.6%	2135.31
S & P COMP (£)	664.92	34.6%	493.86

APPENDIX 3:

Nils Taube

This is the way that Nils Taube's top performing unit trust looked at 31 May 1998. The portfolio reflects the strong bias towards financial shares which was one of his main investment themes at the time. Note also the relatively high proportion of cash and gilts, an indication of Taube's concerns about the level of main stock markets at the time.

REPORT OF THE MANAGER OF ST JAMES'S PLACE GREATER EUROPEAN PROGRESSIVE UNIT TRUST

During the period under review, 1 December 1997 to 31 May 1998 the offer price of St James's Place Greater European Progressive Unit Trust Income units rose by 31.9% from 537.6p xd to 709.1p and the Accumulation units (in respect of which income is reflected in the price rather than distributed) also rose by 32.76% from 843.6p to 1120.0p. On 30 June 1998, the latest available date before the printing of this report, the offer price of the Income units was 690.9p and the

Accumulation units was l092.0p. The estimated yield was 0.96%.

THE TRUST'S PERFORMANCE

The performance of the Trust since its launch in December 1969 and over the period under review is shown below, together with figures for the most commonly quoted indices in comparable markets where the major proportion of the Trust has been invested.

Money Makers

Performance summary

	16.12.69 to 31.05.98 % change	30.11.97 to 31.05.98 % change
St. James's Place Greater European Progressive Unit Trust Income Units (offer to offer)	+ 6,991.0	+31.9
Indices—		
FT Actuaries All-Share	+1,801.9	+22.4
M.S. Capital International (Europe (ex UK))	+1,270.4	+38.6
M.S. Capital International (Europe (inc UK))	+1,213.7	+33.0

Geographical analysis

	31.05.98 %	30.11.97 %
United Kingdom	19.8	28.2
Continental Europe	67.6	58.9
Australia	0.4	–
North America	–	0.6
Net Cash	12.2	12.3
	100.0	100.0

COMMENTARY

Over the last six months European equity markets have continued to perform well. The fund has appreciated by 32.76% while the index has gone up by 32.96%. (MSCI Europe including the UK.)

The fund continues to emphasise restructuring opportunities in Europe. As discussed in previous reports, the financial sector is at the forefront of this process. The coming of a single European currency is a prime motivating factor. At the time of the last report, the fund held 31% of its assets in banks and insurance companies. This is now 27.6%. As they have matured, some of the holdings have been sold, such as Generali and National Westminster Bank, and replaced by others, for example, Aachener und Münchener Beteiligung and Deutsche Bank.

The economic problems of South East Asia and Japan continue to be a matter of concern. As stated in the last report, the fund has avoided investment in industries

296

which may suffer direct competition from a flood of cheap imports from the region.

However, as European economies continue to recover, the fund has made additional investments in service sectors such as television and other media. Canal Plus and Hachette Filipacchi are examples of recent purchases. Central Europe is also an area of interest. It is a region which should enjoy relatively high rates of economic growth in the medium term, both because of its location next to richer neighbours such as Germany, Austria and Italy, but also because of the proposed inclusion of some of these countries in the European Union. The fund has recently invested in Zagrebacka Banka in Croatia, which has both interesting assets and an exposure to the recovery of tourism. Overall, the level of investment in this region remains low at 6.4% of the fund.

The level of cash and short-dated gilts (12.1%) remains high and the temporary use of the futures market to reduce exposure is a reflection of a general sense of caution. As ever, the fund remains poised to grasp opportunities as they present themselves, and over the medium term the prospects in Europe remain extremely attractive.

Taube Hodson Stonex Partners Limited
30 June 1998

Highest offer and lowest bid prices

Year ended November	Income units (p)		Accumulation units (p)	
1993	324.80	189.30	500.80	292.10
1994	382.30	302.90	590.40	468.00
1995	384.50	318.20	597.80	494.70
1996	462.10	346.20	722.20	540.90
1997	583.40	425.40	915.40	671.40
1998	727.80	538.20	1,145.00	845.30

Distributions

Year ended November		Net income per unit		Total income per £1000 invested in November 1986	
		Income p	Accumulation p	Income £	Accumulation £
1993		0.430	0.663	3.40	3.80
1984		2.222	3.432	17.57	19.69
1985		1,842	2.864	14.56	16.43
1996					
FID		0.614	0.959	4.85	5.50
Conventional Dividend		1.161	1.815	9.18	10.41
1997					
FID		0.106	0.166	0.84	0.95
Conventional Dividend	3.579	5.616	28.29	32.22	

Year ended November	Net asset value of trust £'000	Net asset value per unit		Number of units	
		Income p	Accumulation p	Income	Accumulation
1995	78,727	351.1	545.8	6,132,022	10,478,664
1996	112,708	436.4	682.0	5,535,282	12,983,507
1997	155,800	506.7	800.9	5,384.754	16,045,615
1998 to 31.05.98	229,671	670.4	1,059.5	5,254,568	18,351,778

Note: The above figures have been calculated on a mid-market value basis.

Portfolio changes

During the period 1 December 1996 to 31 May 1997 the following changes have been made to the portfolio.

Major sales	Proceeds £	Major purchases	Cost £
Aeroporti Di Roma	4,211,523	Aceralia Corp Side	4,273,275
Alleanza Assicuraz Di Risp	2,181,649	AMB Aach & Munch Bet	3,292,341
Assic Generali	6,363,980	BCA Pop Di Milano	3,802,087
Castorama Dubois	2,880,624	Canal Plus	6,775,983
Computer Services	2,681,215	Deutsche Bank	4,607,500
Deutsche Telekom	6,093,009	Deutsche Telekom	4,718,186
Elcoteq Network	2,820,834	Elcoteq Network	3,128,229
Exchequer 12% 1998	7,431,366	Exchequer 12% 1998	7,276,719
Exchequer 12.25% 1999	7,706,717	Exchequer 12.25% 1999	7,417,266
Exchequer 9.75% 1998	15,600,000	Genset	2,337,899
FIH series 'B'	2,172,448	Hachette Fil Media	3,977,877
Mediaset	3,081,386	Investor	4,010,152
Mediobanca	2,549,405	Kuoni Reisen 'B' (regd)	4,397,084
National Westminster bank	4,075,770	Rolls Royce	2,938,391
NovoNordisk		Saga Petroleum	1,601,411
Peugeot	2,165,751	Sveenska Cellulosa 'B'	4,504,646
SAI (Soc Assic)	1,973,295	Treasury FRN 09.03.1999	24,238,720
Telecom Italia Di Risp	3,055,812	Tryg Baltica	1,651,069
Top Danmark	2,388,156	Valmet	3,299,365
Treasury FRN	12,171,545	Zagrebacka Bank	4,994,578

Statement of assets and liabilities as at 31 May 1998

Holding		Market value £	Trust percentage %
	UNITED KINGDOM 19.79% (28.19%)		
335,700	Amvescap	2,204,710	0.96
375,000	Cable & Wireless 25p	2,599,688	1.13
1,046,594	Cable & Wireless 50p	4,934,691	2.15
394,000	CGU	4,391,130	1.91
179,000	Eidos	2,036,125	0.89
475,000	Great Universal Stores	4,133,688	1.80
593,217	Racal Electronics	2,245,326	0.98
2,626,000	Rolls-Royce	7,658,073	3.33
12,200,000	Treasury FRN 09.03.1999	12,219,520	5.32
666,000	Westminster Healthcare	2,021,310	0.88
116,600	Williamson Tea*	1,020,250	0.44
		45.464.511	19.79
	AUSTRIA 1.02% (1.78%)		
111,940	Julius Meinl International	2,342,013	1.02
		2,342,013	1.02
	CZECH REPUBLIC 0.87% (1.94%)		
19,008	CVM Mokra	314,678	0.14
100,000	Restitucni	1,669,454	0.73
		1,984.132	0.87
	DENMARK 1.50% (5.29%)		
45,000	Kobenhavn Lufthave (regd)	3.453,631	1.50
		3,453,631	1.50
	EIRE 0.00% (0.18%)		
		0	0.00

FINLAND 2.24% (0.00%)

104,980	Elcoteq Network	819,868	0.36
400,000	Valmet	4,310,081	1.88
		5,129,949	2.24

FRANCE 13.64% (9.25%)

86,482	Banque Nat de Paris	4,534,142	1.97
62,000	Canal Plus	6,914,238	3.01
30,000	Europe 1 Comm (regd)	4,354,199	1.90
65,083	Gaumont	3,285,470	1.43
5,285,250	Gaumont conv bonds 3.75 % 01.01.2003	738,046	0.32
88,000	Genset	6,016,339	2.62
29,000	Hachette Fil Media (regd)	4,889,761	2.13
2,700	Infonie	27,260	0.01
51,000	Transgene	566,858	0.25
		31,326,313	13.64

GERMANY 13.24% (7.84%)

48,900	AMB Aach & Munch Bet	3,448,163	1.50
12,187	Baywa (regd)	1,550,204	0.67
128,801	Bayer Verelnsbank	6,468,405	2.82
6,585	Cologne Reinsurance (regd)	4,915,193	2.14
100,000	Commerzbank	2,473,170	1.08
7,142	Commerzbank new	173,317	0.08
100,000	Deutsche Bank	5,276,555	2.30
19,000	Holsten Brau	2,548,844	1.11
22,120	Munich Reinsurance (regd) (50% paid)	6,170,652	2.69
26	Picnic Gastattenge*	8,943	0.00
104	Steigenberg Hotel*	53,660	0.02
(1,400)	Exposure to futures contract Germany	(2,677,490)	(1.17)
		30.409,616	13.24

	HUNGARY 0.77% (0.94%)		
3,200	Budapest Bank HUF 10,000 (regd)*	144,381	0.06
360	Budapest Bank HUF 1,000,000 (regd)*	1,624,289	0.71
		1.768,670	**0.77**
	ITALY 7.85% (14.49%)		
300,000	BCA Pop Di Bergamo	4,343,214	1.89
717,000	BCA Pop Di Milano	3,976,292	1.73
301,807	IFI	4,224,519	1.84
752,000	Mediaset	2,972,102	1.29
360,000	Mediobanca	2,975,062	1.30
2,780,000,000	Mediobanca 2% conv 01.07.2002	1,561,074	0.68
400,000	SAI	1,944,280	0.85
164,000	SAI savings	1,312,371	0.57
1,044,500	Telecom Italia savings	3,459,105	1.51
(720,000)	Exposure to futures contract Italy	(8,754,914)	(3.81)
		18,013,105	**7.85**
	NETHERLANDS 1.00% (0.99%)		
260,807	ABC Medicover*	799,678	0.35
143,550	Fulcrum	1,496,505	0.65
		2,296.183	**1.00**
	NORWAY 1.44% (1.10%)		
320,000	Saga Petroleum 'A'	3,315,151	1.44
		3,315,151	**1.44**
	POLAND 0.94% (0.58%)		
82,993	Fastfood Development (restricted)*	323,178	0.14
42,500	Fastfood development pfd*	304,149	0.13
136,707	Warta (regd)	1,536,897	0.67
		2,164,224	**0.94**

SPAIN 1.93% (0.00%)

500,000	Aceralia Corp Side	4,427,569	1.93
		4,427,569	**1.93**

SWEDEN 10.41% (7.26%)

400,000	Astra 'A'	4,925,645	2.14
25,000	Investor 'A'	847,207	0.37
127,868	Investor 'B'	4,358,260	1.90
152,868	Investor 'B' (SAAB)	126,294	0.05
500,000	Lundbergforetagen 'B'	4,884,533	2.13
300,000	Noble Biocare	2,766,271	1.20
70,000	Oresa Venture	487,866	0.21
687,700	Scania 'B' Wts 10.09.1999	1,192,310	0.52
258,000	Svenska Cellulosa 'B'	4,343,808	1.89
		23,932,194	**10.41**

SWITZERLAND 6.22% (4.63%)

1,500	Kuoni Reisen 'B' (regd)	4,953,446	2.15
3,000	Nestle (regd)	3,955,292	1.72
594	Roche Holdings	3,748,837	1.63
10,000	Sulzer Medica (regd)	1,642,336	0.72
		14,299,911	**6.22**

OTHER EUROPEAN 3.76% (1.50%)

264,000	BTC	1,092,782	0.48
13,631	LEK series A (regd)*	2,449,807	1.07
1,000,000	Manezhnaya Plosh*	1,330,104	0.58
286,000	Zagrebacka Bank	3,748,850	1.63
		8,621,543	**3.76**

AUSTRALIA 0.40% (0.00%)

202,600	Coca Cola Amatil	912,031	0.40
		912,031	0.40

CANADA 0.00% (0.02%)

		0	0.00

EURODOLLAR BOND 0.81 % (1.14%)

3,200,000	Stalexport 4.5% conv bonds 03.04.2002	1,864,230	0.81
		1,864,230	0.81

UNITED STATES 0.00% (0.61%)

		0	0.00

Portfolio of investments	**201,724,976**	**87.83**
Net current assets	**27,946,251**	**12.17**
Net assets	**£229,671,227**	**100.00**

All holdings are ordinary shares unless otherwise stated.

Comparable figures (shown in brackets) are as at 30 November 1997.

*Unquoted/illiquid and suspended securities.

Statement of total teturn

for the period ended 31 May 1998

	01.12.97 to 31.05.98		01.12.96 to 31.05.97	
	£	£	£	£
Net gains on investments		56,146.172		11,227,998
Other (losses)/gains		(4,762,738)		484,285
Gross income	2,829,658		1,673,585	
Expenses	(1,623,419)		(1,091,295)	
Net income before taxation	1,206,239		582,290	
Taxation	(355,600)		(207,325)	
Net income after taxation		850,639		374,965
Total return for the period		52,234,073		12,087,248
Distributions and equalisation		7,821		3,283
Net increase in unitholders' funds from investment activities		52,241,894		12,090,531

Statement of movements in unitholders' funds

for the period ended 31 May 1998

	01.12.97 to 31.05.98		01.12.96 to 31.05.97	
	£	£	£	£
Net assets at the start of the period		155,800,195		112,555,502
Movements due to sales and repurchases of units				
Amounts received on creation of units	23,005,833		14,671,175	
Less: Amounts paid on cancellation of units	(1,376,695)		(804,551)	
		21,629,138		13,866,624
Net increase in unitholders' funds from investment activities (see above)		52,241,894		12,090,531
Retained distribution on accumulation units		–		–
Net assets for the end of the period	229,671,227		138,512,657	
The prices per unit at 31 May 1998 were:		**Bid**		**Offer**
Income units		670.1p		709.1p
Accumulation units		1,058.0p		1,120.0p

NILS TAUBE'S INVESTMENT PHILOSOPHY

THS Partners are global stock pickers. We believe that, whilst stock markets in individual countries are often efficiently priced, significant valuation anomalies continue to exist between comparable companies quoted on different stock markets. Extending this concept, THS believes that successful business ideals in one country are often subsequently successful elsewhere.

With the catalyst of ever cheaper and better communications, these anomalies will increasingly come into focus as the globalisation of industries progresses, and as the investment community restructures itself to exploit them.

THS's investment process aims to identify the most glaring inter-market valuation anomalies, and to disclose attractive opportunities for cross-border fertilisation of business ideas. The central tenet of the process is, therefore, to compare company valuations on a global basis. If a valuation differential is sufficiently large and there is no good reason for it, then further investigation is warranted. The track record and motivation of management as well as the regulatory environment in which they operate is extremely important. We place greater weight on these factors than on the macro performance of individual stock markets.

THS Partners pays close attention to investment themes. Themes highlight the sectors to avoid as well as those in which to invest. This leads us to steer clear of commodity industries unless a management or restructuring story is sufficiently strong to overcome the inherently lower profitability of those sectors.

An example of a sector on which we have concentrated has been communications and the media. We investigated the telecommunications industry when it was entering a period of global growth to cope with the information explosion. Our search led us to the Italian telecoms industry, which was grossly undervalued compared with other countries. We took a substantial holding in Telecom Italia, which appreciated sixfold over a six-year period.

Other themes which we are currently pursuing can be broadly characterised as ageing (including saving), technology users (not producers), pan-European consolidation and the development of the consumer in emerging markets.

For example, savings have become much more important in developed countries where people now expect to live longer but recognise that they cannot rely solely on state or public pension contributions. With this as a back-drop, asset management companies, including the banking and insurance sector, have been and remain a significant area of concentration.

We have focused almost exclusively on Europe for our theme of 'developing consumer markets in emerging economies'. The rate of increase in the economic well-being of consumers in parts of Eastern Europe is much faster than that for most developing economies.

We have largely avoided investments in the emerging economies of the Far East because historically they have been priced at a premium to both Eastern European and the developed market opportunities. This has not recognised any discount for poor corporate reporting nor the fact that, in those markets, shareholders are very low in the order of priorities.

In Eastern Europe, however, THS understands the culture and is confident that those consumers are hungry for exactly the same things as their Western European counterparts. Supermarkets, shopping malls and fast food chains are examples of the many Eastern European investments that we have made.

Before making our investments we investigate potential target companies in detail. We lay great importance on managers with successful business track records, high levels of motivation and businesses with solidly growing cash flow. We are greatly helped in this pre-investment stage by our immense range of contacts whose specialist knowledge can accelerate the decision-making process. Although efficient global players will often be the first companies to follow, we look for soundly managed local companies who can exploit these new opportunities.

PERFORMANCE

In the recent CAPS survey of 84 pension fund managers the J Rothschild SJP fund, managed by THS, ranked 4th overall in 1997 and 4th over five years to December 1997. Professional Pensions awarded the

SJP pension managed fund first place in the large funds category (£200 million +) for its five-year performance to 31 December 1997.

Value Realisation Trust recorded the best performance for an international investment trust in 1997. The St James's Place Unit Trust Group, where THS manages 50% of the funds, was awarded second place in What Investment's 1997 Annual Awards – unit trust company category.

A long-term track record is important to us and we are pleased to have won on three consecutive occasions the premier Micropal award for the best smaller unit trust group over ten years. Other previous awards were for best ten year performance in Europe (SJP Greater European Progressive) and International Equity (SJP International).

By way of contrast, the following extract from the 1997 annual report of the St James's Place UK and General Progressive Unit Trust summarises Nils Taube's views on the UK market in early 1998. Note his concerns about the Asian economic crisis and his build-up of shares in the properties sector.

We were pleasantly surprised with the performance of the UK market last year in the face of uncertainties about the policies of a new Labour government and the continuing strength of sterling. Strong cash flows into UK savings institutions no doubt helped. Foreign investors, particularly Americans, have become increasingly active in Europe in general and the UK in particular. European integration continues, which has led to increased business consolidation both within the UK and across borders with other companies in Europe.

Sterling's strength has meant that the market's bias has tended to be towards domestic blue chip companies and large multinational concerns. Traditional exporters, especially engineering companies, have been harshly treated. The fund has only two holdings which come into this category, Rolls Royce and Oxford Instruments, and in both cases we think they have a good long-term future as they produce world beating products. Financial companies have been one of the main drivers of the market, the fund's major holdings being National Westminster Bank and Commercial Union, both of which have performed very well. We have also built up the exposure to the property sector with holdings of Great Portland Estates, London Merchant Securities and Quintain Estates.

The UK economy has continued its strong performance driven by the service sector. However, the labour market is now tight and there is upward pressure on wages, especially for skilled workers. With this classic sign of overheating, the Bank of England, in its new independent form, now has the delicate task of slowing down economic activity without increasing interest rates too far, which would make sterling destructively strong for many manufacturing businesses. The now well-publicised problems in the Far East look as though they may dampen world economic growth by some 1.5% on latest estimates, and this may be enough to help take the steam out of our economy, when coupled with the modest rise in short-term interest rates which we have recently experienced.

In the short term we are fairly cautiously positioned. At the time of writing the Fund has 19.5% in cash and short government bonds. It is too early to tell exactly what effect the Far East financial crisis will have, but we are now beginning to see disappointing earnings and words of caution from a number of US companies which may result in a mild set-back in Wall Street, which, as the world's lead stock market, would probably be mirrored in the UK. We wish to be positioned to take advantage of such an eventuality.

Taube Hodson Stonex Partners Limited
29th January 1998

APPENDIX 4:

Colin McLean

It has taken 60 years for value investing to become an overnight success. Only recently in the UK has it been recognised, although in the US, it has been a winner for decades – since establishment in the 1930s by Graham & Dodd, and subsequent adoption by Warren Buffett and many others. But I am not here to present a eulogy on value investing. To allow you to make a balanced assessment of the approach, I intend not only to describe its characteristics, but to put these in the context of other investment approaches. For, despite the enthusiasm with which value investing has been stuck as a marketing label on funds and management houses in recent years, the last three years have been tough for many UK value investors.

The first issue is defining the term 'value'. There is no single label that fully describes it. It is often viewed as contrarian, versus consensus approaches based on anomalies and possible surprises, rather than efficient market pricing. Many attempt to reduce it to simply a matter of yield versus growth. And, in style terms, we now have investors somewhere in-between value and growth, described as 'growth at the right price'. Do all these labels really matter? Surely every investor wants to buy undervalued stocks, in the hope they will go up?

Those who believe the stockmarket is efficient do not need an investment manager. Index funds were created for these people. And, indeed, for anyone else who thinks that shares might not always be correctly priced, but believes all investment managers are bad, and incapable of taking advantage of this. They can all take a random walk to the cheapest index fund. I have never believed that the stockmarket is efficient, but it is only in recent years that the academic evidence has mounted to put my faith on a firm foundation.

There is now considerable evidence that there are many systematic mispricings of shares, creating opportunities for investors. These opportunities are available to all – the question is just which style of investing captures more of these, more systematically, and with lower risk. In doing this, value investing must compete with other investment styles.

To describe the value investor's approach to these anomalies, I would like to start by setting aside current labels, and go back to the foundations of the discipline as explained by Benjamin Graham. Graham set out ten criteria for an undervalued stock, including low price to book value, low P/E ratio, low gearing and above-average yield. The factors were designed to ensure that a company was growing, did not have too much volatility in its earnings, and was not expensively priced compared to those earnings. There is ample evidence from public funds that this approach worked very well during the 1950s, 60s, 70s and 80s. But today many have, I believe, wrongly picked out individual value characteristics as epitomising the style, rather than recognising that Ben Graham was describing an overall approach to investing. Value investing requires many tools – it can not just be reduced to book value, yield or cash flow.

At the root of the value investing approach is the recognition that the stockmarket does not efficiently price all shares, all of the time. That is, on the basis of public information, it is possible to find shares where the current market consensus is simply wrong. Often there is a significant difference between stockmarket value and true worth. As our yardstick of true worth, valid measures would include current break-up value or the discounted present value of the likely future stream of earnings and dividends.

We do not need detailed academic studies to demolish the hypothesis of stockmarket efficiency. Each day there are share prices which fall by 25% or more. Yet even though this may be triggered by profit warnings or dividend cuts, there is rarely any evidence that true underlying worth in a substantial business can change to this extent in a matter of hours. In May, 1997, the biggest stock on the London market, HSBC, gained 9%, or £4 billion, in just two days. We do not need long-term studies to tell us what is plainly obvious from examination of any individual day's trading – much of what happens in the stockmarket does not make a lot of sense.

If share prices move around more than underlying company values do, we need some measures of underlying worth as our benchmark. Too many would-be value investors have assumed that, even though share prices may be wrong, they need look no further than stockmarket ratios to pick out 'Value stocks'. Rather than doing the right fundamental work on company values, they focus on screens, relative P/Es, and even what is published as 'cash flow'. I believe that this focus on relative value, rather than absolute worth, is the reason for so much disappointment from investment groups that claim to be value investors.

Thus, we know that the stockmarket sometimes gets it wrong. But we need to value companies on the basis of their future earnings streams, to establish whether the company is a bargain at its market price.

There is no single yardstick for this, but the most important underlying principle is that value investors view investment as part ownership of a business, not just buying shares. Good businesses are not necessarily ones where the share price has been going up, or which pay out a large dividend. Value investors look for companies that are generating enough cash flow to maintain their enterprises and renew productive capacity. Surprisingly, some businesses that appear to be cheap on price to cash flow are over-distributing. British Gas before its 1997 reconstruction was a good example of this. Growth is best organic, and should be funded from a company's own retained profits.

Value investors' analytical techniques are therefore business driven, much like those of a trade investor, with little emphasis placed on *per share* data. Earnings per share and price/earnings multiples are poor indicators of fundamental value – post tax earnings are distorted by taxation policies and capital structure. Share prices often reflect market perception rather than facts. By contrast, analysing

companies as businesses involves gaining a detailed understanding of profit margins, organic growth and strategic value – in other words the core business franchise.

The value investing perspective involves a focus on different accounting data than most investors. Value investors are more interested in operating profits than post tax profits. It is necessary to closely examine the constituents of turnover growth, separating real volume growth from transient pricing effects. Analysis also involves assessing margin trends, both for the individual company and the sector in which it operates. For example, it is more useful to look at return *on total* capital employed, than simply equity returns. It is also important to establish that returns on new capital invested are attractive. Only then is it possible to make a realistic assessment of long-term profits progression.

The key to any business is real sales growth, and a predictable margin pattern on that turnover. Where this can be cross-referenced to valuations by trade investors, then a realistic picture of fundamental worth, expressed as a multiple of sales, emerges. This value is adjusted for net debt or surplus cash within the business, to arrive at an estimate of the true worth of the enterprise which is directly comparable to stockmarket capitalisation. It is the difference between true worth and the stockmarket price that provides an opportunity for the value investor.

This approach will highlight anomalies, or bargains for the value investor. But, we all know that shares can remain cheap for some time. To convert the opportunity into performance for clients, there has to be a dynamic that releases the hidden value, and leads to a re-rating of the company's shares.

For example, where an undervalued situation has been caused by a violent swing in stockmarket sentiment, then we can expect that this pricing anomaly will self-correct once facts and fundamentals are re-assessed. Where the difference is due to an underperforming company which has an otherwise solid franchise, then new management, or a takeover, can be the catalyst for the release of value. In any event, share buy-backs and special dividends will often look attractive to companies that are focused on shareholder value, where their equity is too cheap. I have found that this form of value release, where a company takes action itself, to be the most frequent catalyst to market recognition of value.

It may well be that the opportunities identified by this value-based analysis are of growing companies. The stockmarket frequently fails to understand the ingredients of growth, and underestimates its persistence in good businesses. There are some undervalued growth businesses, just as there are many over-rated ones. That is why the perceived contrast between value and growth approaches misunderstands value investing. Where value investing does differ, is in its handling of risk, style of portfolio management, and time horizon. The prescription may be simple, but it is not easy for most investors to stick to – not least because there are usually a whole variety of other short-term pressures on the investment process.

Typically, value investors are less concerned with stockmarket risk, in the sense of month-by-month volatility. They are also usually less distracted by short-term relative performance of their portfolios to the stockmarket. After all, commercial risk is usually measured by the chance of losing money absolutely, over the medium to long term, rather than by what price a forced seller would get today. Instead, value investors aim to reduce risk primarily through intensive research, rather than mere portfolio diversification. Real risk lies within companies, and needs to be dealt with in the analytical process, whereas stockmarket risk usually diminishes with the passage of time. Sentiment is not an important factor in long-term capital accumulation. By focusing on the downside, value-based methods address risk *intrinsically* – aiming to ensure that shares are underpinned by real value. Rejecting bad businesses is an important part of value investing's control of risk.

Fundamental to value investing is what Graham called the "margin of safety". This is not just a matter of believing that the odds are in your favour when you make an investment. Instead, it is the extent to which an investment is supported by existing value. That is, a value investor should not buy an investment that requires a significant projection of future new business to justify its share price.

My own view of this established value differs from many of the North American practitioners, to the extent that I believe adjustment is needed for application in the UK. There has historically been far too much flexibility in the UK on accounting treatment. Even today's tougher accounting regime still carries over a legacy from past distortions. For example, in the UK, book value is a less useful guide to worth. Indeed, book values also fail to recognise the characteristics of the UK's dominant service sectors, where there are some good businesses based on relatively low investment of financial capital. It is important to understand the dynamics of businesses driven by know-how and human capital. Similarly, cash flow is frequently cited as a valuation yardstick, yet this is not usually cash at all, but just derived from profits figures.

There are more useful investment tools. If a single measure does characterise value investment, it is probably price to sales. (Given information on margins, this is a simpler alternative to relating enterprise value and operating earnings.) The normal ratio of market capitalisation to sales will vary from sector to sector, depending on average operating margins. But there is much less risk involved in buying, say, a manufacturing company whose profits growth will come from improving margins from 6% to 8%, than in buying one attempting to move from an existing above-average position of 12% up to 16%. Similarly, improving returns from existing sales and customers is usually easier than winning new business. Thus the risk framework of value investors is drawn directly from business principles.

Fortunately, although value investing is easy to *describe*, many become frustrated in *applying* it. The other half of value investing, after the analyses, is to do with the buying and selling discipline. Investors with a firm view of value should have the confidence to average down if the market takes a long time to agree. The size of the initial purchase should allow for this, but we should also remember that a fall creates an opportunity by itself. One illustration of this was a purchase by our funds last summer of Railtrack shares. We put a 4% position in each portfolio in Railtrack, which quickly fell to 3.6% as last September's party conference season hit the shares. The discipline of topping up the holding by 10%, to take advantage of this fall, also highlighted that, in fact, very few shares were available. The fall had taken place on low volume, and I became even more convinced that little remained to prevent the stockmarket from recognising the value of this business. In fact, within six months, the shares gained 60% – a remarkable re-rating for a FTSE 100 stock.

On both buying and selling, value investors must be driven by their own discipline and analyses. This is the best way of avoiding the reaction to events that is almost human instinct. Unfortunately, many investors' dealings are triggered by events or news, and this usually ensures that others are trying to do the same thing at the same time. To exploit the weakness of human nature in reacting to events, and its tendency to push share ratings to extremes in both directions, requires the discipline of dealing when there does not publicly seem to be any good reason to do so. Remember that individual shares can make money for some investors at certain times, but leave others with losses. Indeed, a short-term perspective and lack of patience can almost guarantee that a bad investor can lose money in any stock. Value investing is not just a type of share analysis, but encompasses an entire approach to portfolio management.

While I have mainly described share analysis, the value approach also works well in buying other investment trusts. In March last year, Scottish Value Trust purchased a stake in Kleinwort European Privatisation Investment Trust, 'KEPIT'. These shares were purchased at an average discount of 18% and, in November, SVT was rewarded with a liquidation close to asset value. What highlights the value investment characteristics of this, is that over that period KEPIT's net asset value actually fell slightly. It was the changing market valuation of the assets, rather than underlying portfolio growth, that generated SVT's 15% return.

In 1991, SVT started buying into Ensign Trust, a one time star investment trust that had dramatically fallen from favour, with continued downward revisions in its asset value. SVT started building up a stake at 20p, and found plenty of willing sellers. Indeed, SVT was still buying at 15p, and the price was continuing to fall. By this time, 15% of SVT's assets were committed to Ensign, and we seemed to be the only ones who believed the 40p net asset value. Indeed, we had done detailed work ourselves on Ensign's unquoted holdings, which included several good investments

as well as many bad ones. I think it was just as well that SVT was closed-end, because from the phone calls I was getting, it was clear that not all SVT's shareholders shared my faith in the value of Ensign as an investment. Fortunately, what happened next was that, within three months, Ensign was liquidated at 43p, and SVT's net asset value jumped 15% overnight. I think it illustrates well the application of value investment principles to investment trusts.

Value management is not just something that can be bolted on and applied by any organisation. For long periods, the reason why shares are cheap is all too plain to see. Building up a stake in a neglected and unpopular company can be very lonely. I think that it is important that a value investor has the right psychological disposition to take a contrarian stance, and hold shares for longer periods. To exploit the market's extremes of sentiment, a dispassionate attitude to investment is essential.

The entire value approach requires an attitude of mind and business structure to match it. Strong decisions are required, and usually the fewer people involved in the decision, the stronger the resolve can be. There is no point in structuring an investment management business merely to reach a consensus decision on value – by its nature such a consensus will rarely differ much from the stockmarket herd.

To sum up, the investment approach I have described has enjoyed outstanding long-term success but is not easy to apply. Over the short term, it will frequently lose to momentum investors, particularly in strong markets. Yet, while human nature should ensure that the stockmarket always offers opportunities for value investors, the unique demands of the discipline make it unlikely that it will ever be universally adopted. Thus, I see all the ingredients for value investing to continue its success in future.

APPENDIX 5:

Michael Hart

It is always interesting to look over a professional investor's shoulder and see how he keeps tab on his holdings. Michael Hart likes to put all the key facts on the economy or on specific companies down on a single sheet of paper, as the two examples given here show. Note the simple and straightforward style. One gives Hart's view of the world the way it looked shortly after the Thatcher government took power in 1979, which was still some three years before the global bull market in equities finally took off in earnest. The second is an update on one of Hart's longest standing holdings, Rentokil. The company has proved an outstanding growth share: its market value has risen from £301 million when Hart wrote his note, to £6500 million in mid-1997. The Appendix also gives the Foreign & Colonial portfolio as it stood at the end of December 1996, together with some interesting comparisons of how the investment trust's shares have performed over time against the components of the old FT 30 Index (now largely supplanted by the FTSE 100 Index). Note the wide disparities in performance over time.

UK REPORT (1979)

The last report was on 12 October. Quite a lot has happened including the ending of exchange controls, terrible money supply figures and M.L.R. shooting up three points.
– The index has fallen from 475 to 427 (-10%).
– The pound has risen from 215 to 220 (+2%).
– M.L.R. is up from 14% to 17%.
– Inflation progression 15.6%, 15.8%, 16.5%, 17.2%, 17.4%.

Bull

Weight of money despite no exchange controls.
North Sea
– self-sufficient
– surplus 1982 peaks 1983
– importing again by 1990

Conservative Government
– determined anti-inflation policy
– further spending cuts
– signs of success on labour front, miners, B.L., Shell drivers, Chrysler

Money supply
– M.3. 13% creeping back to 7-11% target

Strong Pound
Lower interest rates in New Year – New York trending down 500 share index P/E 6.8, yield 6.9% but gilts yield 14%.

Bear

Weight of money:
– can now go anywhere
– public sector disposals only £500m?
– rights issue

World trade prospects dull

Trade figures (1980)
- £1-2b. deficit
- large non oil deficit
- large N. Sea oil financial deficit 1980 and up to mid-1980s
- propensity to import

Negative UK growth (1980 – 2%?)
Inflation – rising trend until mid year, peaking 20%, 17% for year
Tough budget – £2b – deflationary measures.
OPEC?

Unions
- high level of settlements
- post Xmas confrontations
- steel industry strike on top of engineering strike
- rising unemployment and attack on benefits will raise the temperature 1½-2m.

Conservative Government
- high risk strategy
- PSBR, money supply, bank lending doubts
- U Turn
- 30 OFT investigations per annum

Profits
- only 5% increase 1980
- company liquidity
- firm pound
- dividends 5%

Inflation is still on a rising trend and wage settlements have been far too high. However, powerful groups of workers have stopped short of all out strikes.

M.L.R. is probably at its political limits and the money figures in January and February may give the Government an excuse to get rates down. Provided this happens gilts should be a reasonable market and equities may well respond. However, if the Government sticks to its guns and money is kept tight the pressure on balance sheets could result in shocks.

Company RENTOKIL
Date 20 March 1986
Final results to 31 December 1986

Price	FTA Index	Year to 31.12	Pre-tax profits	EPS	P/E	Yield	
157p	807.79	1985	£26.0m	8.0p	19.6	2.2	
		1986	£30.5m	9.6p	16.4	2.5	Buckmaster
			£32.0m	10.1p	15.5	2.7	Scrimgeour
		1987	£35/37m	11/12p			
High/Low	Relative performance from:		1.1.85	1.1.86			
182/127p			-26.6%	-3.1%			
ROE 25.5%							

Mkt cap £301.4m		% change	Profits		% change
UK Sales	£148.3m		£15.9m		+3%
	-2				
Pre-tax profits	£26.0m	+5	Overseas	£10.1m	+9%
Net profits					
EPS	8.0p	+9			
Dividend	2.44p	+15	Sophus Berendsen owns 55%		

Comment

Worse than expected results. The problem in the UK was the Property Care division which failed to pick up as expected in the second half. Contract services did very well. Overseas companies produced a 26% gain in local currencies but exchange rate movements reduced this to 9%.

Bull

1. Pest Control and other Contract Services continue to show good growth with profits rising by 15% per annum plus.

2. Overseas margins beginning to move up as Rentokil increases its share of individual markets.

3. Strong balance sheet – net cash of around £10m.

Bear

1. Monopolies Commission is to investigate the UK Pest Control industry where Rentokil is the dominant operator with a 30% market share. This will probably take two years.

2. Outlook for Property Care is still uncertain.

3. Increasing competition in UK Pest Control.

4. Rating is still high though the premium has been greatly eroded over the past few years.

Recommendation

Buy on falling prices. High quality growth company with some little local difficulties.

Holdings

F. & C. 1,250,000 @ 21p

FOREIGN & COLONIAL INVESTMENT TRUST
THIRTY LARGEST EQUITY HOLDINGS AT 31 DECEMBER,1996

1 (2) Shell Transport & Trading, UK
Leading international oil exploration, production and marketing group, which has a strong balance sheet and an attractive yield. 3.2%

2 (1) Robert Fleming Holdings, UK
An unquoted UK merchant bank with diverse operations and a strong presence in the Far East. 2.9%

3 (3) Hypo Foreign & Colonial Management, UK*
Unquoted holding company for our investment in the fast growing fund management business, Foreign & Colonial Management. 2.7%

4 (4) B.A.T. Industries, UK
Diversified group with cash-generative international tobacco interests, and financial services through Allied Dunbar, Eagle Star and Farmers Group in the US. 1.5%

5 (6) Glaxo Wellcome, UK
Large annual research and development expenditure has led to a wide range of new products coming on to the market, and the takeover of Wellcome has produced greater economies of scale. 1.5%

6 (8) British Telecommunications, UK
Long-term growth in demand should be boosted by falling prices, better marketing and a range of new services. The proposed merger with MCI will add to BT's international capabilities and reduce further the proportion for regulated earnings. 1.3%

7 (10) British Petroleum, UK
Major integrated oil group with an excellent record of performance improvement. 1.3%

8 (5) BTR,UK
Major international manufacturing group. The new management team is expected to improve on recent lacklustre results.1.2%

9 (12) Rentokil Initial, UK
International environmental services and healthcare group with an excellent record of growth and profitability. The acquisition of BET should continue this rate of growth. 1.1%

10 (9) General Electric Company, UK
Major electronics group with a strong balance sheet, some interesting new ventures and an attractive yield. 1.1%

11 (17) Foreign & Colonial Portfolios Fund – American Smaller Companies – Luxembourg
Specialist fund that gives exposure to growth companies which are too small for the Company to invest in directly. 1.0%

12 (7) Roche Holdings, Switzerland
Switzerland's second largest pharmaceutical and chemical company. Pharmaceuticals are by far its most important activity and prospects here remain excellent. The acquisition of Genentech added a new dimension to the group's traditional research work. 1.0%

13 (24) Walgreen, USA
An aggressive store opening programme and increasing contributions from prescription business provide Walgreen, the nation's largest drug store retailer, with strong growth potential. 0.9%

14 (18) Abbott Laboratories, USA
Diversified healthcare firm with strong market positions in pharmaceuticals, nutritional products, diagnostic tests and hospital instruments. 0.9%

15 (16) RTZ, UK
A world leader in the mining industry concentrating on the development of large, high-quality mineral deposits.0.9%

16 (27) Legal & General Group, UK
A leading UK life assurance company, which should benefit from favourable demographic trends, while the restructuring of the life fund should allow a good rate of dividend growth.   0.8%

17 (22) BAA, UK
Long-term growth in air travel, and the further development of retailing give good prospects for the operator of Britain's major airports.   0.8%

18 (2) Automatic Data Processing, USA
A provider of data processing services to a wide range of industries. It has a good track record and generates a significant cash flow.   0.8%

19 (15) Allied Colloids, UK
Manufacturer of speciality chemicals which should benefit from the acquisition of a similar company in the US.   0.8%

20 (21) United Utilities, UK
The merger of North West Water and Norweb should create substantial efficiency savings to underpin good dividend growth.   0.8%

21 (11) Foreign & Colonial Emerging Markets Investment Trust, UK
Specialist fund giving exposure to fast-growing emerging economies across the world.   0.8%

22 (-) Bayer, Germany
One of the largest chemical companies in the world and has strong positions in its markets. By concentrating on its core business units and a continuous cost cutting programme it should see strong earnings growth.   0.7%

23 (-) Illinois Tool Works, USA
Leading producer of industrial components and equipment with a strong track record of earnings growth, which looks set to continue.   0.7%

24 (-)VNU, Netherlands
Leading Dutch publisher of newspapers and consumer magazines. Having divested its printing business, the group is enjoying a strong recovery in profits as advertising in the Netherlands and elsewhere picks up, and it benefits from its recent acquisitions in the US.   0.7%

25 (-) Kingfisher, UK
Strong recovery in profits being led by B&Q, Comet and Woolworth, while consumer spending is expected to rise further.   0.7%

26 (19) Southern Electric, UK
The largest regional electricity company in the UK with a strong balance sheet and above-average dividend prospects. 0.7%

27 (25) British Gas, UK
Value is expected to be realised by the demerger of the company, and the resolution of outstanding contracts with other major gas producers.   0.7%

28 (-) Booker, UK
International food distribution and agribusiness group which should see gains from the takeover of Nurdin & Peacock.   0.7%

29 (30) Provident Financial Group, UK
A leading provider of personal credit in the UK, with a record of consistent growth in earnings and dividends.   0.7%

30 (-) National Westminster Bank, UK
Further rationalisation of the core banking business should help to push earnings ahead.   0.6%

Share price of Foreign 7 Colonial compared with the FT30 Share Index and its present constituents

5 years to 31.12.96	% change	10 years to 31.12.96	% change
Asda Group	+274.58	Reuters Holdings	+446.55
GKN	+246.63	Smithkline Beecham	+353.16
Reuters Holdings	+191.00	EMI Group	+292.76
British Airways	+172.34	GKN	+275.83
EMI Group	+148.79	Glaxo Wellcome	+261.14
NatwestBank	+147.47	Tate & Lyle	+236.77
British Petroleum	+139.08	Guinness	+215.52
Vodafone	+96.15	British Petroleum	+189.06
Lucas Varity	+93.48	Royal & Sun Alliance	+175.66
General Electric	+91.00	**FOREIGN & COLONIAL**	**+175.06**
Smithkline Beecham	+84.13	Marks & Spencer	+171.27
Marks & Spencer	+76.30	Cadbury Schweppes	+171.08
FOREIGN & COLONIAL	**+75.73**	Boots	+164.25
Blue Circle Industries	+67.41	Natwest Bank	+150.18
Royal & Sun Alliance	+54.88	BOC Croup	+134.81
FT ORDINARY SHARE	+48.74	Blue Circle Industries	+118.88
BOC Group	+43.20	FT ORDINARY SHARE	+114.14
Boots	+40.44	General Electric	+106.49
Peninsular & Oriental	+37.85	Grand Metropolitan	+103.08
Imperial Chemical Industries	+29.10	Lucas Varity	+90.99
British Telecom	+20.09	British Telecom	+82.64
BTR	+19.61	BTR	+80.95
Tate & Lyle	+18.20	Courtaulds	+53.52
Cadbury Schweppes	+16.98	British Gas	+49.17
Glaxo Wellcome	+11.14	Imperial Chemical Industries	+46.27
Grand Metropolitan	+4.08	Allied Domecq	+43.11
BICC	-3.14	Peninsular & Oriental	+21.26
Guinness	-9.94	BICC	+8.69
British Gas	-15.28	Hanson	-3.98
Courtaulds	-22.08	Asda Group	-4.66
Allied Domecq	- 25.32	British Airways	n/a
Hanson	-31.95	Vodafone	n/a

20 years to 31.12.96	% change	30 years to 31.12.96	% change
Glaxo Wellcome	+7390.37	Glaxo Wellcome	+31,290.73
BTR	+5161.14	Hanson	+24,048.15
Smithkline Beecham	+2036.89	Asda Group	+22,677.78
Grand Metropolitan	+1942.56	BTR	+20,332.00
Hanson	+1886.04	Smithkline Beecham	+8272.34
Marks & Spencer	+1883.84	Grand Metropolitan	+4634.17
Royal & Sun Alliance	+1822.16	General Electric	+4581.54
FOREIGN & COLONIAL	**+1815.54**	**FOREIGN & COLONIAL**	**+3528.68**
BOC Group	+1372.09	Marks & Spencer	+3517.47
Guinness	+1318.60	Royal & Sun Alliance	+3278.76
Cadbury Schweppes	+1302.10	Boots	+2777.61
General Electric	+1253.97	BOC Group	+2698.23
Natwest Bank	+1155.94	British Petroleum	+2610.87
British Petroleum	+975.60	Natwest Bank	+1983.88
Boots	+904.17	Guinness	+1933.33
EMI Group	+857.82	Tate & Lyle	+1516.14
Blue Circle Industries	+835.42	EMI Croup	+1193.31
Asda Group	+730.61	Peninsular & Oriental	+1134.68
FT ORDINARY SHARE	+693.23	Cadbury Schweppes	+1032.04
Tate & Lyle	+658.09	Allied Domecq	+890.55
Allied Domecq	+645.57	Lucas Varity	+882.56
Courtaulds	+449.99	FT ORDINARY SHARE	+809.08
Peninsular & Oriental	+407.28	Imperial Chemical Industries	+800.15
Lucas Varity	+359.21	Blue Circle Industries	+781.99
Imperial Chemical Industries	+356.76	GKN	+539.92
GKN	+285.41	Courtaulds	+484.47
BICC	+248.93	BICC	+146.49
British Airways	n/a	British Airways	n/a
British Ga	n/a	British Gas	n/a
British Telecom	n/a	British Telecom	n/a
Reuters Holdings	n/a	Reuters Holdings	n/a
Vodafone	n/a	Vodafone	n/a

JJB SPORTS

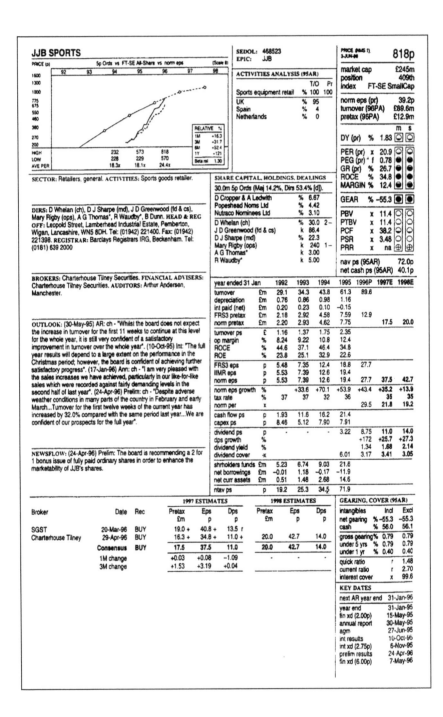

PRICE (p)	5p Ords vs FT-SE All-Share vs norm eps				(Scale 1)
	92	93	94	95	96 97 98
1600					
1300					
1000					
775					
675					
550					
460					
380					
270					
200					

HIGH	232	573	818
LOW	228	229	570
AVE PER	18.3x	18.1x	24.4x

RELATIVE	%
1M	+16.3
3M	+31.7
6M	+52.4
1Y	+121
Beta rel	1.30

SECTOR: Retailers, general. ACTIVITIES: Sports goods retailer.

DIRS: D Whelan (ch), D J Sharpe (md), J D Greenwood (fd & cs), Mary Rigby (ops), A G Thomas*, R Waudby*, B Dunn. HEAD & REG OFF: Leopold Street, Lamberhead Industrial Estate, Pemberton, Wigan, Lancashire, WN5 8DH. Tel: (01942) 221400. Fax: (01942) 221398. REGISTRAR: Barclays Registrars IRG, Beckenham. Tel: (0181) 639 2000

BROKERS: Charterhouse Tilney Securities. FINANCIAL ADVISERS: Charterhouse Tilney Securities. AUDITORS: Arthur Andersen, Manchester.

OUTLOOK: (30-May-95) AR: ch - "Whilst the board does not expect the increase in turnover for the first 11 weeks to continue at this level for the whole year, it is still very confident of a satisfactory improvement in turnover over the whole year". (10-Oct-95) Int: "The full year results will depend to a large extent on the performance in the Christmas period; however, the board is confident of achieving further satisfactory progress". (17-Jan-96) Ann: ch - "I am very pleased with the sales increases we have achieved, particularly in our like-for-like sales which were recorded against fairly demanding levels in the second half of last year". (24-Apr-96) Prelim: ch - "Despite adverse weather conditions in many parts of the country in February and early March...Turnover for the first twelve weeks of the current year has increased by 32.0% compared with the same period last year...We are confident of our prospects for the full year".

NEWSFLOW: (24-Apr-96) Prelim: The board is recommending a 2 for 1 bonus issue of fully paid ordinary shares in order to enhance the marketability of JJB's shares.

SEDOL:	468523
EPIC:	JJB

PRICE (p&s 1) 3-JUN-96	818p
market cap	£245m
position	409th
index	FT-SE SmallCap
norm eps (pr)	39.2p
turnover (96PA)	£89.6m
pretax (96PA)	£12.9m

ACTIVITIES ANALYSIS (95AR)

		T/O	Pr
Sports equipment retail	%	100	100
UK	%	95	
Spain	%	4	
Netherlands	%	0	

			m	s
DY (pr)	%	1.83	◐	◐
PER (pr)	x	20.9	◐	◐
PEG (pr)	† f	0.78	●	●
GR (pr)	%	26.7	●	●
ROCE	%	34.8	●	●
MARGIN	%	12.4	◐	●
GEAR	%	-55.3	●	●
PBV	x	11.4	○	○
PTBV	x	11.4	○	○
PCF	x	38.2	○	○
PSR	x	3.48	○	○
PRR	x	na	⊞	⊞

nav ps (95AR) 72.0p
net cash ps (95AR) 40.1p

SHARE CAPITAL, HOLDINGS, DEALINGS
30.0m 5p Ords (Maj 14.2%, Dirs 53.4% [d]).

D Cropper & A Ledwith	%	6.67	
Popeshead Noms Ltd	%	4.42	
Nutraco Nominees Ltd	%	3.10	
D Whelan (ch)	%	30.0	2-
J D Greenwood (fd & cs)	k	86.4	
D J Sharpe (md)	%	22.3	
Mary Rigby (ops)	k	240	1-
A G Thomas*	k	3.00	
R Waudby*	k	5.00	

year ended 31 Jan		1992	1993	1994	1995	1996P	1997E	1998E
turnover	£m	29.1	34.3	43.8	61.3	89.6		
depreciation	£m	0.76	0.86	0.98	1.16			
int paid (net)	£m	0.20	0.23	0.10	-0.15			
FRS3 pretax	£m	2.18	2.92	4.58	7.59	12.9		
norm pretax	£m	2.20	2.93	4.62	7.75		17.5	20.0
turnover ps	£	1.16	1.37	1.75	2.35			
op margin	%	8.24	9.22	10.8	12.4			
ROCE	%	44.6	37.1	46.4	34.8			
ROE	%	23.8	25.1	32.9	22.6			
FRS3 eps	p	5.48	7.35	12.4	18.8	27.7		
IIMR eps	p	5.53	7.39	12.6	19.4			
norm eps	p	5.53	7.39	12.6	19.4	27.7	37.5	42.7
norm eps growth	%		+33.6	+70.1	+53.9	+43.4	+35.2	+13.9
tax rate	%	37	37	32	36		35	35
norm per	x					29.5	21.8	19.2
cash flow ps	p	1.93	11.6	16.2	21.4			
capex ps	p	8.46	5.12	7.90	7.91			
dividend ps	p	-	-		3.22	8.75	11.0	14.0
dps growth	%					+172	+25.7	+27.3
dividend yield	%					1.34	1.68	2.14
dividend cover	-x				6.01	3.17	3.41	3.05
shrholders funds	£m	5.23	6.74	9.03	21.6			
net borrowings	£m	-0.01	1.18	-0.17	-11.9			
net curr assets	£m	0.51	1.48	2.68	14.6			
ntav ps	p	19.2	25.3	34.5	71.9			

	1997 ESTIMATES			1998 ESTIMATES		
Broker	Pretax £m	Eps p	Dps p	Pretax £m	Eps p	Dps p
SGST	19.0 +	40.8 +	13.5 r			
Charterhouse Tilney	16.3 +	34.8 +	11.0 +	20.0	42.7	14.0
Consensus	17.5	37.5	11.0	20.0	42.7	14.0
1M change	+0.03	+0.08	-1.09	-	-	-
3M change	+1.53	+3.19	+0.04			

Broker	Date	Rec
SGST	20-Mar-96	BUY
Charterhouse Tilney	29-Apr-96	BUY
Consensus		BUY

GEARING, COVER (95AR)

		Incl	Excl
intangibles			
net gearing	%	-55.3	-55.3
cash	%	56.0	56.1
gross gearing	%	0.79	0.79
under 5 yrs	%	0.79	0.79
under 1 yr	%	0.40	0.40
quick ratio	r		1.48
current ratio	r		2.70
interest cover	x		99.6

KEY DATES

next AR year end	31-Jan-96
year end	31-Jan-95
fin xd (2.00p)	15-May-95
annual report	30-May-95
agm	27-Jun-95
int results	10-Oct-95
int xd (2.75p)	6-Nov-95
prelim results	24-Apr-96
fin xd (6.00p)	7-May-96

APPENDIX 6:

Jim Slater

How does Jim Slater use his own statistical service, REFS, to pick shares? At first sight, the data looks dauntingly difficult to read but remember the information is intended for serious investors who are already familiar with the terminology of investment. Here is how Slater himself describes the process that led him to buy one of his greatest recent successes, the sports retailer JJB Sports. The different elements he refers to are labelled for easy cross-reference. In the key on the right-hand side of the page, the darker and fuller the 'moon', the more highly a share rates on that particular valuation criterion.

PEG = Price/earnings/growth rate factor

PER = Price/earnings ratio

PBV = Price/book value multiple

PCF = Price to cash flow multiple

PSR = Price/sales ratio

'BOTTOM UP' INVESTING

For bottom-up investors the individual company entries are the first port of call. After analysis, any company of interest can be put in context by referring to the Tables Volume.

All investment analysts have their own investment beliefs, preferences and particular ways of analysing an investment. I will demonstrate my approach by taking JJB Sports, a company I have recommended in the past, to show how I decide whether or not a growth share is a worthwhile candidate for my portfolio. I will work from the June 1996 issue of REFS, because I do not want the illustration to be construed as a current recommendation. The company has since had a two for one bonus issue and the share price, the company's circumstances and market conditions have changed a great deal since June 1996.

I might notice the shares of JJB Sports in the table of growth companies with very high growth rates or more likely in the table of shares with low PEGs. Alternatively, a broker might draw the company to my attention stressing that with its chain of sports stores and out-of-town stores, it could be a major beneficiary of BSkyB's increased coverage of football and a growing public interest in sports and leisure activities. The broker would probably add that the company has a vigorous expansion programme opening about 30 new stores a year and that like-for-like sales are also increasing substantially. My appetite whetted, I want to check the financial statistics in some detail.

First, I glance at the graph. It gives me an instant overview of a share that has performed exceptionally well since it came to the market in late 1994. EPS have been growing at a heady pace which seems set to continue. Relative strength has been excellent at +121% over the last 12 months, +52.4% over the last six, +31.7% over the last three and +16.3% last month. Clearly the strong momentum is continuing.

The average PER over the last three years has been 18.3, 18.1 and 24.4, so the company usually commands a high multiple. The present prospective PER of 20.9 is just above my normal limit of 20, but JJB Sports has obviously grown at an extraordinary rate, so I am prepared to soften that criterion a little provided other factors like cash flow and balance sheet strength are well above par.

Next I check the KEY STATISTICS. The market capitalisation of £245m is near the top end of the SmallCap Index. Promotion to the Mid 250 would be very positive, so I take a quick look at the Index Promotion Candidates in the Tables Volume. The table tells me that it is not yet a candidate for promotion, but is well within striking distance. I reckon that with its present rate of growth the company should be promoted to the Mid 250 Index within the next year or so (Note – JJB Sports was promoted to the Mid 250 Index on 24 March 1997).

The almost white moons show that the dividend yield of 1.83% is low compared with both the market and the sector, but this is not a major drawback for a great growth share, especially as dividends are forecast to increase rapidly.

The PER is definitely high and offputting. However, the PEG is very attractive indeed at 0.78, as evidenced by the almost full black moons against the market and the sector.

The growth rate of 26.7% seems low in relation to the past. It is four months since JJB Sports financial year began, so the 26.7% is a blend of the 1997 consensus forecast of 35.2% for 1997 and 13.9% for 1998.

Now I look at the individual brokers' forecasts. In this instance, there are only two – Strauss Turnbull's of 40.8p for 1997 is much higher than Charterhouse Tilney's 34.8p.

I check past increases in EPS in the large panel of historic figures. In 1993 – 33.6%, 1994 – 70.1%, 1995 – 53.9% and 1996 – 43.4%. I ask myself why the forecast growth for EPS has fallen off to 35.2% in 1997 and only 13.9% for 1998. I check the OUTLOOK statement and see that so far this year turnover is up 32%. I can also see that operating margins have been rising steadily with increased sales. During 1993 and 1994, a similar percentage increase in turnover resulted in a 70.1% increase in EPS. Turnover in 1996 was £89.6M, so a 32% increase in 1997 would put it up to about £117M. If operating margins increase by say, a further 1.6% to 14%, that would result in a pre-tax profit for 1997 of £16.4M – almost spot on the company broker's forecast of £16.3M. It therefore looks to me as if the 1997 forecast is okay, so the problem now is with the 13.9% forecast for 1998 – that is what is pulling down the forecast future growth rate.

Not unnaturally, the company broker expects growth to taper off. However, I believe that fast-growing companies tend to keep surprising analysts and anyway it is extremely difficult to forecast that far ahead. I look back nine months to the September 1995 issue of REFS to see what was being forecast then. For 1996 the consensus was 23.7p against the actual result of 27.7p and for 1997 it was 31.2p against the current consensus forecast of 37.5p. Clearly, JJB Sports makes a habit of surprising analysts. I therefore conclude that the 1997 forecast will at least be met and the 1998 forecast is more likely than not to be beaten substantially. Even if 1998 growth was only 25% this would increase EPS for 1998 to about 47p. The prospective PER for the 12 months rolling ahead would, as a result, fall to about 20. The growth rate would increase from 26.7% to 32% and the PEG would fall to a very attractive 0.63. Put another way, it is easy to see that if in 1998 EPS are 47p the PER will be a very moderate 17 in comparison with an attractive growth rate of 25%.

As the black moons indicate, both ROCE and margins are excellent. The five-year historic results panel shows clearly that margins in particular have been growing at a very attractive rate. This is a very healthy sign and is almost certainly an ongoing feature as turnover is increasing by leaps and bounds.

Gearing is negative (-55.3%) and the black moons show that the cash position is extremely comfortable. A cash mountain is always very reassuring.

JJB Sports is not an asset situation, so I am not concerned with the PBV or PTBV. The PCF of 38.2 is high but this is a historic figure. With fast-growing companies the current PCF is always much more pertinent. I am far more interested in the cash flow per share in comparison with EPS, so I look closely at the panel of historic figures and in particular the norm EPS line and the Cash Flow ps line. As you can see, since 1993, cash flow has been substantially ahead of EPS every year.

As indicated by the white moons, a PSR of 3.48 is definitely very high. High PSRs often accompany the high margins of companies with a very successful selling formula. With a growth share of this calibre, 3.48 is not a complete turn-off. It is more of a factor to be borne in mind and to keep an eye on in future years in case it gets completely out of hand.

Next, I look at the panel of historic figures and, in particular, at turnover and turnover per share. The growth in both is extraordinarily strong and consistent. I have already checked the excellent and growing operating margin figures. ROCE and ROE are also consistently well above average.

I check the FRS3 EPS against normalised EPS and I am pleased to find that there is very little difference between the two. The tax rate is normal, which is also reassuring. It means that creative accounting is unlikely to have been at work.

The JJB Sports company entry in the June 1996 issue was prior to a recent REFS improvement – extra lines have now been introduced to show PEGs and provisional PEGs. These give a helpful general idea of the likely level of PEGs in future years.

Cash flow per share is well above EPS and Capex is fine. I like to see a company spending money on expansion but, on the other hand, I do not like to see all available cash being absorbed year in year out. In the case of JJB Sports, the proportions are very healthy leaving a substantial balance of 'owners' earnings' each year.

My next point of interest is SHARE CAPITAL, HOLDINGS, DEALINGS. As can readily be seen, David Whelan, the chairman is the dominant shareholder. A quick reference to directors' dealings in the Tables Volume shows that he reduced his shareholding by a trivial percentage in April and an executive sold 32,560 out of 272,560. This is a very long way removed from cluster selling, so no alarm bells ring.

Now I look at the GEARING, COVER panel. Borrowings are almost non-existent and there is a very healthy cash balance. Also the quick and current ratios indicate great financial strength.

A final look at NEWSFLOW shows that the board is recommending a two for one bonus issue. This should be very well received by the market as the June 1998 share price of 818p is a relatively heavy one.

The KEY DATES panel tells me that the AGM is due on 27 June 1996. There will probably be another bullish statement then which should provide a further boost to market sentiment.

All in all, I conclude that JJB Sports meets all of my criteria and is a strong candidate for my portfolio. The next step is to obtain the Annual and Interim Reports, brokers' circulars and press cuttings before coming to a final decision.

APPENDIX 7:

Mark Mobius

One of the best features of Mark Mobius's emerging markets funds are the clear and candid reports that he writes for his shareholders and investors. The extracts that follow are taken from the annual reports of Templeton Emerging Markets Investment Trust and give a flavour of some of his recent commentaries on specific countries and markets. They are included here together with a summary of the trust's holdings at 30 April 1997.

LETTER FROM SOUTH AFRICA
(16 December 1996)

We arrived in Johannesburg after a flight of less than an hour from Gabarone, Botswana's capital city. Our principal purpose for visiting South Africa was to evaluate the prospects of adding new companies to our South African portfolio, but also to gauge the extent of political and economic change in the country. The trip took us right across this beautiful country from Johannesburg in the north-east to Cape Town, the judicial capital of South Africa, in the south-west. While I was in Johannesburg I interviewed many candidates for new analyst posts in our

South Africa representative office. We are currently expanding the office to meet the need for a larger analytical capability, commensurate with the increasing number of opportunities in South Africa and across the African continent. I decided to hire a local South African with a banking background and a Kenyan with experience in Kenya's Capital Markets Authority, the Kenyan equivalent of the SEC in the US.

Today, as we speed along the highways towards the airport in Cape Town I take the time to admire the view of Table Mountain and the bay, where Dutch settlers landed to found the city in 1652.

The Cape Town region is probably the most spectacular and beautiful part of South Africa, although people from Johannesburg and Durban may not agree. On this October day, the sky is blue and clear and the weather, although a little cool, is invigorating.

On the surface, everything seems peaceful and orderly in this country of 45 million people, but there is a strong undercurrent of tension here. The promises made by the ruling African National Congress, headed by Nelson Mandela, have not been fulfilled. Mandela makes speeches telling people to be patient. But in a country where the majority of the people have been waiting so long for basic resources, let alone prosperity, many are naturally impatient. Mandela has limited resources to spread around. Where he puts it is crucial for South Africa's economic prospects. In my view, the problem of inadequate education is of paramount concern since there is a shortage of skilled, and educated, workers among the black population able to undertake sophisticated, and productive, jobs. Government resources diverted into the education sector are likely to have the highest return. The numerous language barriers that exist in South Africa are also a major problem undermining the mobility of labour and the individual's ability to secure productive work. There are four main language groups amongst the black population of South Africa: Xhosa, Zulu, Sotha and Tswana. In each group there are many subsidiary languages.

Despite language difficulties, many economic migrants have travelled to Johannesburg from all over the republic. Johannesburg is South Africa's largest city with a population of nearly 2 million – and rising – and is situated at the heart of the gold mining district. It is a magnet for people all over the country seeking economic betterment. However, the dislocation that many migrants have felt after leaving tribal lands, and the inability of many to secure work have led to discontentment. As a result crime rates in Johannesburg have shot up. On the radio we hear advice to motorists not to make any sudden moves if their car is hijacked, because the hijackers may shoot nervously if they see the hands of their victims moving. In one part of Cape Town, vigilante groups have been formed to execute common criminals. The government's reconstruction development programme is designed to alleviate the problems of housing, education, electrification and fresh water. As we drive past the slums on the outskirts of Cape Town – which are a huge conglomeration of huts, built from scraps of wood, tin, rock and other materials – we can see just what a monumental task it is. Despite these problems, the basic infrastructure in South Africa is excellent compared to any other part of Africa and to many other parts of the world. The highway along which we are driving is evidence of this. It is a beautifully built, four-lane, tarmacadam road, which enables speeds of up to 120 km per hour to be reached.

The key questions for us as investors are: 'Is it safe to invest in South Africa and does South Africa have a long-term future?' Our answer is YES. The transition from white minority rule to black majority rule has been achieved relatively successfully and has confounded all the critics who predicted chaos and bloodshed on the streets. The fact that the crime problem is talked about so much and is attacked in the press is evidence that people are aware of it and are trying to do something about it. Another sign of progress is that the press is now quite free to criticise their government and parliament.

Although the adjustment process to a more equitable society in South Africa has been a difficult one for the country, its peoples, the economy and many companies, it has been a boon for some exporters. The abolishment of Apartheid has led to the opening up of many new markets to South African goods. In Durban, we visited a major tyre producer that was facing poor domestic demand and had begun to explore opportunities abroad. They had recently obtained the licence to sell their product in 70 countries around the world and had begun a big export drive. In the long term they expected stronger domestic demand for tyres. They said that in South America the average car age was 10 years whereas in South Africa it was 20 years so that there is good potential for growth in tyre demand as higher incomes allow upgrading of car ownership.

The next company that we visited was also looking abroad for new opportunities. This company, which had a diversified business base, was looking for opportunities in Angola, Zimbabwe, Zambia and Namibia and had established sales centres there. The company was also helping black businessmen to get started in the caterpillar contracting business. They said that they had sold 160 tractors to one-man contractors and that they helped them in the areas of finance, maintenance and a whole range of activities.

We currently hold 2.0% of the fund in South Africa equities. I believe that the future for the South African economy and its diverse peoples is bright. It could become one of the major emerging markets in which we invest, as well as the driving force for strong economic growth in sub-Saharan Africa.

Dr J B Mark Mobius

LETTER FROM PORTUGAL
(8 May 1996)

It is always a pleasure coming to Portugal since the people are so hospitable and the general atmosphere so genteel. When I first visited the country in 1988, it was very much a backwater and the country was still shaking off the cobwebs of many years of dictatorship and military rule. Now the cities and villages around the country are vibrant with life and activity. Most evident is the growth in modern retail distribution networks and a wider selection of consumer goods in the shops.

We started our trip to Portugal with the emerging markets, in general, experiencing a bull run and Portugal was no exception to this. The Lisbon BVL General Index was up about 15% from January to May 1996. In fact, the last ten years have seen a rapid expansion in the

Portuguese stock market. In 1985, there were only 24 listed companies on the exchange but that number had increased to 169 by 1996. Although Portugal's economic growth rate has not matched the spectacular rates of growth seen elsewhere in the emerging markets, growth has still exceeded that for many developed countries over the last ten years.

The Portuguese economy is more and more affected by developments in the rest of Europe, and less by domestic political and economic considerations. Just prior to my visit Portugal had had two elections: one for the Parliament and one for the Presidency. The Socialist Party won the parliamentary elections, although they fell short of obtaining an absolute majority by four seats. However, it is clear that whichever party is in control, the government remains committed to meeting the Maastricht criteria so that Portugal can participate in the European Monetary Union (EMU) and eventually share a common currency with the rest of Europe. Accordingly economic policies are aimed at ensuring convergence with the rest of the European Union (EU) on inflation and interest rates and there is considerable determination to override domestic issues, such as unemployment and welfare, in order to meet this goal of monetary convergence. This political will is reinforced by Portugal's proximity to Spain, its EU neighbour. It is difficult for Portugal to ignore developments that are occurring just across its border. For example, a 10% difference in the VAT charged on soft drinks between Portugal and Spain results in large retailers in Portugal purchasing international brands of soft drinks from Spain.

There are two factors that should prove favourable for the continued expansion of Portugal's stock market. First, and foremost, the government is looking to step up its privatisation programme. The proceeds from privatisation are expected to reach approximately US$2.4 billion in 1996. The list of companies in the government's privatisation programme includes banks, a cement company, a petroleum company, a shipyard, a power company, additional shares in Portugal Telecom, two tobacco companies, a mining company and an agricultural company. The second factor that should help growth in the stock market is the significant corporate restructuring that has taken place in recent years in order to cut costs and improve corporate earnings. This is a process which is likely to continue.

In recent years, there has been considerable consolidation in the banking sector which is still the most important sector of Portugal's stock market. In 1995, Banco Portuguese Do Atlantico (BPA) was purchased by Banco Comercial Portugues (BCP). Also, Antonio Champalimaud, a Portuguese who returned from Brazil, reassembled his financial empire, which was nationalised in the 1970s, and combined Banco Portugues Sotto Mayor (BPSM), Mundial Confianca, an insurance company, and Banco Totta & Acores. The merger of large groups in the insurance and banking sectors has resulted in a number of cost savings and improved efficiency. One company told us that it was able to save significantly in the bulk-buying of both supplies and services. For example, by hiring one security company, instead of several, to pick up cash from different branches of their various subsidiaries, it was able to make significant savings. In another case-savings of 6% were achieved on total telephone bills through larger scale and more effective purchasing. However, company restructuring in Portugal can be an expensive process due to the high cost of dismissing workers. If a company fires a worker, then the cost of dismissal is typically one month's wages for every year of employment. Although bank margins are quite healthy averaging between 2.5% and 3.7%, taxes are high and banks have tried to reduce their tax burden by moving some operations to tax havens such as Madeira.

Another interesting transformation that is taking place in Portugal is in the retail market. Over the last decade, traditional retail outlets were overtaken by large retail chains. As a result, hypermarket and supermarket sales now represent over 30% of the total market. The country currently has about 35 hypermarkets, 680 supermarkets and 280 furniture discount markets. Shopping centres are now common across most parts of the country. However, supermarket operators are being hampered by restrictions on the size of stores that are allowed. These regulations were designed to protect small retailers who have gradually been squeezed out of the market by the entry of larger entities. One supermarket and hypermarket operator mentioned that since 1994 larger stores had to obtain special licences to

open. The company solved this problem by dividing its large shopping centres into separate units of less than 2000 square metres each which are run as single stores but from a legal and tax point of view are regarded separately.

In the communication sector the merger of three government-controlled telecommunication companies into one single organisation, Portugal Telecom, has transformed the sector. Portugal Telecom has the exclusive right to operate fixed lines until the year 2003. As domestic and international call tariffs decline, it is expected that traffic will rise. One obvious efficiency improvement is that before this reorganisation there was a long waiting list for telephone lines but now lines are being installed much more quickly.

While Portugal may not show the explosive economic growth that some Asian economies have, there are nevertheless strong reasons for optimism. The pace and direction of structural economic reform is clear and this will allow Portugal to catch up with its more developed European neighbours. At the same time the corporate sector has been transformed and large efficiency gains have been realised through the application of more modern management techniques. *Dr J B Mark Mobius*

MEXICO CITY, MEXICO
(26 July 1995)

Mexico was the worst-performing emerging market for the 12 months ended 30 April 1995: following the massive 45% devaluation of the Mexican peso against the US dollar, the market showed a fall of 49%. In Mexico, as in other emerging markets, significant political and social changes are taking place which will have an inestimable impact on the overall development of the economy. One party, the Partido Revolucionario Institucional (PRI) has been in power since the 1920s. However, recently its position has been weakened as a result of the ongoing Zapatista uprising in Chiapas, the unsolved murder of presidential candidate Luis Donaldo Colosio in March 1994, and the September 1994 assassination of Jose Francisco Ruiz Massieu, the PRI's secretary general.

In February 1995, Mexico's attorney general announced that one of the leaders in charge of security on the day candidate Colosio was shot, had hired a former colleague to assassinate Massieu. Even more shocking was the accusation of Massieu's brother, Mario Ruiz Massieu, that the chain of command led back from the gunman to a PRI deputy, arousing suspicion that others in Mexico's ruling party might be involved. Then, in March of this year, Raul Salinas, brother of former Mexican President Carlos Salinas, was arrested on suspicion of being the mastermind behind Massieu's assassination. Since the families of former heads of state have had an unspoken immunity for more than six decades, this was a brave move for President Ernesto Zedillo and Attorney General Antonio Lozano.

Mexico's currency problems started in September 1994 when Massieu was assassinated as reserves fell from US$29 billion in September to US$17 billion in October. But even though money was leaving Mexico at an astonishing rate, the market continued to rely on the ability of the new government to defend its currency and cover it deficits.

When President Zedillo took office on 1 December 1994, the exchange rate was 3.438 pesos to one US dollar, Zedillo's inauguration speech was less than impressive and did nothing to allay the market's fears that something was amiss. When he went to Chiapas on 8 December, he was not well received by the populace and the rebels questioned the legitimacy of the newly inaugurated governor.

On Friday, the 16th, the Treasury Minister announced that he would hike interest rates to defend the peso. Two or three billion US dollars left the country that day. At that time, the exchange rate was 3.462 pesos to one US dollar. The outflows continued and by 20 December, reserves were down to US$9 billion. Finance Minister Jaime Serra Puche and the Pacto Group, comprised of business, labour and government officials, held an emergency meeting and agreed to raise the ceiling of the US dollar to peso trading band from 3.4712 to 4.0016. The next morning Jaime Serra Puche went on radio and television to say that this was not a devaluation. With that, the panic was on. By the evening, reserves had declined to US$3 billion. On 21 December, the exchange rate had fallen 3.977 pesos to one US dollar. On 22 December, the Pacto Group held another meeting and decided to float the currency. The exchange rate plummeted to 4.70 pesos to one US dollar and ended the year at 4.90. Between 1 December and 31 December, the peso fell in value by 43% versus the US dollar. The government was paralysed.

During this period, we witnessed the extreme reaction you would expect under such conditions. The world was shocked by the devaluation, and the credibility of the central bank was greatly damaged. Investors remembered that just a few months before, Mexican officials had assured them that such a devaluation was out of the question. Some said they felt betrayed. While just a short time before Mexico was praised almost unanimously, now market commentators questioned whether the Mexican financial system was sound enough to resist pressures from the aftershocks of devaluation. Fears surfaced that US$25 billion in peso denominated Cetes (Treasury Bills) or Tesobonos (US dollar denominated government obligations) maturing within six months would create a crisis and threaten the remaining central bank reserves and the credit lines from the IMF and the United States.

Why did so much go wrong in such a short time? I believe that over-consumption, low domestic savings, an unfavourable trade balance and a huge current account deficit were the root causes. In my opinion, the Mexican government was too complacent about its large trade imbalance. The salinas Administration believed that the imbalance was caused by companies importing capital goods and that these goods would eventually improve productivity and result in GDP growth

and increased exports. Instead, the economic growth resulted in higher inflation and an overvalued currency, making exports less competitive and leading to an even worse trade situation.

An additional problem was caused by the heavy reliance on portfolio inflows as opposed to direct investments. Finally, the US government, multilateral institutions and others, did not issue warnings which could have led to a more effective and orderly adjustment. Major institutions were emphasising short-term profit opportunities and encouraged short-term investments into Mexico in a search for higher profits.

What can we learn from the Mexican experience? It shows that events in one market can quickly spill over to other markets as international investors increasingly view markets as part of a global whole. As we have seen, investors all over the world reacted to the Mexican situation: Brazil, Argentina and other markets fell rapidly in sympathy with Mexico, despite fundamentally different economic frameworks and experiences. In such cases, investor psychology dominates and if many investors become bearish about Latin America, emerging markets in general may turn down, even though the financial and economic realities do not warrant it. Over the long term, however, we can expect to see significant divergences between different markets. Some will go up while others go down and it is important not to confuse the macroeconomic picture with the microeconomic picture.

Another important point to remember is that the best opportunities to purchase stocks at bargain prices may arise when a country's debt provision, trade balance and other indicators seem disastrous. Taking advantage of such opportunities, of course, requires considerable research, a willingness to take risks and an ability to take a long view. Those who are impatient and afraid of short-term movements should not invest in emerging markets such as Mexico. For those prepared to take a longer-term view we believe there will be ample rewards. Although the net asset value per share of your Company fell by 3.1% over the year the long-term record remains encouraging. Net asset value per share has grown by 241.1% since its first publication on 31 July 1989. This compares favourably with the rise of 166.0% in the IFC Investable Composite Index over the same period and contrasts with a rise of 44.0% in the Morgan Stanley World Capital Index, an indicator of developed market performance. Based on wide-ranging socio-economic factors we believe future long-term out-performance by the emerging markets is likely, although the level of this outperformance cannot be expected to be as large as in the last six years.

Dr J B Mark Mobius

MADRAS, INDIA
(1 August 1994)

After a fast-paced week of meetings here, I can safely say I've seen a country that offers far greater investment potential than immediately apparent although it will take some time before this potential is fully realised.

Much of the emerging market community's attention lately has been focused on the exciting new opportunities in China, and rightly so. Admittedly, India today poses colossal headaches for interested fund managers with money to invest, but if it succeeds in capital markets reform – and there are some absolutely critical steps to be taken – it will offer just as much long-term growth potential for foreign shareholders. It's a process that's well worth watching for our projections at Templeton show that over the next two decades the Chinese and Indian stockmarkets will grow to become the two largest in the world, well ahead of the US and Japan.

Ask about India and many people will think first about negatives. They'll cite its extreme poverty, low adult literacy, headline-grabbing communal violence and terrorist incidents, and tradition of highly bureaucratic government intervention in the economy that generally hinders free market development. Of course, this is a highly distorted, simplistic picture.

For one thing, as I've noticed in my travels this week to Bombay, New Delhi, Goa, Madras and other cities, India already has the world's largest middle class. It's a well-educated, more than 200 million-strong segment of society showing a strong appetite for consumer goods. They live in a country of more than 900 million people, the world's second most populous after China – whose recent fast pace of economic and political liberalisation has had a noticeable impact on India. Business and government leaders here might be the last to admit it, but they've seen the dizzying pace at which international capital has poured into China in response to its ongoing reforms, and know they can no longer afford to risk being left out of these opportunities.

Taken by itself, this middle-class block is already larger than the entire populations of all other emerging market countries save for China. By some estimates, it's growing at 12% a year – or six times faster than the Indian population at large. Its buying power is being aided by an annual inflation rate that has fallen to about 8.5% (about half what it was two years ago). In the overall economy, fiscal deficits as a share of Gross Domestic Product (GDP) have been cut from about 8.5% to 6% in the last two years. Today's 3.5% annual GDP growth rate could soon reach about 6% a year and stay there for the rest of the decade, depending on agricultural production and other factors. That's not China-style growth, but as personal incomes rise, well-managed local companies with quality products to sell to 200 million or so middle-class Indians deserve more than a fleeting look from foreign investors.

Take, for example, one Bombay pharmaceutical manufacturer I visited. This company expects to benefit from one of the government's new market-orientated reforms decontrolling the price of many prescription drugs. Its sales have already increased dramatically over the previous year's figures, and should rise again in response to this policy decision. But that only begins to touch the surface of its potential, for in India per capita consumption of drugs is well under what it is in developed countries.

Or consider an agrochemical firm I saw in New Dehli. This firm is owned by one of the country's top industrial groups, and is building a highly efficient mega-plant in Rajasthan to supplement its impressive existing operations. At this point, agriculture-dominated India is a net importer of fertiliser and with the need for food production rising, those domestic producers that can compete with foreign suppliers have no trouble selling. This firm has a good image and sales network, and should do well in the years ahead.

Of course everything is not perfect. We have to deal, in some cases, with poor information flow and very difficult travel conditions. India's largest stock market, the Bombay Stock Exchange (BSE), has been in business since 1887, making it the oldest one in the developing world. It boasts a market capitalisation of US$70.8 billion, making it the seventh largest in the developing world after Malaysia, Mexico, Taiwan, South Korea, Thailand and Brazil. The BSE has shown about an eight-fold increase since 1987 and today is more than twice the cumulative size of the Chinese markets – which have only been around since 1991.

The Bombay Sensitive Index, comprised of 30 companies representing 18 industries, has climbed steadily in the past year, rallying last fall to hit an 18-month high, and some experts say divestiture of large state-owned enterprises and existing corporations who need to expand their capital base could add billions of dollars to its value in the next few years. But, foreign investors will probably not be the key players as they were in some other emerging market countries. India already has 15 million shareholders – more than any other country in the world except the United States. Bombay expects to have at least 50 million of them by the year 2000. This comes in a country that has a sustained savings rates of better than 20% of GDP, high for the developing world, and on a par with far more developed countries like South Korea.

Until recently, middle-class and wealthy Indians have put only a tiny share of their savings in the stockmarket, but this has begun to change rapidly. The government's recent moves are fostering a boom in the private mutual fund industry, which should greatly increase the efficiency of domestic investment on the markets. All this spells rising domestic demand for equities.

Prime Minister Narasimha Rao and Finance Minister Manmohan Singh have broken with tradition and allowed foreign institutional investors to start buying directly on the local markets. Since they did so in September 1992, about US$800 million has flown into Indian equities, and much more is lying in wait. There are also billions of dollars in potential investment from wealthy Indians abroad that most observers say has yet to come home. Return of similar flight capital helped fuel the boom in the Latin markets a few years back, and is doing the same in India.

India isn't getting as much attention in the international press as its faster rising neighbour, China, but it has a much deeper tradition of private sector activity,

capital markets and democracy, and a universal use of English. The potential is vast, but unfortunately, so are the problems, which is why the Templeton Emerging Markets Investment Trust has not had many Indian holdings in its portfolio.

Liquidity and access to reliable financial information are major problems. Far worse are the settlement and clearance delays that bog down India's exchanges. Continued use of outdated settlement and clearance practices often make exchanges a nightmare to foreign investors who find them much tougher to access than markets in Asia and Latin America. To reach its potential, capital market reforms are urgently needed. The entire system must be upgraded, starting with a central depository system and computerisation. We expect that the necessary reform steps will eventually be taken, and when the right climate exists, we will be interested in adding to our Indian portfolio. In the meantime, we will monitor the pace of change closely.
J B Mark Mobius

CHIANG MAI, THAILAND
(30 July 1993)

Chiang Mai has changed considerably since I first visited it in the 1960s. At that time I was living in Thailand and Bangkok, the capital, was just an emerging city profiting from an American-financed Vietnam War boom. Thailand allowed the US to develop several army bases within the country to support the Vietnam War and Chiang Mai the 'northern regional capital' was little more than a backwater town. Today it is a thriving and bustling city. At that time I purchased shares in the first international class hotel in Chiang Mai, the Rincome Hotel. The shares were purchased on the 'Bangkok Stock Exchange', founded by an American entrepreneur, Willis Bird, and operated out of his finance company office. In those days the concept of purchasing shares in companies on an open market was new to the Thais. However, the idea soon caught on and the Bangkok Stock Exchange was made defunct by new regulations mandating the government-controlled Thailand Stock Exchange. Unfortunately the Rincome Hotel listing was not transferred to the new exchange. This provided me with one of my early lessons of the benefits of stock exchange listings and their role in providing liquidity. But the hotel is still in business and despite past crises and near bankruptcy, now pays dividends to its shareholders.

We came to Chiang Mai on the way to visit one of our more remotely located holdings, Padaeng Industry. The trip from Chiang Mai started at 5.00 o'clock in the morning and after a four-hour drive through peaceful farmlands and brush we arrived at Tak Province and the city of Tak where the Padaeng plant is located. Upon arrival at Tak, Dr Ing. Kitisil Kalayanakoul (Thai names are real tongue twisters) and his colleagues gave us an explanation of operations and tour of the well-managed plant. The zinc mine at Mae Sot near Tak, which provides the raw ore for the plant, was first discovered by Japanese soldiers during World War II who spotted a distinctive plant which turns red when the

earth has high concentrations of zinc ore. Development of the site, however, had to wait until well after the end of the war.

As we moved through the plant, we noticed that the company has begun producing an alloy of aluminium and zinc that is most often used in die-casting for automobile parts, home appliances, toys and other products. Our hosts proudly told us that the automated ingot production equipment which collected molten alloy from the furnace, poured it into moulds, cooled the moulds and then released the ingots and stacked them automatically was produced by the plant's engineers. They copied the technology from the larger zinc ingot production equipment originally imported from Europe. It is another example of what we see so often in emerging markets, the successful transfer of productivity-enhancing technology at a low cost from a developed to an emerging country.

The plant's officers told us that currently in Europe and America investment in new equipment and high costs associated with pollution control requirements were driving many of the producers out of business. They added that the pollution control regulations in Thailand were also very stringent, but with the newer equipment and technology the expense to meet those requirements was not as high as with older plants in Europe. One manager assured us that the pollution control standards in Thailand were every bit as stringent as in other countries. He joked: "Our own pollution control people in government travel around the world to copy all the regulations, combine them and now apply them to us so that we end up with even more stringent pollution controls!" But it was clear to us that the company was up to the challenge. Near the plant was a large settling pond used to store treated waste water prior to releasing it into the nearby river. Large fish were happily swimming in the pond, living proof, the plant officers pointed out, of the adequacy of the purification techniques used. They said they occasionally had a clean fresh fish for dinner from the pond's stock.

We departed the Tak Province plant in the afternoon for Phitsanuluk, passing the historic town of Sukhothai with its famous ruins of one of Thailand's ancient kingdoms. That kingdom was carved out of territories ruled by the Khmers whose Angkor empire stretched from what is now Cambodia. The Sukhothai kingdom declared its independence in 1236 AD and expanded its influence by taking advantage of the declining Khmer power and a weakening Sri vi jay a empire (headquartered in what is now Sumatra, Indonesia) to the south. Sukhothai is considered by the Thais to be the first true Thai kingdom partly because one of the Sukhothai kings, Ram Khamheng, organised a writing system which became the basis for modern Thai script. He is also credited with codifying the Thai form of Theraveda Buddhism, as borrowed from the Singhalese in Sri Lanka (Ceylon). This ability of the Thais to successfully absorb and integrate many cultural influences while remaining unique is testament to the country's strong cultural and religious underpinnings. However, there is a historical wariness of foreigners. The Ayuthaya kingdom which succeeded the

Sukhothai were receiving European visitors as early as the 16th century with the Portuguese establishing an Embassy in 1511, followed by the Dutch in 1605, the English in 1612 and the French in 1662. During the reign of King Narai in Ayuthaya in the 17th century, a Greek, Constantine Phaulkon, became a high official. But he made the mistake of allowing French soldiers to be stationed in the Kingdom and the Thais, fearing a coup d'etat, expelled the French and executed Phaulkon. The word for foreigners of European descent in Thai is 'farang', an abbreviated form of 'farangset', meaning 'French'. The country was sealed from the west for 150 years after this incident. Thereafter Thailand successfully managed to avoid being colonised, while her neighbours were ruled by the British (Burma and Malaysia) and the French (Indochina).

During the years of my travel in Thailand, the most remarkable change has been the considerable improvement in road infrastructure in the historically neglected 'up country' areas outside the capital city, Bangkok. Both the road from Chiang Mai to Tak and the road from Tak to Phitsanuluk are well paved even though they traverse some of the most desolate areas of the country.

The Thai royal family have shown great interest in rural improvements in the less developed area in the north and northeast and spend a considerable amount of time in the rural areas. They often use their palace in Chiang Mai as the base for such activities. Nevertheless, the lifestyles and living standards of 'up country' are a far cry from that found in the capital city.

Even when it comes to plane connections, all routes lead to Bangkok. In order to travel to our next destination in the northeast of the country, we had to fly to Bangkok, stay overnight, and depart our hotel at dawn for the flight to Kohn Kaen, a bustling and dusty rural town. The Indian-Thai venture, Phoenix Pulp and Paper, was originally established to utilise the abundant supplies of kenaf in the area. However, as the company has expanded to a capacity of 100,000 tons per year and is building a new plant which will double capacity, supplies of kenaf are not sufficient and now bamboo and eucalyptus timber have been added to the raw material supply which amounts to a requirement of 400,000 tons per year. In addition to 870 directly employed workers, the company is proud of the fact that they provide work to 30,000 'partner' farmer families who plant bamboo and eucalyptus for the company.

Pollution is topical with the Phoenix executives. The company was involved in a highly publicised case last year when it was ordered by the Provincial Governor to stop operations. Ironically, the company had always been careful to meet government pollution standards and were apparently unfairly blamed for polluting a nearby river. According to Mr S.K. Mittal, the firm's Director and Technology General Manager and Mr A. Ranganathan, General Manager, Administration, in March 1992, molasses were accidentally drained into the Nam Pong River from a nearby sugar mill. Since molasses have a very high biological oxygen demand and as this large block of molasses drifted down the river it consumed all the oxygen and killed the fish, an important food source for the local population. The incident became a national issue when the molasses drifted down the river into the next province. Thinking that the waste water from the pulp plant was the cause, the Kohn Kaen Provincial Governor ordered the plant closed. In the process, the complications of excess bureaucracy came into play since, according to the company executives, the current system of pollution control in Thailand involves 14 different agencies and perhaps 45 regulations, often conflicting. After 39 days and additional expenditure on pollution control equipment to bring the suspended solids in the plant's waste water down to levels even lower than legally required, the plant was given permission to resume operations. The company is now testing a 'wetlands project' where waste water is put into fields with special plants which help purify the water thereby saving on the energy and chemicals normally required to treat waste water. An expert from the United States and a university professor from Kohn Kaen University are working on the project. The company has strong reasons to adhere to strict pollution controls. It has received a ten-year, interest-free US$100 million loan from Finland for new equipment and the Finnish Government requires adherence to stringent pollution controls as a condition for the loan.

The executives said that they felt vindicated when the Finns, knowing the facts in the pollution case, did not cancel their loan.

Dr J B Mark Mobius

TEMPLETON EMERGING MARKETS INVESTMENT TRUST DISTRIBUTION OF PORTFOLIO

Geographical analysis (by country of incorporation)
as at 30 April 1997

Country	Cost £'000	Market value £'000	Capital appreciation (%)	% of portfolio
Brazil	37,969	116,320	206	16.7
Hong Kong*	53,690	82,528	59	11.9
Mexico*	65,066	66,333	2	9.5
Greece	30,112	53,928	79	7.7
Argentina*	28,055	46,022	64	6.6
Turkey	35,266	45,170	28	6.5
Portugal*	30,560	35,103	15	5.0
Malaysia	19,993	27,080	35	3.9
Indonesia*	24,323	25,605	5	3.7
India*	25,320	22,583	(11)	3.2
China* §	18,487	21,921	19	3.1
Thailand*	25,194	19,200	(24)	2.8
South Africa	18,650	18,751	0	2.7
Philippines*	12,517	18,578	48	2.7
Singapore*	14,898	16,067	8	2.3
South Korea*	22,019	14,935	(32)	2.1
Colombia*	8,365	10,711	28	1.5
Czech Republic	14,244	10,688	(25)	1.5
Venezuela*	5,055	8,342	65	1.2
Chile†	2,962	8,293	180	1.2
Hungary*	4,917	8,080	64	1.2
Pakistan*	10,412	6,605	(37)	0.9
Israel	3,953	4,351	10	0.6
Poland*	2,762	3,504	27	0.5
Namibia	1,574	1,665	6	0.2
Zimbabwe*	1,064	1,404	32	0.2
Botswana	837	786	(5)	0.1
Kenya	900	660	(27)	0.1
Sri Lanka	547	264	(53)	0.0
Peru*	171	222	30	0.0
Total investments	**519,882**	**695,699**		
Other net assets		**32,035**		
Shareholders' funds		**727,734**		

Source: Annual Report, author's calculations.
* includes US-listed stocks
† includes UK-listed stocks
§ includes Hong Kong-listed stocks

INDEX

REFS *see* Really Essential Financial
  Statistics
relative strength 212, 214, 221-2, 226
Rembrandt 117
renewal
  commission 54
  fees 54
Rentokil 93-4, 320-1
rerating 138, 215-6
return
  on capital 7-8, 129, 134-5, 214
  on equity 7-8
Return To Go (Slater, J.) 208, 221
Reuters 129
risk 6, 24, 34, 78, 89, 143, 195, 218, 242,
  249, 264, 271
RIT and Northern Investments 97
Robertson, Donald 124, 127
Roditi, Nicholas 102
Rogers, Jim 203
Rolls-Royce 157-8
Rothschilds 98, 100, 119
Rothschild, Lord Jacob 97-8
Rudd, Nigel 186
Rushbrook, Ian 4, 67-96, 261, 265-6
  emerging markets, and 88
  investment report 285-8
  investment techniques 262, 263-4
  models 82-4, 86-7, 90, 94
  Ratios 82-3, 85

St. James's Place Capital 98
St. James's Place Greater European
  Progressive Trust 98-100, 107,
  295-305

sales per share growth 129, 133
Scandinavia 34, 35, 188-9, 192
Schlesinger group 17, 18
Scot Income 73
Scotsman 76
Scottish Value Management *see* SVM
  Asset Management
Scottish Value Trust *see* SVM Global
  Fund
screening 129, 143-4, 222
  computer models 17, 77, 82-3, 84-5,
    136, 148
  REFS 201-2, 263
securities
  diversification 78, 143, 154, 166,
    173, 244, 268-9, 289
  fixed interest 5, 80
security analysis *see* investment criteria
Sergeant, Sir Patrick 157, 207
shareholders' funds 8
shareholdings 104, 163
shares
  blue-chip 158-9, 273
  cyclical 63, 111, 213, 220, 266
  intrinsic value 125-6
  relative strength 212, 214, 221-2,
    226
  returns 8, 153, 266
  selling 65, 91, 95, 137, 219, 226, 265
Sheffield, John 75
Singapore 197
Slater, Jim 184, 185, 197-228
  bottom-up investing 328-30
  charts, and 40, 219
  investment techniques 30

Slater, Mark 201, 217-8, 228
Slater Foundation 200, 203
Slater Growth fund 201, 217-8
Slater Walker 74, 179-80, 184, 198, 204,
    205, 206-9
small companies 16, 23, 64-5, 79-82, 130,
    144-5, 212, 223, 263, 273
Smith, Terry 144
socialism 248
Society of Investment Analysts 101, 107,
    118
Soros, George 11, 109, 110, 168
South Africa 331-3
Spanish Mountain Gold 203
Special Situations 10, 19-20, 24, 29-30,
    35, 41, 45-6, 54-5, 65
    asset proportion by location 37
    China 65
    Global 55
    vs FTSE All-Share Index 43
Spectator 194
sports retailers 224
Spydar 197
Stagecoach 140, 142, 144
status change 182, 215, 218, 220, 245
steel companies 111, 213
Steer, George 177-8, 180
stock market 1-8
    see also crashes; efficient markets;
        emerging markets
    bear market 46, 109, 114-5, 145,
        158, 167, 183, 184, 266
    bull market 41, 45-7, 57, 144-5, 155,
        266, 267
    capitalisation 212
    corrections 114-7

overseas 35, 36-7, 155, 188-9, 192-3,
    234, 244
timing 83, 85, 86, 145, 165, 170, 190,
    220, 222
stockbrokers 16, 73, 271
    Angus, R. 87-9, 90-1, 96
    Bolton, A. 13-4, 27-8, 30
    Carrington, J. 185-6, 187, 194, 196
    Hart, M. 157
    Rushbrook, I. 79, 88-9
    Slater, J. 200-1, 216
    Taube, N. 107-8, 120
Stonex, Cato 98, 102
Sunday Business 11
Sunday Telegraph 204, 206
supermarkets 103-4, 139, 187, 270
SVM Asset Management 123-4
SVM Global Fund 124-5, 127-8
SVM UK Growth Fund 124
Takeover Code, The 207
takeovers 20, 25-6, 32, 33-4, 60, 104, 119,
    124, 138, 207
Taube Hodson Stonex Partners 98, 122
Taube, Nils 97-122
    investment techniques 257, 262,
        264, 268-9, 306-7
    Nils Taube Investments 122
    ratios 114
tax charge 135
technical analysis 39-41
    Bolton, A. 13, 16, 40
    Carrington, J. 191
    Mobius, M. 251
    Slater, J. 40, 219
    Train, J. 39-40
television companies 26, 40-1, 49, 224